Educational Policy for Effective Schools

Editors:

Mark Holmes, Ontario Institute for Studies in Education

Kenneth A. Leithwood, Ontario Institute for Studies in Education

Donald F. Musella, Ontario Institute for Studies in Education

Additional Contributors:

John Davis, Ontario Institute for Studies in Education

Joseph P. Farrell, Ontario Institute for Studies in Education

Linda LaRocque and Peter Coleman, University of Alberta and Simon Fraser University

Karen Seashore Louis, University of Minnesota

Les McLean, Ontario Institute for Studies in Education

Edward A. Wynne, University of Illinois

OISE Press
Ontario Institute for Studies
in Education

Teachers College Press
Teachers College,
Columbia University

SOCIAL SCIENCE & HISTORY DIVISION
EDUCATION & PHILOSOPHY SECTION

The Ontario Institute for Studies in Education has three prime functions: to conduct programs of graduate study in education, to undertake research in education, and to assist in the implementation of the findings of educational studies. The Institute is a college chartered by an Act of the Ontario Legislature in 1965. It is affiliated with the University of Toronto for graduate studies purposes.

The publications program of the Institute has been established to make available information and materials arising from studies in education, to foster the spirit of critical inquiry, and to provide a forum for the exchange of ideas about education. The opinions expressed should be viewed as those of the contributors.

©The Ontario Institute for Studies in Education 1989
  252 Bloor Street West
  Toronto, Ontario M5S 1V6

All rights reserved. No part of this publication may be reproduced in any form without permission from the publisher, except for brief passages quoted for review purposes.

Canadian Cataloguing in Publication Data
Main entry under title:

Educational policy for effective schools

Rev. chapter discussed at a conference held in spring, 1987.
Includes bibliographical references.
ISBN 0-7744-0328-4

1. Education and state. I. Holmes, Mark, 1935-
II. Leithwood, K. A. (Kenneth Arthur), 1942-
III. Musella, Donald F., 1928-

LC71.E38 1989   379'.2   C89-093833-4

Library of Congress Cataloging-in-Publication Data
Educational policy for effective schools / Mark Holmes, Kenneth
  Leithwood, Donald Musella, editors.
      p.   cm.
Bibliography: p.
ISBN 0-8077-2981-7
1. School management and organization. 2. Education and state.
I. Holmes, Mark, 1935-   . II. Leithwood, Kenneth A. III. Musella,
Donald F.
LB2805.E353   1989   89-4373
379--dc19   CIP

ISBN 0-7744-0328-4   Printed in Canada
1 2 3 4 5 UTP 39 29 19 09 98

Contents

SOCIAL SCIENCE & HISTORY DIVISION
EDUCATION & PHILOSOPHY SECTION

Preface

This book results from discussions Don Musella, Chair of OISE's Department of Educational Administration, held with some of his colleagues in the Department of Educational Administration in the summer of 1986. He was in the process of setting up a Centre for Executive Studies and felt that policy in the area of school effectiveness was one natural focus. Mark Holmes and Ken Leithwood, both of whom were actively working in the area of school effectiveness and educational policy, were enthusiastic about Don's idea of combining a conference and a book.

The idea was that the Department should combine its own expertise with that of others both within and outside OISE to develop a set of papers in the form of chapters looking not at school effectiveness itself but at contemporary policy implications. The chapters were given a preliminary airing at a conference held in the spring of 1987. This book, however, is not in any sense a set of conference proceedings. Quite the reverse — the conference was used both as a vehicle for disseminating ideas on policy and effective schools and as a first trial for the chapters. The chapters were extensively rewritten after the conference.

There is one chapter that does not derive from the conference. We are grateful to two critics who identified a number of weaknesses in the first draft of the book. To some extent, we have repaired them. Both critics felt that the book, as one written in large part by Canadians, lacked Canadian examples. We invited Linda LaRocque and Peter Coleman, who have carried out extensive research on the superintendent and the effective school district in British Columbia, to contribute a chapter which would examine the link between policy and practice. We are grateful that they agreed.

Mark Holmes
Donald F. Musella
Kenneth A. Leithwood

Introduction

This book is about the implications of research into school effectiveness at the levels of the school district and the state or province. It is important to understand what this book is not. It is not a synthesis of research findings on what makes schools effective—although readers of chapters by Holmes, Farrell, and Davis will get a good idea of what that research tells us. It is not a manual, telling administrators how to develop specific policies to bring about school effectiveness, although chapters by Louis and LaRocque and Coleman implicitly address that issue. It is not a book on school improvement, but Leithwood, Musella, Davis, Wynne, and Holmes refer to that process.

The book was planned at a time when school effectiveness research appeared to have reached a plateau. If effectiveness is defined in terms of academic achievement, or even more narrowly in terms of the basic skills, then there is general consensus on the characteristics effective schools have in common: strong leadership aimed at academic achievement, an academic climate of high expectations, instruction focussed clearly on skills improvement, regular monitoring of student achievement, and a safe, orderly, and pleasant environment. But the implications of those findings are much less obvious than they once appeared. School improvement is not a science, and school improvement efforts, mostly still ongoing, are having mixed results. It seems unlikely that the simple application of a recipe will make schools more effective.

Some educators assume that the school is the level where decisions must be made. But schools may not even like the goals of school effectiveness, let alone the implications of applying the recipe apparently necessary for its achievement. In such situations, the recipe, and the goals, may undergo considerable change. Other educators believe that reform must be imposed in some systematic, uniform way. But changing the behavior of educators, who are not necessarily either systematic or uniform, is not easy, and not always even ethical.

Holmes provides an overview of school effectiveness ideas as they have developed in the last twenty or so years. His argument is pessimistic if one has the idea that a grand plan will somehow erase the most serious problems. But it is more optimistic if one believes that all participants in education, parents as well as educators, should be given more opportunity to articulate their choices.

McLean looks at the implications of findings in the Second International Mathematics Study for effective teaching in the Ontario context. However, much of what he reports will have relevance throughout North America. If he is right, many of the curriculum guides and textbooks, based as they are on a spiral curriculum, are fundamentally misguided. Indeed, the whole notion that children learn best when encouraged to learn for themselves, bit by bit, at their own pace, is strongly challenged by his reading of the data.

Farrell takes the reader to the developing world, showing that practice considered irrelevant in the American context is vitally important in other parts of the world. Simply introducing Western notions of improvement into the developing world is likely to be a particularly short-sighted and expensive policy. Farrell speaks to the developed world too — if indirectly. By placing the gains that can be achieved at low expense in developing countries in the context of the much smaller gains achieved at enormous expense by us, he forces us to think again about our penchant for massive, expensive programs of planned change.

Leithwood, Musella, Davis, and Wynne all consider the impact of policy for improved effectiveness at the level of the school. But there agreement ends. Leithwood argues for direct training of principals in patterns of sequential growth so that they will eventually reflect what he defines as the model decision-making principal. Musella and Davis are both cautious as they apply ideas about school change to school effectiveness. Musella argues for a coherent, planned model of change that is sensitive to the people involved. Davis examines the school as the embodiment of cultural norms which are likely to be resistant, even hostile, to outside interference. Wynne, rejecting technocratic, decision-making plans, argues for the development of a moral community, based on a set of traditional cultural values.

In the final section of the book, Louis and LaRocque and Coleman consider the potential contributions of the district itself (as distinct from a policy framework developed for schools at the level of the district). Both chapters are based on extensive empirical research and each makes a strong case that the district superintendent can indeed make a difference.

This book is about the conjunction between knowledge and ignorance: fairly exact but still limited knowledge about a set of relationships and considerable ignorance about what should be done next. This book straddles that divide; it addresses the question, "What does school effectiveness mean for educational policy?"

The book was written in the context of the Western, English-speaking world. It will therefore be of greatest appeal to readers in North America, Britain, Australia, and New Zealand. Educational policymakers, especially those at the district level, will find it particularly useful. It points to the major policy issues and problems that arise from an attempt to improve schools. The book should be helpful as well in the pre- and in-service education of school administrators.

We believe this book fills a gap in the available literature on effective schools. We are aware of the numerous writings which simply urge administrators to disseminate and implement effectiveness ideas — we have not added to that collection. What we have tried to do is address a range, admittedly an incomplete range, of the policy issues raised by the effectiveness research. No single answer or consensus arises from the very different contributors represented here. Quite the reverse; the disagreements among the contributors underline and clarify the complexity of the policy issues. Perhaps at least there is some consensus about the problems and about the policy issues that have to be addressed.

The following is a sample of policy questions raised in this book.

- To which goals should schools give priority? What should they be trying to effect?

- How can continuous improvement be maintained as personnel change?

- Can and should principals be educated to do the right thing as distinct from doing things the right way?

- Are we wasting both time and money by throwing money at either non-problems or problems we cannot cure?

- Can and should we try to change teachers' basic philosophies?

- How can we implement proven instructional strategies?

- To what extent is school culture a barrier to change? Is it manipulable?

- How best can senior administrators work with school principals?

- If change is centralized, are teachers and principals de-professionalized?

- If change is decentralized, who can be held accountable for improvement?

- What happens when there is widespread disagreement about the focus and methods of change?

The discriminating reader may end up somewhat perplexed. The writers not only have different perspectives, sometimes they simply disagree. For example, Linda LaRocque and Peter Coleman suggest that the most effective school districts are those where senior administrators lay on central policies and work closely with principals and other school people to ensure the policies are adhered to in spirit as well as in letter. Louis would not entirely disagree, although she would argue that the idea will not work in geographically large, sparsely populated districts. But Davis argues that the school culture is powerful and able to resist external change unless it is approached with delicacy and diplomacy. Musella, too, suggests that ideas that seem simple and straightforward to senior administrators often seem complicated to those closer to the firing line.

LaRocque and Coleman appear to have empirical research on their side. In a sense, they are likely right — for their small sample of schools in a not very representative part of British Columbia. But suppose we took a sample of urban school districts, even in British Columbia, or a sample of very large, sparsely populated ones. The results within either sample would be much less predictable. Some of the favorable British Columbia data likely result from the interaction of very committed superintendents and compatible school staffs. Even then, will the ethos survive the departure of the particular individuals?

So we come to the question of belief; the successful district administrators believe in what they are doing. Musella and Davis raise questions about what will happen among the disbelievers. Holmes argues that the best plan will go awry if it is carried out mainly by bureaucrats, sceptics, cynics, disbelievers. It is not sufficient to go through the motions. If teachers, like the one he quotes from a popular American book, do not generally put much value on, say, academics and character development, how probable is it that improvement plans in such areas will have a positive effect? Yet McLean makes it sound so simple. We could improve if we reorganized our curriculum and its implementation — more like the Japanese pattern. The Japanese appear to be uniformly successful because they work in uniform ways to achieve the same uniform objectives. But even if we in the West can introduce their ideas, will they work with teachers who do not share a single, homogeneous view of life and achievement? Japanese industrialists have shown us they can produce cars of high quality in North America with North American workers. So perhaps they could produce literate students, too. Leithwood would seem to support that idea as he discusses specifically the kind of training principals should have if they are to become effective leaders.

The explanation of the differences — yes, the contradictions — in the book is not just that you can get an educational expert to support any policy for education. The truth is that there is something of a crisis in Western education, at the very least a dilemma, and no one really knows for sure what we can do for the best. Farrell argues that our problem is one of fortune; we are so well off that there are limits to how much more we can improve; but then again McLean reminds us of the Pacific Rim countries — they seem still to be improving.

In the end, what our schools become depends on human will.

Wynne makes the point indirectly when he describes the qualities of character required in students, and in their teachers and administrators if the students are to acquire them. But what is our will? Once we know what we want, we should work at it directly, cooperatively, firmly, diligently, wholeheartedly, and courageously. But what if we don't know? So the dilemma becomes: either we agree consensually on what we want and work together or we do not agree and we work separately, in different schools in different ways. What we can't afford is a protracted cold war where every advance made by one faction is countered by another.

Some readers may be able to reconcile the different interpretations and starting points of the various authors. There is some fundamental agreement. Not one of the contributors questions the centrality of will. The idea is used in different contexts. The terminology varies: goals, purposes, objectives, consensus, commitment, involvement, philosophy, direction. Perhaps broad agreement is indeed possible. Other readers will see in the agreement on the centrality of will the source of deeper disagreement. Sometimes implicitly, sometimes explicitly, different ideas of educational purpose emerge. Holmes and Wynne, and perhaps LaRocque and Coleman, speak from more traditional, absolutist perspectives. They either argue for or assume some given ends, essentially traditional goals related to academics and moral conduct. Farrell, too, appears to assume some legitimate ends — although his are more egalitarian in nature. In contrast, Musella and Davis appear to imply that the educational process is at least as important as what happens as a result of it. McLean, Leithwood, and Louis take a more pragmatic stance — not that ends are less important than process, but that the important policy question concerns the selection of appropriate means to address whatever ends have already been selected by the legitimate authority.

It is important to realize that, although we have deliberately provided a broad set of perspectives, none of the writers lies outside the educational mainstream of Western democratic society; there is no laissez-faire voice for deschooling, no Marxist voice calling for revolution. So, it will be understandable if readers reach the conclusion that the writers reflect the three major strands of thought in contemporary education — conservative, liberal progressive, liberal technocratic. If these three strands of the mainstream cannot agree on purpose or process, perhaps that explains why public school systems have difficulty in undertaking meaningful, purposeful, consensual, directed plans for school improvement.

Mark Holmes

Part One

EFFECTIVENESS AND IMPROVEMENT IN THE DEVELOPED AND DEVELOPING WORLDS

1/School Effectiveness: From Research to Implementation to Improvement

Mark Holmes

In this survey, Holmes argues that schools will improve most when the public can make informed choices and when schools serve consensual communities. Questions to consider include: What are the ethics of professional change? How can communities choose their priorities? Which decisions should be made by educators and which by lay people?

The Problem

Over the last thirty years, a consensus has developed among researchers about school characteristics related to effectiveness in achieving academic goals, in particular the basic skills of reading and mathematical computation. More recently, a plethora of school improvement projects has been undertaken, mainly in the U.S. It is too early to judge the general success of these efforts, but it is already clear that some are doomed to failure.

The school effectiveness bandwagon, which is how it is defined by outsiders and many insiders, is attacked on several grounds. Most centrally, the overarching significance of the criteria of effectiveness implicitly or explicitly adopted is not accepted by those who prefer goals related to social transformation (Giroux and McLaren 1986 pp. 217–219), to self-concept and personal fulfilment (Howe 1983 p. 172), or to a liberal renaissance (Barrow 1984). In addition, there is widespread doubt about whether school effectiveness reforms can be generally implemented and there is even some residual doubt about exactly what it is that school effectiveness researchers have discovered.

It is important to understand both how we have reached our current situation and how we can best use the available knowledge.

In the early '70s, there was some feeling that it was impossible to identify important, school-based characteristics that are clearly beneficial to students. Coleman et al. (1966) were interpreted as suggesting that the effects of differences among schools were substantively inconsiderable compared with the massive effects of differences among homes. Today, it seems probable that there are some school characteristics related to academic effectiveness, but for various reasons we remain uncertain as to whether we can and should develop them and even if we do whether they will then reproduce the desired result.

School Effectiveness in Historical Perspective

It is reasonable to trace the beginnings of school effectiveness to the muckraking investigations into the outcomes of the American common school begun in the 1940s. As early as the 1930s, Counts (1963) had argued that schools should serve a social construction purpose. He distinguished himself from Deweyan progressives, who were interested more in school processes than in the outcomes of schooling, as well as from the mainstream. By the '70s, Bowles and Gintis (1976) saw the liberal, progressive reformers as now part of the mainstream, balanced within that stream by the technocratic reformers, with whom the school effectiveness movement can generally be identified. In contrast, Marxist reformers, in which group Bowles and Gintis themselves fall, following Counts, wanted transformation of both school and society. At the same time, conservatives, sometimes understandably confused with the technocratic reformers — technocrats and conservatives both emphasize the basic skills — wanted to restore the force of tradition in education.

Hollingshead (1949) helped uncover the reality behind the illusion of a "democratized" common school by showing how the school effectively sorted students according to their social origins; the academically successful came predominantly from the right side of the tracks, hewers of wood and drawers of water from the wrong. Other studies followed. In Canada, Seeley, Sim, and Loosely (1956) showed the complementary contributions of home and school in a Toronto suburb. In Britain, Jackson and Marsden (1962) showed not only the difficulties and limitations in rising through the social classes by means of Britain's "sponsored" as distinct from the American "contest" mobility but also the price paid in family and social relationships. Not only do schools tend to serve as a conduit for the inheritance of social class, but the many exceptions to the rule often pay a heavy price. Hargreaves (1967) went on to show that the broad stratification effected by the economic system is reproduced in microcosm even in a school serving only a portion of the population. His case study of a secondary school serving a population excluding the upper and most of the middle classes showed sharp stratification between those who would be relatively successful and those who rejected the school's norms and demands.

By this time, Coleman (1961) and Stinchcombe (1964) were researching the internal ethos of the American high school in attempts to understand and interpret the adolescent youth culture. Going beyond simple divisions by social class, they found that academic success was not generally a criterion of peer respect. Conservative critics of the progressive, life adjustment approaches to schools of the '50s (e.g., Hutchins 1952, Neatby 1954) and technocratic, post-Sputnik critics of the '60s argued that the schools had become anti-academic. If schools do not have an academic thrust, a plausible explanation for the school's relative ineffectiveness in intervening between home background and academic outcomes emerges. If achievement is not an important criterion of success within school, it is hardly surprising if pupils' work and aspirations are related to the conditions and expectations they experience at home.

By the time Coleman (1966) undertook his seminal study of equal opportunity in the mid-'60s, concerns about the academic nature of the school and social class were compounded and overtaken in the U.S. by concerns about racial differences. Abandoning his earlier focus on school climate, Coleman investigated the relationships among: a variety of attitudinal and material inputs from the home; material but not attitudinal inputs from the school; and a range of low-level cognitive outcomes. As Coleman was funded by a federal department, it is tempting to infer that he was expecting to show that the differences in achievement among racial groups, particularly between blacks and whites, could be offset by large-scale federal intervention to improve the material and teaching conditions in the schools in which minorities were educated. If that was the purpose, the study was totally unsuccessful, for Coleman concluded that differences among schools, in terms of the selected school variables, account for only a small portion of the variance in achievement of individuals. Some of the conclusions of this highly controversial study remain largely unchallenged: in developed countries, differences in home culture, of genetic and social origin, explain considerably more of the variance in academic achievement than do differences among schools; material conditions in schools (buildings, pedagogical training of teachers and principals, libraries, laboratories, school size) have little independent relationship with outcomes; the social context of other pupils in the school and the verbal ability of the teachers may be significant if small school factors.

Some of the shortcomings of Coleman's study provided a rationale for subsequent studies which have given force to the school effectiveness movement. By avoiding control variables which might be seen as being prejudicial to blacks, notably of ability, Coleman developed measures of home background that are at once so all-embracing and so unclear in their conceptual meaning that their import, origins, and value are difficult to define. For example, to what extent are parental attitudes and collections of books a consequence of experiences within a school and to what extent do they derive from the background culture, as Coleman assumed? Coleman avoided all non-material school measures, such as school climate, perhaps because they are not amenable to financial enhancement. And he used as criteria of school outcomes measures of verbal ability and general knowledge which are not the subject of instruction in many school grades and which are, one may reasonably assume, learned as much outside the school as within. If homes in developed countries vary more than schools, then we should not be surprised that home variables explained more of the variance in general measures of learning than did school variables.

In contrast to Coleman's expensive failure, McDill and Rigsby (1973), having controlled student ability and socioeconomic status, concluded that the school academic climate explained some of the differences in individual achievement. In Canada, Holmes (1971) reached similar conclusions. What seemed to differentiate more successful from less successful schools was the level of academic expectation of both teachers and fellow students — the more achievement is expected, respected, demanded, and appreciated the more it is realized. This has become the core belief of the effective schools movement.

While Coleman was completing his major study, the first round of international studies of achievement (the IEA studies) was also underway. Like Coleman, the international researchers were interested in discovering school-based variables related to differences in achievement. Unlike Coleman, they focussed on subjects actually taught in most schools at the level tested. A major underlying concern of these studies was the effect of school organization on opportunities for social mobility. In short, does more (i.e., mass schooling) mean worse? In particular, Husén (1967) wanted to discover if the American, "democratic" approach of "contest" mobility, which was being imported to his native Sweden, was superior to the "elitist," "sponsored" mobility practised at that time by most of the western European countries in their segregated, selective secondary systems. Overall, the findings of the IEA studies were disappointing in terms of school effectiveness and supported opposing answers to Husén's question. Selective and non-selective (comprehensive) systems seem to do equally well with the top 9 percent of academic achievers. Husén argued that this showed the superiority of the non-selective (Swedish) system, which provided mass education at no cost in achievement (1975 pp. 131–132). However, it could be argued equally by a West German that the German system of early selection provides just as good an academic elite, while non-elite youth, instead of struggling unsuccessfully for years as in American, Swedish, and Canadian systems, are provided a useful technical education leading directly to productive employment. If the selective systems really lost all the "late bloomers," a West German might argue, how was it that Sweden and the U.S. did not outperform those selective systems in academic excellence?

One important finding that did emerge was that subjects like mathematics and French and English as second languages are relatively sensitive to instructional time while subjects like reading, literature, and civics are quite insensitive, being related largely to home-background characteristics. This finding was confirmed in Ontario, Canada, where achievement in French as a second language, geography, and mathematics was found to be substantially related to instructional time while achievement in English, civics, and science was not positively related among 14-year-old elementary students (Holmes 1979). Drawing from the empirical research and from ideas of Wiley (1976) and Karweit (1978), Holmes suggested that learning is most sensitive to allocated academic time under the following conditions: a new skill or set of ideas is being learned; opportunities for learning are mainly within school; and direct sequential instruction is provided. Those conclusions have important if indirect implications for the administration of effective schools. Allocation of time is largely an administrative responsibility, particularly when differentiated staffing becomes more common after the early grades. In contrast, the use of time (conceptualized as time on task or engaged time or academic learning time) is largely a pedagogical activity over which administrators have much less influence.

The research on effective instruction, including the idea of time on task, is not explored here because it is less open to direct influence by means of policy. Suffice it to say that positive findings about effective instruction in the classroom tend to be consistent with the ideas developed about effective schools. The emphasis is on direct approaches to the achievement of clear goals. Thus it seems likely that the most effective schools will be using the approaches defined in both bodies of research.

Much of the more recent research in school effectiveness has been based on small samples of schools and case studies where the data can be more carefully assessed. Observational and survey data have been used in the same study. Brookover and Lezotte (1979) pioneered the use of outliers, in a comparison of notably successful with notably unsuccessful elementary schools in the same geographical area, with emphasis on school variables related to administrative behavior and school climate. Orderly climate, careful and frequent monitoring of student achievement, with high demands made by teachers and pupils characterized the most successful schools.

Probably the single most important study in the school effectiveness literature remains *Fifteen Thousand Hours* (Rutter et al. (1979). This study looked at twelve secondary schools in London serving a fairly homogeneous working-class population. Four criteria of effectiveness were used — academic achievement measured by examination results, delinquency, in-school behavior, and attendance. With the exception of delinquency, all variables were found to be strongly related to administrative and broadly measured instructional differences among schools. The level of academic expectations, the level, frequency, and types of reward for good work, the use of consultative as distinct from centralized or participatory decision making, universalism as distinct from pastoral patterns of discipline, and close supervision of teachers' work habits were all seen to be positively related to outcomes. Although Rutter and his colleagues tend to overinterpret their data, these core ideas of effectiveness have been substantiated in several other studies. A good, appropriately sceptical summary of the research may be found in Purkey and Smith (1983).

A study by Ramsay et al. in New Zealand (1983) is notable for its ethnographic methodology and for an unusual claim. Although it too found that the successful schools were orderly and characterized by a demanding academic climate, it claimed that the successful schools were those that emphasized the special culture of the predominantly Maori population. That finding is opposed to Rutter's finding with respect to universalism — a finding also reported by Wynne (1980) and by Coleman, Hoffer, and Kilgore (1982). However, as Ramsay's study was essentially observational, it is difficult to verify the data on which his conclusions were reached.

Although Rutter's findings are among the most radical and most encouraging and go furthest in refuting the pessimism generated by Coleman's 1966 study, some caution is necessary. Rutter's loglinear analysis is far from conservative. It is not possible to be sure whether it is the school variables measured or some unknown correlate of them that is significant in explaining the different levels of success of his schools.

The second Coleman study (Coleman, Hoffer and Kilgore 1982) has also been the subject of controversy (see, for example, *Sociology of Education* 1982). Three major claims are made, of which the first and most publicized is probably the most questionable. They are: (i) private and Catholic schools are more successful than are public schools serving students of the same social background; (ii) private and Catholic schools are most likely to use effective school ideas (high academic climate, high expectations, academic atmosphere, frequent monitoring of achievement, clear expectations of teachers); and (iii) private and Catholic schools not only achieve better outcomes but also produce less variance in the achievement variables. This study has been criticized for, among other things, relying on verbal ability as an educational outcome and making invalid comparisons between private and public school home backgrounds; the very fact that some parents choose to pay in itself makes them different from those who choose not to, argue the critics. However, the third and possibly most interesting finding is consistent with Rutter's claim that his best school did better academically with the lowest social class band of students than did the worst school with the highest, always remembering that his schools served a fairly small band of the social class continuum. That is to say, by demanding high standards of all students, with reduced differentiation of program and expectations, schools achieve both better overall results and less differentiation among students.

Notably missing from the school effectiveness studies has been interaction between gender and school effectiveness. That question has been left to specialist scholars outside the mainstream who argue persuasively, for example, that girls are systematically discriminated against within the school (Delamont 1980). One would expect future studies to examine the school differences apparently related to differentiation of achievement by gender in relation to factors related to other measures of school effectiveness.

Coleman and Hoffer (1987) have raised important issues for school improvement as they confirm many earlier generalizations about effectiveness. They go on to argue convincingly that the greater effectiveness of private Catholic schools in the U.S. stems from their participation within a "value community," a community which lives, plays, and prays together within a set of assumed beliefs. The Catholic school can more easily develop a common, agreed mission than can the public school, which must be sensitive to a wide range of individual purposes, or the non-religious private school, which, although it may form a community of common values, has little overarching authority to stem individual dissent. The authors remind us that good schools are microcosms of larger, working, successful communities.

Overall, there is convincing evidence that there are considerable differences in schools' effectiveness in helping young people achieve specific goals in the basic skills and success in academic examinations. While it would be unwarranted to claim that the differences among schools approach, in their total effect, the differences among home backgrounds, the evidence is overwhelming that the degree to which the school aggressively works toward academic goals is related to its success in achieving those goals.

The Problem Facing School Effectiveness Studies

Certain empirical conclusions may be reached from the effectiveness studies. The following factors seem to be related to school effectiveness with respect to academic achievement: academic climate of high expectation on the part of teachers and students; universalistic discipline; an orderly atmosphere; frequent and immediate rewards for good performance; regular monitoring of achievement; strong community support; strong leadership. All successful schools do not of course possess all those characteristics.

The central, practical problem facing the movement today is one of implementation. It is one thing to discover relationships between certain school variables and certain output variables in existing environments. It is another thing entirely to reproduce such characteristics in other schools, let alone the changes in outputs, in very different situations. There are two separate questions. Can the school effectiveness ideas be successfully implemented? If they are implemented, will they produce the desired changes in outcome? It will be seen that the two conceptually separate questions are closely related.

Before turning to the question of implementation, it may be valuable to make some cautionary comments on the preceding brief history. The level of success of the school effectiveness studies is not substantively high. Statistical significance should not be confused with substantive significance. Differences among schools are usually believed to explain somewhere between 10 percent and 30 percent of the variance in achievement among individuals; in my judgment, the truth is likely to be closer to the former than to the latter within a modern, economically advanced society. As Western societies become more economically advanced and as families become more differentiated, the proportion of variance explained by the school is more likely to decrease than increase. However, it is no more sensible to suggest we should therefore not bother about school improvement than it would be to urge a farmer to ignore the scientific research on fertilizer because the effects in the long run will be small in comparison with those of other variables, such as characteristics of climate, seed stock, and soil. Nevertheless, even the completely successful implementation of school effectiveness ideas will not transform either schools or society. The more we make schools equally successful the more we transfer responsibility for social distribution to the home. Home cultures are not equal, and indeed are probably becoming increasingly different.

It may be argued that we should therefore give low priority to attempts to make schools more effective, in the limited sense of the word employed in most of the literature. The practical arguments are these: (i) more effective schools will not reduce social inequality; (ii) there are more important things we could be doing with the enormous effort required; and (iii) we do not know if effective schooling ideas can be usefully transferred to other schools. The first argument is relevant only to the extent that increased social equality is used as the fundamental rationale for making schools work better. Part of the rationale for school improvement projects has indeed been that disadvantaged children seem to be particularly sensitive to effective school practices; improving the skills of the disadvantaged will not transform the social structure but it may slightly improve the chances of success among some of the disadvantaged. The second argument is the one most generally heard; for example, "I am more interested in helping Jennifer feel happier with herself than with raising her math score two points." This argument is not without logic; we should deploy limited resources to best effect. However, before we cast aside the idea of school improvement in favor of schemes for raising self-concept, three further points should be considered. First, the public is very concerned about the basic skills and it is surely unreasonable to announce that we experts think we know how to improve them but have decided not to bother. Second, there is less evidence that the school can provide lasting increases in self-concept than that it can improve scores in mathematics. Third, it is highly likely that the positive self-concept most parents want in their children (i.e., self-respect, understanding of self) is closely associated with or dependent on success in other school endeavors — intellectual, aesthetic, moral, and physical. As for the problem of implementation, I leave that until later, merely noting that the fact that we do not know whether something can be done is an argument for research not surrender.

The opposition to school effectiveness is not limited to practical questions. The ideas themselves are open to significant criticism. Traditional conservatives consider them of secondary significance. Fundamentalist Christians, for example, whose schools, ironically, are effective in the basic skills, will not want to undertake any project that might detract from their central, spiritual purpose (Peshkin 1986). Progressives oppose most effective school reforms for the good reason that they reflect practices and purposes totally opposed to their own. Certainly, codes of behavior, universalistic treatment, direct instruction, high expectations of all, and monitoring of achievement by standardized tests are anathema to progressives, who have a very different agenda for education. Marxists oppose the effective schools movement because they see it as being irrelevant to the major outcome of schooling, which to them is the structural succession of social and economic status. Indeed, reforms that appeal to populist sentiment may be harmful to their cause of radicalizing society generally and schooling in particular — revolution must be built on popular discontent with the "system." The technocratic mainstream provides the movement with the strongest moral support. But technocrats are nothing if not pragmatic. Their patience is short; they may decide that some other set of reforms, for example, instructional effectiveness, deserves higher priority if school effectiveness fails to produce good results fast.

Most practising educators are probably unaware of opposition to the idea of school effectiveness. After all, no one favors an ineffective school, any more than one favors an adult-centred as distinct from a child-centred school. In this chapter, I am using the term school effectiveness, unless otherwise stated, to refer to the ideas associated with the main body of effectiveness literature (summarized by Purkey and Smith 1983) and with such researchers as Brookover, Coleman, McDill, Rutter, and Wynne. When ideas about effectiveness become translated into programs for improvement, the effectiveness research is often left to one side as educators differ about what it is they wish to improve.

Implementation of School Program: Implications for School Improvement

The translation of school effectiveness ideas into school improvement means the bringing together of two very different bodies of research. School effectiveness, as I have operationally defined it, implies the primacy of academic achievement as a goal, together perhaps with some emphasis on behavior or character. While I do not attempt to provide a comprehensive review of the implementation literature, I do believe it is important to demonstrate some fundamental differences between the two streams of research. It is not sensible to think we can simply use the implementation literature to institutionalize school effectiveness reforms and thereby bring about school improvement in a formalistic way.

Fullan, who is frequently referenced by implementation people, suggests that there are four factors to be taken into account in implementation: (i) characteristics of the change; (ii) characteristics at the school district level; (iii) characteristics at the school level; and (iv) characteristics external to the local system (1982 p. 56). Examples of change characteristics are: need, clarity, complexity, and quality of materials. Examples of district characteristics are: history, the adoption process, administrative support, and in-service training. Examples of school characteristics are: the principal, teacher-teacher relations, and teacher characteristics. External characteristics are the role of government and forms of other external assistance.

There are several difficulties with Fullan's approach to change, difficulties which are identifiable within most contemporary school change models. They can be summarized under three headings: lack of clarity about goals; lack of clarity about the ethical use of authority; and doubtful empirical support.

Lack of Clarity About Goals

The earlier review of the effectiveness literature suggests there is an underlying assumption about what education is for. Generally, it is about changing students. Typically, the changes involve some external specification of academic competence. The evidence of change is necessitated by the word "effect." In the implementation literature, it is generally assumed that the desired change is anything that the legitimate authority determines. On the surface, this problem may be a slight one to both school effectiveness and school change people; after all, the solution is simply to slip the effectiveness characteristics into the category of desired changes to be implemented.

However, if a problem with the effectiveness stream is its only implicit reference to desired educational goals, a problem with Fullan's statement of the implementation stream is that he avoids the problem of good and bad change altogether: "We can never know absolutely what are the good changes" (1982 p. 142). Coleman's Catholic schools appear to be successful precisely because they do believe they know what is good (Coleman and Hoffer 1987); similarly, Bronfenbrenner's (1970) Soviet schools also thought they knew what was good, and they were much more successful in achieving their goals than were the more open American schools with which he compared them; and even in the U.S., fundamentalist Christian schools often seem spectacularly successful (Peshkin 1986). One may counter that the examples of Catholic, communist, and fundamentalist views of truth merely illustrate the validity of the dictum that there can be no absolute knowledge of good. Bloom (1987) is one of a number of contemporary philosophers who demur. It is precisely the cult of openness and relativism, he argues, that presages the decline of education. And it is simply illogical to argue that because people differ on exactly what constitutes the good there can be no absolute good. It is like saying that because scientists have different views about what was the "missing link" between man and ape there can be no such thing. So, two points are being made with respect to goals. First, it is not unreasonable to believe in an absolute good, in which case good goals are to be preferred to bad. Second, in a good society, good goals will also enlist moral support. It matters what goals are in terms of the strength of collective community commitment. The mainstream implementation literature ignores the first argument and understates the second.

Lack of Clarity About the Ethical Use of Authority

Fullan fails to come to terms with authority. He argues that teachers should be given a sense of ownership and should be encouraged to change other teachers; thus, the teacher "can become one of the most powerful forces of change" (1982 p. 125). What this logically leads to is attempts by administrators to manipulate teachers and other subordinate staff. It is at least possible that crude attempts at manipulation and their apparent legitimation by educational leaders have contributed to the pervasive cynicism among teachers concerning educational change. Neither ethics nor morality is listed in Fullan's comprehensive index (1982).

The ways in which teachers may be changed can be categorized under three headings. They may be ordered to change, they may be manipulated into changing without their consciously recognizing the process, and they may be openly persuaded to change. There are many contexts where orders are legitimate. For example, educational goals are usually and legitimately established by an authority higher than the teacher. Program content is often developed by a level of bureaucracy inside or outside the school — to assure continuity and comparability of learning. Student evaluation is usually and reasonably not a matter of individual choice by the teacher. And teachers should not be allowed to teach, explicitly or implicitly, immorality.

Persuasion, if it is both intellectually and personally transparent and honest, is nearly always legitimate. Indeed, it is ethical, desirable, and respectful to attempt to persuade a professional colleague to adopt a better way. However, persuasion that is not transparent, that is accompanied by vague or illicit pressure, becomes manipulation, whereby the manipulated individual is treated as an object to be changed in the most efficient manner possible, and in whom intellectual, moral, and ethical arousal is to be feared as a barrier to change. (This argument is developed more fully in Holmes and Wynne [1989].)

Manipulation, typified today by much advertising and public relations, is frequently effective and often not resented even by professional teachers, although it does make them cynical and suspicious. Thus the lack of clarity about authority is not necessarily a barrier to implementation, but it is a barrier to good (i.e., absolutely good) education because it is itself miseducative. Manipulation corrupts the teacher; even more drastically it corrupts the administrator who is led to believe that manipulation is a legitimate act of administration.

Doubtful Empirical Support

Although there is abundant research on educational implementation which generally serves to support Fullan's generalizations, there is a lack of clear-cut, large-scale empirical evidence. That lack is understandable. Educational change is so variable — in goals, in processes, in evaluation, in involved personnel, and in communities — it would be surprising indeed if a useful predictive formula could be researched and comprehensively assessed.

Kirst and Meister (1985) have examined the history of educational innovations and argue that a simple variable that would best predict effective implementation is the *regulatory* nature of the proposed change. Regulatory changes are the most enduring. Regulatory changes, of course, do not require the elaborate processes laid down by the implementation mainstream. Regulatory changes (for example, changes in school scheduling, introduction of school leaving examinations, changing the school year) are very difficult for schools to avoid. Above all, they do not require changes in the professional, instructional behavior of the teacher (although they may well indirectly lead to such change).

Probably the most successfully implemented educational innovation in Canada in the last twenty years, excluding changes of a purely regulatory nature, is French immersion. By successful implementation, I here mean widespread, thorough utilization. By success, I mean the achievement of the program's stated goals. (I am not arguing that the innovation was a good one, that the valuable goals achieved outweigh the negative and largely unresearched side effects.) Almost everywhere it has been implemented, French immersion has been characterized by strong initial demand by parents, indifference or resistance by teachers, absence of in-service training, absence of specialized teaching materials, and generally "inappropriately" qualified teachers often ignorant of local conditions and instructional methodology. How easy it would have been to explain failure.

Having surveyed the history of most of the major innovations in Canada over the last twenty years, I can only note that it is almost impossible to make generalizations except in the case of regulatory changes. Certainly, parental support or its lack is sometimes key, as in the case of French immersion. The open school ideas of the early '70s were abandoned, partly in response to parental opposition (e.g., North York, Ontario). "Value-free" sex education programs focussing on such topics as abortion, homosexuality, and premarital sex have been abandoned or heavily modified (e.g., Durham and Simcoe Counties, Ontario). In other cases, parental interest is insignificant. The post-Sputnik, inquiry-based approaches to biology, physics, and chemistry have generally persisted in Canada in modified form; in-service, materials, and texts were unquestionably important, but there was no grass-roots involvement, no sense of ownership, and little parental knowledge or interest. On the other hand, the thrust of the new mathematics, which was also supported by in-service and copious materials and which had somewhat more local involvement (most provinces quickly produced their own materials), is much less evident today. Parents were equally uninvolved in that innovation.

I am not suggesting that the mainstream implementation variables are totally irrelevant. Some are on occasion truths by definition. If one has a program (e.g., PSSC physics) that is defined in a written text, clearly the availability of the text is required. If one has a program (e.g., synthetic phonics) that requires specific knowledge and skills, clearly the knowledge and skills must be acquired somehow by the teachers carrying out the instruction. Even French immersion, which seems most immune to the implementation variables, will not be successful if the teachers directly involved are not fluent in French. But the implementation variables provide neither a useful set of predictors for successful implementation of change nor a sufficient set of check points for the planned introduction of a school improvement project. They leave to one side, as I have noted, important questions relating to the worth of the innovation. They also understate the political realities of education. Every innovation is different. The relative success of PSSC physics could not have been usefully used to predict success for the social science program "Man: A Course of Study." PSSC reflected the meaning of physics; "Man" reflected an ideology not universally accepted, although its developers doubtless believed it reflected the core values of the disciplines as they saw them.

The progress of educational change is not mysterious and incomprehensible; observers can usually explain reasonably adequately what has happened after the event. Prediction is more difficult because of the large number of interacting factors. In some cases, even interpretation after the event may vary with the ideology of the interpreter. Were open, progressive elementary schools rejected because parents did not understand them or were they rejected because the innovations represented an ineffective and undesirable approach to child upbringing?

Barrow (1984) argues that our knowledge of instructional methodology is so limited and incomplete that it is entirely inappropriate for professionals to tell other professionals how to teach. Teaching should be left to teachers. In place of never-ending implementation schemes, there should be thoroughgoing discussion about educational content. What ought the substance of education to be? For Barrow, implementation is a non-problem. Teaching should be like medicine or law, with concerned professionals making professional judgments based on the best available information.

I am not counselling despair. Quite the contrary; I am relieved that attempts to package and sell educational change are frequently conspicuously unsuccessful. I remain hopeful that schools can be improved if we agree on what we are about, if we treat fellow professionals with respect by being intellectually open and honest, and if we determine how best we can go about achieving desirable goals.

Implementing School Improvement

School effectiveness efforts are cautiously welcomed in most parts but at the same time the meaning of school effectiveness reform is changed to encompass a much wider range of goals than that on which the research is actually based. Researchers in school change typically adopt a pragmatic perspective where the type and objective of change is a matter for the legitimate authority.

Thus school improvement efforts are often not tied closely to the school effectiveness research. One of the best known attempts to study school improvement in a number of locations is described by Huberman and Miles (1984), for neither of whom, it should be noted, had school effectiveness been a major focus of research. When they asked users (teachers) what made them most likely to adopt an innovation, most frequently mentioned reasons were: administrative pressure (mentioned by 35 out of 56 respondents), improved instructional practice (mentioned by 16 out of 56), and the novelty value or challenge (mentioned by 10). Unmentioned were prospects of improved achievement scores (1984 p. 48). Similarly, only one out of forty-five administrators asked about their motives for change referred to improved achievement scores, and that was the only reference of any kind to positive change in students. It would be a major error to assume that, in general, school change efforts, even when labelled school improvement, are geared to improved effectiveness, that is, to better student outcomes. But this is not to deny that teachers similarly believe that their chosen projects will be good for kids.

However, to their credit, Huberman and Miles did try to assess the impact of the projects on students and concluded, on the basis of a series of case studies (not on statistically validated survey techniques), that the factors most important for impact on students are: user commitment, program fidelity, strong assistance, practice of mastery, and stabilization of use (1984 p. 229). Administrative pressure was useful if it was used to supply assistance and to maintain program fidelity.

In a summary account of the same "DESSI" (Dissemination Efforts Supporting School Improvement) research, Crandall and Loucks (1983) emphasize forceful leadership as well, and they warn against local development, which detracts from fidelity to the innovation; protracted planning; and so-called capacity building, that is, developing the school's own ability to handle its problems.

Although the case study methods used imply cautious interpretation, it is worth noting that there is some consistency with Coleman's emphasis on commitment, with Fullan's emphasis on assistance to the user, and with an earlier finding by Leithwood, Holmes, and Montgomery (1979) that a grass-roots, local emphasis leads to easy implementation but to lack of fidelity to the innovative idea — implicitly, therefore, to ineffectiveness. Thus, the mutual adaptation, admired by most implementors, is likely to be negatively related to effectiveness.

The task then is to bring together ideas from school effectiveness, implementation of change, and school improvement in such a way that legitimate and desirable goals can be best achieved. Before turning to that task, I shall pull together some characteristics and weaknesses of the three strands of research.

The great strength of the effectiveness literature is that it has collated a number of effectiveness factors that appear to be international correlates of certain, desired school outcomes. Shortcomings of the research are:

> 1. The emphasis on strong leadership is well documented but badly sustained. Unknown is the extent to which a leader in a successful school looks good simply because the school is successful. For example, in at least one case in the New Jersey Demonstration Schools Project (Holmes 1988), an extremely successful school is propelled by one each of the principal's superordinates and subordinates. In only one of three most effective schools (out of fifteen) is the principal a strong leader.
>
> 2. The research is based essentially on interrelationships among factors. Rutter et al. (1979) found, for example, that their ef-

fectiveness factors collectively explained a very high proportion of the differences among schools' effectiveness, but that any one or two factors could be deleted from the package with little effect on the explanatory power. This finding raises the question as to whether the enumerated factors are really important in themselves at all or whether they are really proxy variables for a more deep-seated underlying factor. If they are mere correlates of "it," what is the mysterious "it"? A likely candidate is the common purpose found in the functional or values communities to which Coleman and Hoffer (1987) refer. Another possibility is that effective schools establish norms of continuous improvement (Rosenholtz 1985).

3. Even if it is accepted that the effectiveness factors are, at least to some extent, genuine factors in themselves worth replicating, there is no guarantee that they will be equally effective or effective at all if they are spuriously implanted rather than spontaneously developed.

4. Although some goals of education are implicit in effectiveness research, they are usually assumed rather than argued. No plan for school improvement makes sense unless there is reasonable clarity not only about what change is involved but more importantly about what constitutes "better."

The strength of the implementation and improvement literatures is their emphasis on the complexity of change and on the numerous factors that may impede it. Their major shortcomings are:

1. They fail to come to terms with the contrasting values of tradition and change, usually making the implicit judgment that change is generally good and tradition bad. This failure often becomes crassly technocratic in the hands of administrators who adopt the posture that their only job is to follow orders, to implement — frequently in the face of negative or neutral evidence — whatever the current fad happens to be.

2. They also fail to come to terms with a reasonable definition of ethical practice. Thus there is usually no discussion of what it is reasonable for administrators to ask of teachers, and what unreasonable. Frequently this leads to the ironic situation in which administrators assume it is the teacher's "right" to teach immoral behavior by example (in terms of a lifestyle evident to the school community) but not the teacher's right to choose the most effective methodology to teach students certain agreed upon skills. This of course is just one example of the absurdity of imposing the industrial model on the school.

3. An adequate conceptual and empirical base is lacking. Not only is there no conceptualization of what constitutes desirable and undesirable change, but the alleged findings are based on

series of case studies whose applicability to different changes in different circumstances with different actors is of unproven validity.

4. School improvement research is a recent field of study whose claims must, at least for the present, be considered with care. In particular, there is a danger that the labels change — the now suspect expression educational "innovation" is simply replaced by the more congenial expression "improvement." Everyone now knows that change and innovation are often unhelpful and dangerous, but who can oppose improvement?

Improving Schools — Can It Be Done?

The Nature of Improvement

Change and innovation are not necessarily improvements. Indeed, returning to an old and abandoned idea may sometimes constitute improvement. An improved school is a better school. But better in what way?

In the context of the effective schools movement, improvement must mean increased effectiveness. That definition excludes many, probably most, examples of proposed school improvement projects. It requires that there be demonstrable effects as a result of the improved efforts and they must be demonstrable among students. Thus projects which involve change in administrative or instructional methodology do not usually denote improvement in themselves, however successfully the changes are implemented. There must, in addition, be strong evidence of or a strong presumption of improved outcomes among students.

All this is likely to be self-evident to non-educators. How can there be a medical improvement that is not helpful to clients? In education, however, improvement projects frequently involve changes whose relationship to improved outcomes is improbable or imaginary. A variety of explanations is offered: we shall never do anything if we wait for empirical proof (doing anything is very important in large bureaucracies); teachers and administrators are a part of education too, and improvements for them eventually lead to improvements for students (improved comfort for educators is sometimes negatively related to improved outcomes for students); many important outcomes cannot be measured by tests (in which case, considerable evidence for presumption of improvement should be developed); tests often do not measure the results of new teaching methodologies (then tests with clear criteria should be developed and justified which do measure the results); large-scale testing and measurement fail to capture the differences among individual teachers (the objective is to measure outcomes among students not differences among teachers).

Improvement should meet a second requirement. A change in student outcomes does not necessarily denote improvement. Negative changes, for example, reduced competence in the basic skills and lower levels of physical fitness, are not improvement even when they are accompanied by other positive changes. Improvement should mean that the positive changes outweigh the negative.

No attempt is made here to detail a philosophy behind educational improvement, as the purpose of this chapter is to discuss how policies for improvement can be developed. Nevertheless, the difficulty of the task is daunting. Improvement is not what anyone happens to say it is. Words do not mean whatever anyone using them says they mean.

We cannot even fall back on the idea that improvement necessarily relates to stated educational goals. Many jurisdictions do not have stated goals. Lists of stated goals vary greatly in quality and utility. Some were developed in a moment of enthusiasm and lie forgotten. Some, like the Province of Ontario's, were developed by educators without the benefit of public discussion and are seriously lacking in quality and utility. For example, Ontario's omit important goals (namely, acquisition of a second language, pursuit of the disciplines of knowledge) that are actually clearly reflected in legitimate and compulsory courses, notably the sciences. And they are of little practical use because most are vague and ambiguous (Ministry of Education 1980 pp. 4–7).

Even widely quoted and approved goals have their problems. The development of self-concept is one example. There are practical difficulties. First, the term self-concept is variously defined in the literature, sometimes as self-concept of ability (addressing the concept of the individual's own assessment of his or her intelligence), more often as self-esteem or self-respect. Second, it is possible that self-concept (qua self-respect) is mainly a consequence of the achievement of more traditional goals, for example, academic achievement or character development, and not an outcome of specific experiences intended to develop self-concept. More fundamentally, the value of the independent development of self-concept — outside a context of traditional goals of education — is likely to be negative rather than positive. Conceitedness, selfishness, and putting a higher value on one's own abilities than on others' are signs of neither virtue nor maturity. Thus a school improvement project based on raising self-concept may, if successfully implemented, have a negative impact. Desirable self-respect comes from an understanding of one's strengths and weaknesses, an appreciation of one's virtues and one's failings, and above all from the leading of a good life.

School improvement should be based on the strengths of our cultural inheritance. We should be trying to do better what is most fundamental to our nature. Without elaborating the philosophical and sociological thought lying behind the conclusions that follow, I note that it is drawn from Durkheim (1961), Shils (1981), Bloom (1987), and, particularly, MacIntyre (1981).

Education has numerous purposes but at its centre lies a search for truth and the good; it seeks to move us individually and collectively toward good lives in an ideal society. Fact and value are ultimately indivisible when truth and good merge. The truth of good outweighs infinitely the truth of a billion, trivial facts. School improvement projects should be concerned with one or more of the following goals:

- the development of good character — exemplified by truth, justice, courage, friendship, compassion;
- the development of the basic skills;
- the pursuit of truth through the disciplines of knowledge, including the exploration of languages and literature;
- the development of aesthetic appreciation and aesthetic expression;
- the development of physical fitness;
- the development of good citizenship — punctuality, reliability, industriousness, good manners;
- the development of the spirit, whereby good character transcends virtue and individuals accept personal responsibility within larger communities;
- the development of appropriate habits, attitudes, and knowledge for everyday life in our society;
- the development of individuals so they may continue formal education or become productive members of society.

Unsurprisingly, those goals are a restatement of traditional and conventional goals of education. Even if they appear obvious, it is important to keep before us a clear idea of what we should be about when we devote resources to alleged improvement schemes.

The first criterion a school improvement project should meet is that of moral worth, and the test of that is its compatibility with a set of goals such as the one set out above. The second criterion is qualitative and quantitative evidence of success. If the project is to be widely adopted, there must already be in existence compelling evidence that it will indeed bring about the desired outcomes in students. If it is to be conducted experimentally, then evidence of possible change must be collected quickly and continuously to ensure that harm does not exceed any likely benefit.

Policy for the Implementation of Improvement

Once these two criteria have been satisfied the problem of appropriate policy development for implementation remains. The mainstream approach to implementation is likely to have, at best, only occasional success in terms of worthwhile criteria, which is probably one reason why worthless criteria are so frequently used. It is not unknown for teachers to be resentful of changes clearly intended to bring about measurable differences in students. Welsh (1986) is not unusual in reacting negatively to "words and phrases . . . better suited to a directive from a factory manager" (p. 178). The memorandum in question came from an ex-principal for whom Welsh and his colleagues had had respect; but, now that he is a senior administrator trying to change their practices and their philosophy, the conclusion is, "Tony's gone over to the other side" (p. 178). The simple fact is that, as Welsh candidly states, he and his colleagues do not give a very high priority to the improvement of academic achievement.

If the proposal for change comes "top down," it may be dismissed as being inappropriate for local conditions. In the words of the mainstream implementors, there would be no sense of "ownership." Of course there is no possibility of a sense of ownership when the effectiveness ideas have been clearly developed and outlined in the literature for a number of years. And it is not an ethical solution to try and manipulate teachers into believing the ideas are really their own creation.

The alternative is euphemistically known as "grass-roots" change, where implementation and development are left to the individual school. I have already noted that this approach typically leads to the transformation of the idea and to low levels of effectiveness, at least in terms of the original criteria. Instead of high expectations, there may be expectations related to the individual circumstances of each child; instead of regular monitoring of achievement, there may be informal, individualized assessment of progress by the teacher; instead of consistent, universalistic discipline, there may be expectations of behavior in accordance with the norms appropriate for children of different backgrounds interpreted by different teachers; instead of emphasis on direct instruction of sequential skills, there may be encouragement and support for every child so that he or she may generate a high enough self-image to embark on academic endeavor; and instead of community involvement, there may be public relations designed to put what the school is already doing in a favorable light. Many readers, depending on their own values, may well prefer the hypothetical alternatives to the prescriptions for school improvement derived from the school effectiveness literature; the point is that teachers' values and interests may radically change the nature of the implementation program.

It will be useful to divide policy development for implementation into two component parts: first, broader administrative policies about criteria and strategy and, second, precise steps to be taken once the grand strategy has been determined. Often, school districts move directly to the less important second component, having given little thought to precisely what constitutes the improvement, how it will be measured, and what general approach makes the best sense.

Questions to be addressed as part of the first component are: To what extent is the improvement project to be imposed? Are schools to be left entirely or largely to develop and implement their own plans to meet the centrally established objectives? Are sites for the project to be chosen randomly, administratively, or by self-selection? How exactly is improvement to be assessed? Will the criteria vary from school to school? Will the results be public or private? If private, who will see them? Once schools are involved, will participation be compulsory for all or for specific groups of teachers? The second component, relating to precise methodologies for use in implementation, becomes less important, sometimes even redundant, once the more strategic questions have been addressed.

There can be no simple formula to answer those strategic questions in all substantive areas in all political circumstances. However, one issue is of fundamental importance. Fullan emphasizes the importance of "ownership" of the change. I suspect he misinterprets or overinterprets the evidence on that point. What is very often required for effective change of teachers' behavior and beliefs within the classroom is a new or revived commitment; a feeling of ownership is one but only one source of commitment. The pragmatic advantage to researchers of conceptualizing the idea as "ownership" is that it permits change agents to manipulate teachers into believing the idea is theirs. Developing commitment from a wide range of teachers is a forbidding prospect. If the manipulative approach is ruled out on ethical grounds, we are left with the crucial problem of how commitment can be developed. As Welsh has illustrated all too clearly, some teachers are far from being committed to the likely substance of effective school reforms: basic skills, academic achievement, unambiguous character education, and so on.

If one were to reduce the school effectiveness findings to one phrase it would be the centrality of school climate. Effective schools are those which have high expectations (about achievement, about character, about behavior, about all the school's goals). Now one could try to implement this central idea by so ordering, persuading, or manipulating teachers that every day they chant the mantra, "We expect all pupils to work hard, behave well, and become virtuous." The likelihood of that practice being effective would appear to be close to zero. If the mantra were chanted with sarcasm, humor, innuendo, irony, or in a tired monotone, a negative effect would be unsurprising. One should not underestimate the ability of the intelligent and the educated to ridicule virtue, a property which is after all as accessible to the humblest peasant as to the world-renowned expert. I have heard professional educators read the section of the Ontario *Education Act* on the inculcation of virtue to a group of teachers for humorous effect. Indeed, the only times I have heard reference being made to that section in public addresses have been for humorous effect.

If commitment is a necessary but insufficient condition of success, a rapid movement from a broad approval at the state or provincial level to in-school implementation is unlikely to be successful. Success will be most achievable in those situations (i) in which educators are already committed to the school effectiveness goals but are not using the best approaches, perhaps because they do not know them, perhaps because their professional environment discourages them, and (ii) in which educators have an incoherent or a lapsed set of professional goals and can be persuaded that the school effectiveness goals are the right ones. I cannot comment on how widespread those two situations are. However, I do know many situations in which educators are committed to alternative goals (for example, individual development, freedom of choice for pupils, improvement of self-concept) or are committed to instructional methodologies that are inimical to school effectiveness reforms (individualized instruction, heterogeneous grouping for the teaching of skills, acceptance of the child's "own" rate of progress, the teacher's monopoly on assessment of academic progress).

It is difficult then to see how a strategy can or should be developed for implementing school improvement plans in schools where many or most teachers are philosophically opposed. In areas where such schools exist, it would seem wise to implement programs only in those schools that are receptive, ensuring at the same time that there is regular monitoring of progress in all schools. With open enrolment, parents and students will vote with their feet. Alternative schools that work well on their own terms and receive strong public support will continue to flourish. But parents will have the opportunity to send their children to schools dedicated to school effectiveness. If I am right in supposing that what most parents want for their children is effective schooling, as defined in this chapter, the pattern of education in the district will gradually change. If school effectiveness reforms are forced on all schools, the resultant failure will be attributed to the poverty of the effectiveness ideas rather than to the lack of commitment on the part of those who reluctantly went through the motions of chanting mantras.

The specific administrative and instructional methodologies associated with the good outcomes of effective schools are precisely those one would logically expect. If we want young people with a strong, straightforward moral code and of high intellectual standing, then it makes sense that we put them in an environment characterized by clear expectations, regular checking of behavior, regular monitoring of achievement, and so on. In-service should be provided in a number of areas. Some teachers have never learned how to teach directly for mastery. Some have never learned to test regularly to see what progress has been made. Many principals have little or no experience in organizing schools based on a competence model. The idea that all student work, regardless of quality, should be praised and publicly shown is all too widespread. However, in general, it will be more useful if teachers choose the in-service they feel they need as distinct from being drafted into it. To impose a single instructional and organizational methodology on all teachers and ad-

ministrators would be to repeat the errors of the child-centred learning movement, admittedly on a much stronger research base.

Two basic principles of implementation appear to be somewhat
inconsistent with one another. Principals and teachers are professionals, who ought to have discretion in their daily professional
behavior. (Independent schools with small or non-existent
bureaucracies outside the school seem to be no less successful than
public schools with enormous bureaucracies.) On the other hand,
successful implementation seems to require a degree of fidelity to
the original idea. Those two principles can best be met in the following ways: (i) ensure there is strong, committed leadership; if the principal does not provide it, ensure it is provided in some other way,
from inside or outside the school; (ii) ensure the program objectives
are crystal clear and ensure there is full knowledge by all concerned in advance of how the objectives will be evaluated; (iii) provide
strong informal as well as formal support for the improvement project without trying to control or monitor it beyond the publicly an-
nounced methods of evaluation.

The approach briefly outlined here is more feasible in densely
populated urban and suburban regions than in rural areas where
parents realistically have little choice of school or teacher. But lucki-
ly the problems are much more serious in urban and suburban areas.
It is in those latter areas that educators' collective clout is strongest,
where the influence of parents on patterns of schooling is least, and
where school effectiveness practices are most likely to be absent.
Even in rural areas I would advocate implementing school effectiveness projects on a school by school or even classroom by classroom
basis, wherever possible leaving it to the schools themselves to decide
to adopt the improvement practices. In rural areas, where consensus is stronger, perhaps all will choose to come in.

Consideration should be given in advance to how the evaluation
of school improvement efforts will be judged. There is sometimes
an assumption that school improvement projects are like a horse
race. They begin at a particular moment and the amount of improvement is measured over a set period. That approach fails to take into account the very differing starting points of schools. In New Jersey,
some of the schools in the project have been improving steadily for
several years, others have not. The following scenario is not unlikely.
School A is doing a very good job with a very difficult population
of students. Its achievement results are poor compared with all other
schools but good compared with other schools with comparable
populations. Over the project period School A manages to effect very
little or no further improvement. School B is doing a rather poor
job in terms of its population, but gets better overall results than
School A. It shows steady improvement during the improvement project. Great sensitivity is required to interpret these results in a way
that is not grossly unfair to School A — which is still at the end
of the project more effective than School B.

Conclusion

It will be evident that I expect many school improvement projects to fail, because the ideas are wrong, because the research is incomplete, and because it is often unethical and ineffective to try and force radical change on professional educators. Philosophical commitment to an alternative set of values is as or more important to educators than self-interest when they oppose school effectiveness ideas. The combination of both philosophical opposition to school effectiveness and self-interest is powerful.

A philosophical and moral disagreement lies at the heart of the current crisis in education. There is widespread uncertainty about the purposes of public education. I have addressed that disagreement only indirectly, but, just as it is myopic for school change agents to ignore the ethical and moral implications of their work, academic commentators on school effectiveness will be blind indeed not to confront the evident lack of educational consensus in modern society. Compounding this overall lack of consensus is the fact that educators, much more than the general public, are unsympathetic to both the goals and the methods required to improve school effectiveness. Evidence of this dichotomy is dramatically provided by a recent educational Gallup Poll carried out in British Columbia (Provincial School Review Committee 1985). Respondents were divided into separate groups of educational professionals and the general public. The former were much less in favor of clear, traditional standards, standardized testing, and provincewide curriculum and much more favorable to progressive change, varied curricula, and varied standards. This example is extreme, but similar splits between educators and the public can be found in Ontario and Great Britain.

Top-down enforcement of school effectiveness ideas, imposed by state, provincial, or school district fiat, is unlikely to be very effective in unsympathetic environments, not only because top-down change is unfashionable (except where the change is something educators want) but because large numbers of teachers will resist the changes for sincerely held, philosophical as well as self-serving reasons. Many educators simply do not believe that virtue and the three Rs are the most important goals of elementary education; and many more do not like to be held accountable for their students' progress in these areas. Grass-roots change is likely to be ineffective because those same educators are unlikely to develop plans to implement proposals they heartily dislike. Either little change will take effect or the substance of the change will be radically altered.

School effectiveness cannot be effectively marketed like a VCR, like peace and AIDS education, or like a two hundred schoolday year. It does not meet an expressed desire of educators; it is not a trendy, new idea with which the alert educator can be first on the block; and it is not a regulatory change.

There is no simple answer, but the following are practical and ethical avenues:

• Publicize the research findings and persuade educators to adopt both the goals and the effectiveness approaches. Many teachers will like to do the right thing and will gladly adopt effective approaches if they understand the rewards that both students and they themselves will reap.

• Encourage voluntary school improvement projects where there is genuine commitment. Special support in terms of student and program evaluation and visits to improved and effective schools and appropriate conferences will reward and reinforce those educators who are attempting to make the positive changes.

• Develop a system for the regular monitoring of achievement and other educational outcomes in all schools. Many ineffective schools have staffs and principals totally oblivious to their ineffectiveness. As long as they can conceal their limitations, even from themselves, there is no incentive for them to review their ineffective practices and dubious philosophies.

• Permit genuine open enrolment. Many school systems allow limited open enrolment, the limit being administrative convenience. The unpopular school is guaranteed survival and the popular school has its enrolment capped. Genuine open enrolment would mean the possible demise of some schools and subsequent reopening under new management. Popular schools might take over unpopular schools as an alternative to the latter's closure. For open enrolment to work well, full disclosure of school performance indices, with respect to achievement and behavior in relation to student intake, must be public. Differences in school goals should also be made public.

• Encourage competition among schools by permitting alternative approaches to education within the system. If the schools respond to public demand, most will strive for effective school goals. Few parents will knowingly choose schools which are publicly disclosed to be uninterested in their poor standards of behavior and their poor academic achievement.

• Move to reward teachers and administrators financially for all-round excellence in education. This does not necessarily mean a simple merit pay plan. A differentiated staffing model has promise providing the criteria for promotion are very clearly established in terms of changes brought about in learners. Currently, teachers are rewarded by promotion to administrative ranks for compliance with administrators' likes and whims rather than for producing educational excellence in the school.

• Be open and accountable to the public. Ensure that research findings and school performance indices are readily available, but ensure that the school composition is taken into account.

Provide forums whereby public demand can be clearly voiced and channelled.

There have always been and always will be some schools that are more effective than others, just as some teachers are more effective than others. Over the last twenty years, however, the evidence has accumulated to suggest that the more effective schools tend to have certain characteristics in common. There are no great technical or financial problems in implementing effective school strategies and the public is generally supportive.

Superficially, then, there would appear to be no problem. And indeed there would appear to be countries, such as Japan and Singapore, where most schools are effective, in basic, academic terms. Better utilization of "implementation" ideas is not the main answer. It is not that we do not know *what* to do and not that we do not know *how*. The problem is one of *will*. Some educators genuinely believe that school effectiveness means adopting the metaphor of the industrial enterprise. They do not believe that raising academic standards is particularly important. Or they do not realize that their standards could readily be raised. Many educators are not interested in inculcating virtue, even claiming that it would be unethical. They see school effectiveness as a bandwagon, and one on which they have no desire to climb. Empirical evidence, persuasion, and even direction will have little effect on such people. They are often uninterested in empirical data, not susceptible to persuasion, and they remain secure behind the school or classroom door.

The mass implementation of school effectiveness ideas requires open, public accountability for results, coupled with some freedom of choice of school. Given the opportunity, most parents, rich and poor, will choose schools which emphasize good character and high levels of intellectual skills. For those who don't? Well, there is no shortage of schools for them. The task for policymakers is to make the opportunities for children to attend effective schools genuinely available to all. But do policymakers want to be accountable?

References

Barrow R 1984 *Giving Teaching Back to Teachers*. Wheatsheaf Books, Brighton, Sussex

Bloom A 1987 *The Closing of the American Mind*. Simon and Schuster, New York

Bowles S, Gintis H 1976 *Schooling in Capitalist America*. Basic Books, New York

Bronfenbrenner U 1970 *Two Worlds of Childhood: U.S. and USSR*. Russell Sage, New York

Brookover W B, Lezotte L W 1979 Changes in school characteristics coincident with changes in student achievement. Michigan State University, College of Urban Development, East Lansing, Michigan

Coleman J S 1961 *The Adolescent Society.* Free Press, New York

Coleman J S et al. 1966 *Equality of Educational Opportunity.* U.S. Department of Health, Education, and Welfare, Washington, DC

Coleman J S, Hoffer T 1987 *Public and Private Schools.* Basic Books, New York

Coleman J S, Hoffer T, Kilgore S 1982 *High School Achievement.* Basic Books, New York

Counts G S 1963 Dare the school build a new social order? In: Gross R (ed.) *The Teacher and the Taught.* Dell Publishing, New York

Crandall D P, Loucks S F 1983 *The Study of Dissemination Efforts Supporting School Improvement,* Vol. X: *A Roadmap for School Improvement.* The Network, Andover, Massachusetts

Delamont S 1980 *Sex Roles and the School.* Methuen, London

Durkheim E 1961 *Moral Education.* Free Press, New York

Fullan M 1982 *The Meaning of Educational Change.* OISE Press, Toronto

Giroux H A, McLaren P 1986 Teacher education and the politics of engagement: The case for democratic schooling. *Harvard Educational Review* 56(3): 213–238

Government of Ontario 1981 *Education Act.* Queen's Printer for Ontario, Toronto

Hargreaves D H 1967 *Social Relations in a Secondary School.* Routledge and Kegan Paul, London

Hollingshead A de B 1949 *Elmtown's Youth.* John Wiley, New York

Holmes M 1971 A critique of neo-progressive trends in Canadian education. *Interchange* 2(3): 63–80

Holmes M 1979 *Instructional Time and Academic Achievement.* Ministry of Education, Toronto

Holmes M 1988 The principal's leadership and school effectiveness: Implications of the New Jersey demonstration schools project. OISE, Toronto

Holmes M, Wynne E A 1989 *Making the School an Effective Community: Belief, Practice and Theory in School Administration.* Falmer Press, Sussex, England

Holmes M in press Curriculum as ethics. In: Husén T, Postlethwaite N (eds.) Supplement to *The International Encyclopedia of Education.* Pergamon, Oxford

Howe H II 1983 Education moves to centre stage: An overview of recent studies. *Phi Delta Kappan* 65(3): 167–172

Huberman A M, Miles M B 1984 *Innovation Up Close: How School Improvement Works.* Plenum Press, New York

Husén T (ed.) 1967 *International Studies of Achievement in Mathematics: A Comparison of Twelve Countries,* Vols. I and II. John Wiley, New York

Husén T 1975 Implications of the IEA findings for the philosophy of comprehensive education. In: Purves A L, Levine D U (eds.) *Educational Policy and Instructional Assessment.* McCutchan, Berkeley, California

Hutchins R M 1952 *Some Questions About Education in North America.* University of Toronto Press, Toronto

Jackson B, Marsden D 1962 *Education and the Working Class.* Routledge and Kegan Paul, London

Karweit N 1978 The organization of time in schools: Time scales and learning. Centre for Social Organization of Schools, Johns Hopkins University, Baltimore

Kirst M W, Meister G R 1985 Turbulence in American secondary schools: What reforms last? *Curriculum Inquiry* 15(2): 169–186

Leithwood K A, Holmes M, Montgomery D J 1979 *Helping Schools Change.* OISE Press, Toronto

McDill E L, Rigsby L C 1973 *The Academic Climate of Schools.* Johns Hopkins University Press, Baltimore

MacIntyre A 1981 *After Virtue.* University of Notre Dame Press, Notre Dame, Indiana

Ministry of Education 1980 *Issues and Directions.* Ministry of Education, Toronto

Neatby H 1954 *So Little for the Mind.* Clarke, Irwin, Toronto

Peshkin A 1986 *God's Choice.* University of Chicago Press, Chicago

Provincial School Review Committee 1985 *Let's Talk About Schools,* Vol. III: *Gallup Survey.* Ministry of Education, Victoria, British Columbia

Purkey S C, Smith M S 1983 Effective schools — A review. *Elementary School Journal* 83: 427–452

Ramsay P, Sneddon D, Grenfell J, Ford I 1983 Successful and unsuccessful schools: A study in southern Auckland. *Australia and New Zealand Journal of Sociology* 19(2): 272–304

Rosenholtz S 1985 Effective schools: Interpreting the evidence. *American Journal of Education* 93(3): 353–388

Rutter M, Maughan B, Mortimore P, Ouston J 1979 *Fifteen Thousand Hours.* Open Books, London

Seeley J R, Sim R A, Loosley E W 1956 *Crestwood Heights: A Study of the Culture of Suburban Life.* University of Toronto Press, Toronto

Shils E 1981 *Tradition.* University of Chicago Press, Chicago

Sociology of Education. 1982 55(2/3)

Stinchcombe A L 1964 *Rebellion in a High School.* Quadrangle Books, Chicago

Welsh P 1986 *Tales Out of School.* Viking, New York

Wiley D E 1976 Another hour, another day: Quantity of schooling, a potent path for policy. In: Sewell W H, Hauser R M, Featherman D L (eds.) *Schooling and Achievement in American Society.* Academic Press, New York

Wynne E A 1980 *Looking at Schools: Good, Bad, and Indifferent.* Lexington Books, Lexington, Massachusetts

2/Lessons for Administrators from Large-scale Assessments of Teaching and Learning

Les McLean

In this application of findings of the Second International Mathematics Study, McLean argues that what most Canadians and Americans are doing in mathematics education is fundamentally wrong. Questions to consider include: Is it possible for the West to change its highly individualized ways? How can we be sure what explains the Japanese success story? Should we get rid of the spiral curriculum?

> Canada's future citizens and decison-makers are in school today. When they leave, they will face a world made daily more complex by rapid scientific and technological developments. To cope with such a world, Canadians must be literate not only in the traditional basics of language and mathematics, but also in the new basics of contemporary society: science and technology.
>
> Science Council of Canada 1984

Few would disagree with the Science Council's assertion. To be literate today means more than being able to read and write; knowledge and skills in mathematics and science are also needed. Schools are required to provide the opportunity for everyone to acquire this basic literacy, and they are also expected to motivate students to take advantage of it. For the most part here in Canada, we let teachers and administrators get on with that job, using report cards and teacher reports to tell us how it is going. Standardized tests are sometimes given and the results kept on file. Five provinces give some form of graduation examination and count the results as 50 percent of every student's final mark, but, with these few exceptions, teachers' evaluations of student achievement are what count.

In other countries, national tests and examinations are more frequent for students going on to higher education.

Large-scale assessments of student achievement are carried out in order to monitor the general level of achievement across a school district, a province or state, or an entire country. They are different from student testing programs in that only group averages are obtained. In order to achieve wide curriculum coverage, different students answer different sets of questions, and the results are then averaged over curriculum topics for classrooms and schools. A provincewide assessment of intermediate divison English and mathematics was carried out in Ontario in 1981, using the Ontario Assessment Instrument Pools (OAIP) (McLean 1982). A similar study of français was carried out in 1984 (Joly and Braban 1987).

The United Nations defines *literacy* as completion of at least eight years of schooling; by that definition, 97 percent of Canadians are literate. The Science Council of Canada's (1984) national study found that "science is rarely taught adequately (*if at all*) in elementary schools across the country" (p. 10, emphasis added). Assessments of senior chemistry and physics in Ontario in 1983–84 gave a somewhat better report on the amount of science taught (McLean 1987a, 1987b). However, these surveys found a dependence on textbooks presenting an image of science as "overly standardized and simplified in order to present a smooth road to scientific knowledge" (Science Council of Canada 1984 p. 37). Canada participated in the Second International Science Study but, as I write, only the curriculum analysis has been published (Connelly, Crocker and Kass 1985).

Large-scale assessment is big business in the U.S., where statewide assessments are routine and where the National Assessment of Educational Progress (NAEP) has conducted surveys of achievement for almost 20 years. Two recent reports covered the 1984 assessment of writing and a comparison of reading achievement over a 15-year period (NAEP 1985, 1986). The Assessment of Performance Unit (APU) has been monitoring school achievement in England, Wales, and Northern Ireland for almost as long, and several independent appraisals have appeared (Cambridge Institute of Education 1985; Gipps and Goldstein 1983; Thornton 1986). In short, several countries are now in the process of digesting and interpreting the results of studies carried out over many years. There is interest in the implications for teaching and learning. The search is on for pedagogical relevance (McLean in press).

The Canadian provinces of British Columbia and Ontario participated with over twenty countries in the Second International Mathematics Study (SIMS), a comprehensive survey of mathematics education that looked at curriculum, textbooks, teaching methods, teachers, students, and student achievement. Figure 2:1 shows the study design, a model containing three curricula — the one we *intend* to teach, the one actually taught (the *implemented curriculum*), and the one students learn (the *attained curriculum*). Two groups of students and teachers were involved, one in grade 8 and one in grades 12 and 13. A report on Ontario and international results has been published (McLean, Wolfe and Wahlstrom 1987), and the full international reports will soon appear in three volumes.

Figure 2:1
Components of the Design of the Second International Mathematics Study (SIMS)

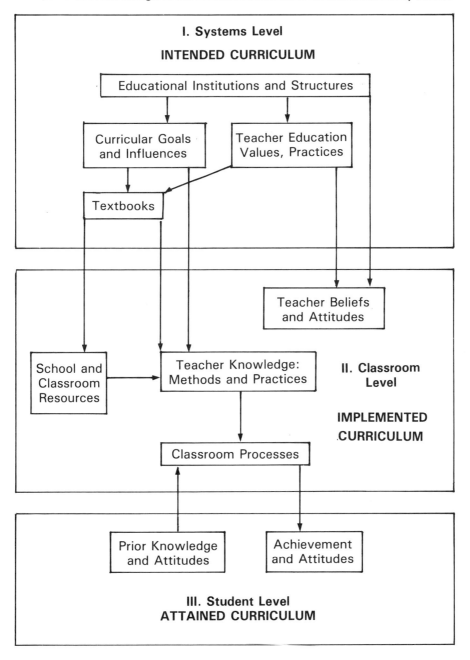

Because of its wide scope and thorough analysis, I shall focus on SIMS, referring to other assessments as appropriate.[1] The search for implications will also extend to the reports from several Ontario school boards where the SIMS survey has been repeated. A number of implications have been drawn regarding the way time is allocated and used in schools, and this will be the first topic addressed.

Organization and Use of Time

How time is used can be more important than the total time allocated to teaching and learning. This message will not come as a surprise to most educators, but the evidence may lead them to organize schools differently. Here are brief references to some findings:

> • At the grade 8 level, three-quarters of the countries showing better mathematics achievement than Ontario allocated less time to the teaching of mathematics than Ontario does. Of those countries with poorer achievement, two-thirds allocated more time than Ontario.

> • At the grade 13 level, Ontario schools organized on a semester system showed lower achievement than schools organized on full-year plans. School characteristics such as social class measures failed to account for the difference.

> • At the grade 1 and grade 5 levels, high achievement was associated with intensive focus on a few topics and low achievement with brief attention to many topics, at least in China, Japan, and the U.S.

The results from grade 1 and grade 5 are just as complex as in the higher grades. On average, teachers spent more time teaching mathematics in Chinese and Japanese classrooms, but the average in the U.S. was dragged down by the 25 percent of the classes where less than 5 percent of the available time was spent teaching mathematics (Stevenson, Lee and Stigler 1986 p. 695). Time on mathematics was estimated from systematic observations at random times over a period of several weeks, so the result is a credible one. I shall concentrate on classes in which significant teaching time is spent on mathematics, attending to organizational and methodological issues.

One implication is that short periods make it difficult to focus and achieve solid understanding, and that very long periods may also make it difficult for teachers to sustain intensity. The international comparisons suggest that "short" be taken as any period less than 40 minutes in length. Few countries organized around very long periods of 80 to 100 minutes. It must be stressed that these results are almost all from mathematics classes, and that there is some evidence from Ontario science assessments that long periods are useful in science. We do not know how the results might apply in language and social studies classrooms, but plausible explanations for the ineffectiveness of short periods seem to apply equally well to them.

Some schools organize around periods as short as 30 minutes, and all schools shorten their periods on some days because of assemblies, sports events, and other special circumstances. The implication for administrators is that they should resist this organization and search for other ways to accommodate special events. The evidence suggests that one good learning period of, say, 50 minutes is markedly superior to two rushed periods of 25. One good period of 40 minutes is likely to be as good or better than two of 25. In other words, when a schedule with 40- to 45-minute periods is disrupted, it may be preferable to schedule half as many classes of regular or longer length. The classes not held can be balanced over the year or negotiated with teachers according to the work under way at the time. I shall return later to the effect on teachers.

Classes in semestered schools are normally organized in long periods, and various explanations have been offered by educators for the lower achievement that has been observed (Raphael, Wahlstrom and McLean 1986). The objective evidence shows that on average less content is covered in semestered classes, but, as mentioned above, that could be an advantage if it were associated with greater intensity. Anecdotal reports suggest, however, that the reverse is true, that semestered classes tend to take up one topic in a long period and then spend class time on homework. There are certainly exceptions, but it would seem that many teachers are not able to make as good use of long periods as they do of somewhat shorter ones. Semestered classes are very popular with students, but the popularity seems to be due more to the flexibility they offer (for early graduation and part-time jobs) than to the mathematics learned. Students in full-year classes have attitudes to mathematics that are as positive as those of students in semestered classes.

The time available is no doubt a factor in determining how time is used, but the most powerful influence is the teacher. The international comparisons revealed that instruction is teacher dominated worldwide, North America being no exception (Travers and Westbury 1987). The studies also revealed, however, that instruction was driven overwhelmingly by the textbook and that teachers employed a very narrow range of teaching methods. Where wider ranges of teaching approaches were found, they were associated with higher achievement. There is apparently no one best method for teaching mathematics. Administrators, especially principals, should exercise instructional leadership in encouraging a greater variety of teaching approaches and use of a greater variety of materials.

One approach to teaching mathematics that was *not* supported was the use of small-group instruction. Such instruction is not common outside North America, but, wherever it was reported, it was associated with lower achievement. A number of explanations are possible, given the nature of SIMS, but the consistent pattern should at least caution us not to advocate the method too quickly. Small-group instruction was reported with classes at all ability levels, not just more- or less-able students, and highest achievement was invariably associated with whole-group instruction. Effective small-group instruction may be more difficult to implement, and students simply receive less instruction. Administrators should ensure that experiments with small-group instruction are carefully monitored and evaluated.

Organization and Content of the Curriculum

The surveys of topics and teacher choices in the large-scale studies suggested that at least two aspects of curriculum design deserve attention: enrichment in the middle school and intensity throughout. The international comparisons have been especially useful in showing us where more can be achieved than we now attempt. The concept of intensity is more comprehensive, so it will be discussed first.

Increasing and Maintaining Intensity of Instruction

The first relevant observation is that much of grade 8 instruction in North America is review. This appears to be generally the case throughout the intermediate division in Ontario (grades 7 to 10). Topics introduced in previous years are still being taught in grade 8, and little growth in achievement is attained. Fractions and percentages are examples, along with two- and three-digit multiplication and division. In contrast, substantial growth in achievement is observed where new material, for example, operations with integers, is introduced in grade 8. It would appear that some arithmetic topics are given a little attention each year, with little success. A few years ago, for example, average achievement was only at about the 30 percent level on percentage problems in grade 10 (McLean 1982 p. 138). Somewhere between 25 and 50 percent of teachers reported that they taught this material as new content in grade 8, and virtually all said they reviewed it (McLean, Raphael and Wahlstrom 1986 p. 55).

This tendency to touch a topic and move on before the majority of students have mastered it is common in North America, but not in Japan and in other countries where high achievement is observed. It comes at least in part from a curriculum that includes many topics but does not stress any one. Figure 2:2 is reproduced from a recent American report, *The Underachieving Curriculum* (McKnight et al. 1987 p. 94). The Canadian data in the figure are from British Columbia, but if Ontario's were there they would almost exactly parallel those of the U.S. Japan puts emphasis on algebra, while the Flemish schools in Belgium and schools in France concentrate more on geometry.[2] In other words, there are two forces tending to reduce intensity — the curriculum itself and the pattern of reteaching or review into which teachers have fallen.

Figure 2:2
Representation of the Even Coverage of the Grade 8 Curriculum in the U.S. (very similar to Ontario) and the Greater Focus on Topics in Most Other Countries

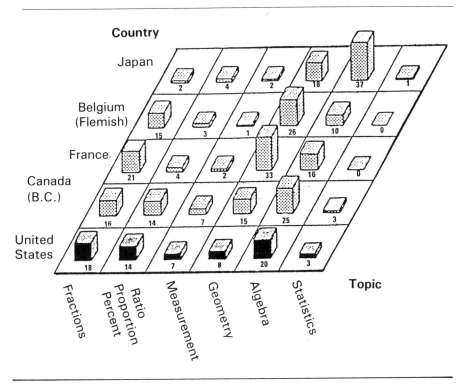

Source: McKnight et al. 1987 p. 94

Dispersal of time over many different topics is not peculiar to mathematics. The Science Council's study of curricula across Canada found a pattern that concerned the researchers:

> Some documents specify as many as 10 different aims for a single science program. Guidelines at the middle and senior years often stipulate a broad range of aims. . . . Can a program enable students to achieve many objectives or can only a few be achieved thoroughly? No guideline document sets out any order of priority of aims. Can one assume therefore that all of the stated aims are equally important? If not, what is the proper balance for many varied aims?
> One way of approaching answers to these difficult questions is to ask: "What practical difference to the day-by-day teaching of science would it make if each one of a ministry's aims were separately dropped?" If the honest answer, in any given instance, is that no difference would result, one may indeed question the function of that particular aim. . . . If there are too many different aims, if they are vague or carelessly stated or if those specified are not perceived by teachers to be attainable, then they will likely be ignored. (Orpwood and Souque 1984 pp. 73–74)

Judging from the evidence of the provincial surveys (McLean 1987a, 1987b) and the international studies (Connelly et al. 1985), the aims are more likely to be taught superficially than ignored. Administrators should encourage teachers to adopt courses of study that sample from the large number of aims in guidelines only those topics that they can teach intensively so that a majority of the students master them. The Science Council's final recommendations make this more difficult by insisting that the historical context be taught and that topics in technology be included, along with an emphasis on Canadian examples, but the general point is valid — pick some topics and teach them thoroughly. Only rarely should topics be introduced and left for another teacher to finish in a subsequent grade.

Enrichment in the Middle School

As noted in the previous section, a finding that has run through the surveys of mathematics education (SIMS in B.C., Ontario, and the U.S.; field trials in grades 7 to 10 in Ontario) is that much of the mathematics instruction in the middle-school years is review. SIMS was able to add the additional information that performance improves very little as a result of this instruction (in grade 8, at least). On the other hand, when new content is introduced and taught intensively, good growth in performance is observed. Figure 2:3 illustrates this pattern in Ontario by a graph that shows three aspects at once — percent correct, percent wrong, and percent omitted, one for each side of the triangle. The lines between pairs of points within the triangle join pretest and posttest and so reveal the amount of growth. The topic is integers, adding and subtracting positive and negative whole numbers (and zero). In other parts of the world, much less time is spent on review, but the students still do well on the items that cover material from previous years. In other words, the content has been learned and retained reasonably well.

Figure 2:4 is the same type of graph for a topic introduced earlier than grade 8 in every country participating in SIMS — common and decimal fractions. Between 80 and 90 percent of Ontario teachers reported that they taught this material in grade 8 (depending on the item); a quarter of those reported that they taught fractions and decimals as new material. Almost 95 percent reported they were "developing the concept" of decimals. There are many aspects of such a topic, of course, and there were only a few items in the SIMS booklets, but the pattern in Figure 2:4 is not encouraging. Little or no growth is the rule, and the level of achievement is not impressive.

The extensive review of numerical methods, and the reports from some teachers that they present the topics as new material, can be attributed somewhat to the curriculum guidelines. The latest guideline for grade 8 suggests eight hours (out of the 120-hour minimum) for "Whole Numbers and Decimals" and seven hours for

Figure 2:3
Amount of Growth in Performance on Items Measuring New Content Taught in Ontario Grade 8 Classrooms

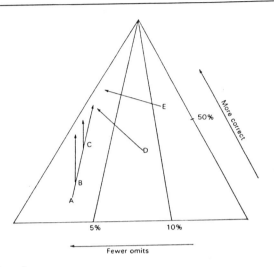

A. $(-2) + (-3) = ?$

B. The air temperature at the foot of the mountain is 31°C. On top of the mountain the temperature is $-7°C$. How much warmer is the air at the foot of the mountain?

C. $(-6) - (-8) = ?$

D. The set of integers less than 5 is represented on one of the number lines shown below. Which one?

E. $-5(6-4) = ?$

Figure 2:4
Amount of Growth in Performance on Items Measuring Content Taught before Grade 8 and Commonly Reviewed in Grade 8 Classrooms in Ontario

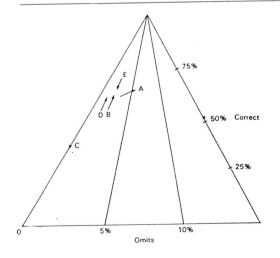

A. $0.40 + 6.38 = ?$

B. $0.004\overline{)24.56}$
In the division above, the correct answer is . . .

C. Which of the following is thirty-seven thousandths?

D. 74.236 rounded to the nearest hundredth is . . .

E. $\boxed{847.36}$ In the number in the box, the digit 6 represents . . .

"Fractions and Decimals." The new topic, "Integers," is allocated seven hours. Teachers choose these patterns in good faith, following common practice and official guidelines. Administrators should discuss the pattern with teachers and encourage them to introduce the new material called for in the guidelines and to make every effort to ensure it is learned in *their* classroom. If numerical methods are to be reviewed, the effort should be intensive, using a variety of methods. Skilful use of calculators should be a teaching goal throughout the intermediate division. The topic is allocated two hours in both grade 7 and grade 8.

Ministry of Education curriculum guidelines still include only a little algebra in grade 8, and teachers offer only a little. Countries similar to Canada teach more algebra, and the students learn it, so this decision might be reconsidered.[3] The implication of these results is that it is better to introduce new material that is learned than to go over and over old material that is still not learned.

Questioning Ability Grouping

Some form of grouping by ability is found in most countries — addressed variously as tracking, streaming, setting, and the like. Officially, separate mathematics programs are not begun in Ontario until grade 9, but evidence from SIMS would suggest that some grouping is happening in grade 8 (McLean et al. 1987 pp. 36–38). In grades 9 and 10, mean achievement differences among the basic, general, and advanced streams are greater than mean differences between grades, but it is also true that there is a large overlap in the achievement differences (McLean 1982). Formal ability grouping at this level has been justified on pedagogical grounds, but problems with general level classes have led some to question it on social and psychological grounds. Findings from SIMS suggest that on balance we must question the value of tracking by ability.

- Countries that succeed in grouping the students by ability have lower average achievement.

- The country with the highest achievement by far, Japan, shows almost no variation among classrooms (no grouping by ability).

- Grouping in many countries is ineffective and inconsistent.

- Where grouping is effective and consistent, the result for many students in the lower-ability classes is a drastic reduction in their opportunity to learn.

In summary, what we have seen is that it is possible to teach mixed-ability classes and obtain very high achievement. It was also documented that less content was presented, that is, there was less opportunity to learn, in lower-ability classes. Often it was new content, the topics intended to be taught as new material, that was omitted. If continued over several years, students in these classes fall farther and farther behind, regardless of how hard they work or how able they might be, particularly when we recall that it is the older material that is usually not learned.

Teachers respond differently to their own perceptions of the ability of their students.[4] A few perceive that they have a lower-ability class and redouble their efforts, while others reduce the amount of material they try to cover. Those that present the new material and maintain the intensity of instruction see satisfactory to excellent improvement, even with lower-ability classes.

There are surely reasons why students will be grouped at some times. Special education regulations may demand special classes under carefully prescribed circumstances — for the very able as well as for the least able. However, the general thrust within special education recently has been to recommend mixed-ability classes as much as possible, and our findings support this direction. In the absence of strong evidence to the contrary, avoid ability grouping and attempt to ensure that all students receive instruction in the prescribed curriculum. Officials should re-examine the rationale for differentiated programs in mathematics in grades 9 to 12. One of the rationales for separate levels of instruction is that teachers find it easier to teach more homogeneous classes. There doesn't appear to have been any careful study of this rationale, but it certainly is plausible.

So how have the Japanese managed to do so well? They have larger classes, each with the full range of abilities (at least the sort of range Ontario would have if the general and advanced streams were mixed), and their achievement is far superior. One answer suggests itself immediately — Japanese teachers have fewer classes per day than do North Americans. The mathematics periods average 48 minutes per day, but a Japanese secondary school teacher has only three or four classes per day (an average of just over 16 periods per five-and-a-half-day week). Japanese teachers spend more time in meetings, but the subjects discussed are different from the typical meeting in North America. Meetings on this side of the Pacific are often devoted mostly to administrative and school policy matters, while on the other side time is spent on the mathematics being taught and on specific instructional problems. North American teachers in the SIMS study said that mathematics was easy to teach, whereas the Japanese teachers said it was difficult and demanding. Teaching large classes of mixed-ability students would be difficult and demanding, but given the time to prepare for such classes (and to mark the homework), teachers can achieve very good results. It would take considerable political will on the part of government and teachers to change organizational patterns to Japanese levels, but some movement in that direction should be considered.

Improving a Good Program — More Intensity for Specialists

Ontario has one of the most ambitious secondary school mathematics programs among the SIMS countries. A high proportion of students continues to take mathematics after the compulsory years, terminating in the three academic courses. Two, and sometimes all three, of these are required for entry into most university programs in mathematics and science. Students taking two or three of the courses made up the Ontario sample of mathematics specialists for SIMS.

Even with this restricted definition of *specialist*, Ontario has one of the highest mathematics retention rates in the world. Among countries with comparable systems (with 13 years of schooling), only Hungary retains more, with Scotland comparable to Ontario. Figure 2:5 shows the precentage of the age group still in school at the end of secondary schooling (as the long bar) and the percentage of those still in school who are specializing in mathematics (as the darkened part of the bar).

Figure 2:5
Bar Charts of Mathematics Specialist Samples (Population B) Compared to Age and Grade Cohort in 10 Countries*

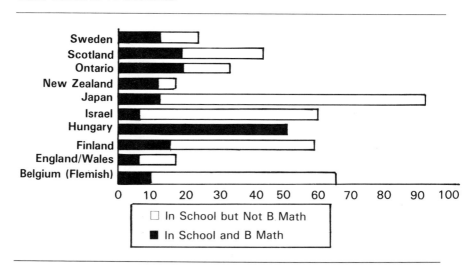

*National school systems differ in so many ways that all comparisons require several qualifiers (see text)

However it is measured, Ontario figures show that a substantial proportion of students stay in school through the university preparation year, and a very high proportion of those take mathematics. For comparison, the percentages of the age cohort in school and also taking mathematics in Ontario and Scotland were 19 and 18, respectively, whereas the comparable figure in England and Israel was 6 percent. Finland was at 15, and Japan and Sweden at 12. In Hungary, 50 percent were in school and *all* were taking mathematics (McLean et al. 1987 p. 10).

Almost all the content of the comprehensive SIMS achievement items was included in the curriculum intended to be taught somewhere in one of the three academic courses. Exceptions were some differential geometry concepts prized by the French and the Belgians. In other words, students taking two or three of the Ontario academic courses almost certainly had an opportunity to learn all the mainstream topics of calculus and algebra and most of the geometry. The opportunity-to-learn (OTL) data did reveal a few topics that received little or no attention (complex numbers almost none, for example, and trigonometry only a little), but these were exceptions. The SIMS items were not only appropriate according to the guidelines, they were relevant to the implemented curriculum.

As was the case at the grade 8 level, Ontario grade 13 achievement results fell right in the middle of participating countries — with Sweden, Belgium, New Zealand, and Israel, and well below England, Japan, and Hong Kong. Students in Finland did very well on the SIMS tests, usually coming third or fourth among the countries. Retention data were not available from Hong Kong, but it is known that they have one of the most selective systems in the world — certainly as low as England (6 percent). Thus, the results from Finland and Japan are especially admirable — high achievement with a relatively high proportion of students continuing to take mathematics.

Each country had to draw some lessons for itself. For example, Ontario might ask, "Why are the results not up there with Finland? Where did our students do less well?" The answer to the "where?" question would be that Ontario students did well on the easier, more straightforward calculus questions but poorly on those questions requiring extension and application of the basic concepts. They fell down on trigonometry items that students in other countries found relatively easy (McLean et al. 1987 p. 30).

A plausible answer to the "why?" question is that teachers report not teaching the trigonometry, and many of them may be giving insufficient attention to applications of the basic concepts. Students did well on algebra questions, reflecting the popularity and strength of the grade 13 algebra course. Some clear lessons emerge — increase the intensity of the advanced courses by (i) more emphasis on applications of the basic calculus concepts, (ii) attention to the trigonometry topics now slighted, and (iii) teaching the complex number topics now neglected.[5]

What happens to the very best students when a high proportion of all students take mathematics? Does it penalize the best when anyone who wants to (and who passes the earlier courses) can take advanced mathematics? We have the examples of Hungary (where everyone takes advanced mathematics), Scotland, Finland, and Ontario to compare with highly selective countries such as England, Israel, and the Flemish region of Belgium. Figure 2:6 shows not only the average for all these countries (the square at the bottom of the lines) but also the average score attained by the top 1 percent (the dark triangles on top) and the top 5 percent (the black circles between the boxes and the triangles) of students in that country.[6]

Figure 2:6
Line Chart of Mean Achievement Levels in Analysis and Estimated Achievements of Top Percents of Age Cohort

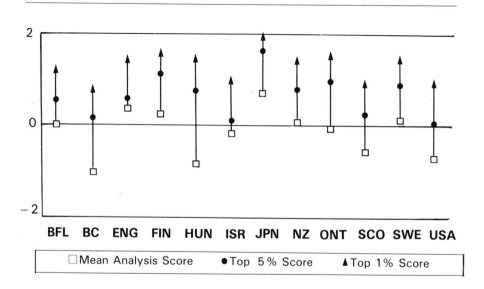

Japan comes out on top again, their top 5 percent scoring higher than the top 1 percent in other countries. This is impressive, since 12 percent take advanced math, but the best students in Ontario and Hungary are as good as or better than the best in England and Belgium. The top students in Israel and Scotland did less well. New Zealand is more selective than Ontario (or Japan), and its students fell just below Ontario's. In short, schools in Japan, Hungary, and Ontario demonstrate that large numbers of students can study advanced mathematics together without penalizing the best among them. Here is evidence in support of a policy that *all* students who demonstrate by their efforts that they want to study at the advanced level should be encouraged to do so.

Monitoring Student Opportunities and Attainments

One of the most striking findings from the large-scale assessments has been the importance and usefulness of measures of growth during a course of study — measuring how much students learn during a course that they didn't know before. School achievement is also related to a host of personal characteristics, so any measure that cannot take these into account is likely to give us a misleading assessment of school effects. Looking only at end-of-year averages can mask a serious failure to learn among able students and cause us to miss impressive progress among the less able or with new learning.

Eight countries tested at the beginning and at the end of the year at the grade 8 level in SIMS, but the rest tested only at the end of the year. Figure 2:7 shows an analysis of learning and forgetting in the countries where a pretest was given. *Learners* were those who answered a question incorrectly on the pretest but answered correctly on the posttest. *Forgetters* did the opposite. The figure tells us that there was relatively little learning in arithmetic (although we know there was lots of reviewing of old content), not much learning in geometry (except for Japan), and quite a bit in algebra in the countries where algebra is taught at that level.

Searching for explanations of school effects is a popular research activity. Speculating about them, or simply declaring what the explanations are, is even more popular. Providing valid explanations from actual measures of achievement is difficult — and rare. New evidence for the difficulty of the quest has come from the attempt to find relationships between school and student characteristics and student achievement measures in SIMS, both between and within countries. There is an embarrassment of riches in both achievement and status variables, but the pretest turned out to play a dominant role.

After an elaborate series of statistical analyses carried out only on posttest results (where data are available from twenty countries), an interesting and complex pattern of relationships began to emerge. The pattern varied by country and topic; no simple summary was possible. One further analysis was then done, in only one country (because of the complexity of the analysis). The data from New Zealand were reanalyzed by adding a single extra variable — the pretest. Here is what the data analysts wrote:

> The effect was massive, at least with respect to the variables measured at the individual student level [where most of the effects were found]. All of the variables found significant in the previously described analyses were not significant in the reanalyses except for gender. Also no variables previously not found to be significant emerged as significant in the reanalysis; in effect the only variables to be consistently significant were the pretest and gender. (Schmidt and Kifer in press)

The analysts go on to report that after taking account of pretest scores, girls had outperformed boys during the grade 8 year. Not only were the previous relationships all erased, but a new finding

Figure 2:7
Double Bar Charts of Percentage of Forgetters and Learners in Three Content Areas at the Grade 8 Level*

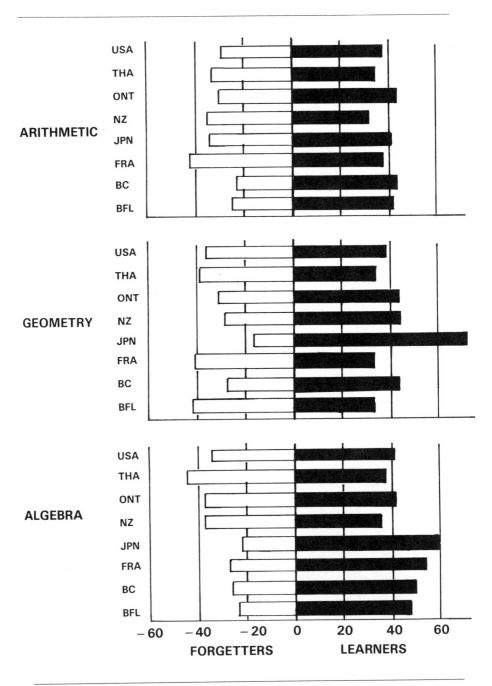

Figures are for: United States, Thailand, Ontario, New Zealand, Japan, France, British Columbia, Belgium (Flemish)

emerged that is contrary to most published research. One has to be cautious with such results. The analysis of the New Zealand data where pretest was included is not necessarily more correct or more valid than the other analyses. The result does tell us that the findings are extremely sensitive to the variables included in the analyses and that no one result should be accepted as definitive. That said, it must be noted that no other variable had such a massive effect as the pretest.

The lesson is that monitoring of school achievement should include measures taken at the beginning of significant periods (such as school years) as well as at the end. Not to do so is to risk missing important and useful findings and to risk being misled by patterns explainable in terms of the entry characteristics of the students. It is worth repeating that testing at a single point, whether beginning, middle, or end, cannot be relied upon to reveal problem areas. Moreover, testing at the beginning and end or testing each year at the same time cannot be relied upon unless there is a way to link the measures to individuals (or perhaps intact groups). This, of course, is why test norms were developed — to supply an intact group with which to compare a set of test scores.

Test norms supplied by publishers are at best an approximate standard because it is not economical to develop norms for each province or system. Obviously, if the norm group is poorly chosen, comparisons can be badly misleading. Test norms reflecting the full range of student achievement in a representative comparison group (good norms, that is) have the same flaw as a single test — they do not allow us to detect growth (or lack of it). Classes that started a year high in achievement relative to others will stay high, whether they learned anything recently or not. Even spectacular progress by high-scoring classes may be missed as they go from the 97th to the 98th percentile. Low classes will still be low, although they might have made real progress, and steady slipping back can easily be missed until it has gone a long way.[7]

As if that were not enough, the large-scale studies have demonstrated conclusively that both the amount and intensity of instruction vary enormously across classes, almost everywhere. Thus, measures of the attained curriculum (student achievement) are much more useful if they can be linked to measures of the implemented curriculum (what teachers actually teach) — opportunity to learn. Figure 2:8 is a display of the range of opportunity to learn across grade 8 classrooms in eight countries. There is a display of these ranges for each of five topics that together cover 95 to 100 percent of the curriculum in those countries. The measure of OTL used to make the figure was derived from teacher responses that told whether they taught the mathematics necessary to answer each of the 156 achievement items common to all these countries.

Look at the ranges for Ontario (third from the left in Figure 2:8). The ranges are shown with boxplots, graphics that show the middle

Figure 2:8
Display of the Large Range of Opportunity to Learn (OTL) across Grade 8 Classrooms in Eight Countries (ranges are shown for five topics that cover the curriculum)

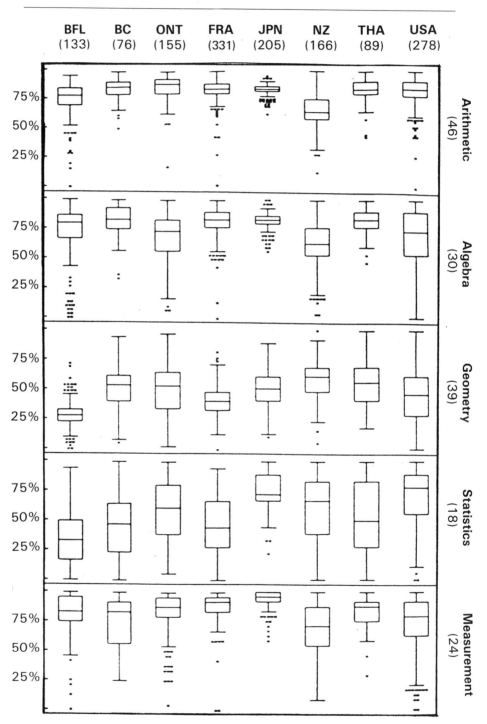

50 percent of the classrooms by a box, with a line across it marking the median (the point above and below which 50 percent of the classes were found). Lines extend above and below the box to the largest and smallest OTL values. Notice the Ontario boxplot for geometry. The largest value was nearly 100 percent (indicating a teacher who taught almost everything) and the smallest was nearly zero (indicating a teacher who taught almost none of the items). The range in the U.S. was from 0 to 100 percent.[8]

Now look at the Ontario boxplot for measurement (bottom of the figure). The box is small and high up, indicating that most of the teachers taught most of the material. There are dots beyond where the line extends downward (below about 50 percent OTL, that is). These represent classes where opportunity to learn was far below the rest — so far that they get a special symbol. Look at the boxes for arithmetic and algebra in Japan. The boxes (half the classes in the whole country) are tiny and the entire range small, reflecting the homogeneity across Japanese classrooms. There was considerable range in OTL responses about geometry items in every country, perhaps reflecting the lack of consensus about what geometry is. The figure is shown to drive home the message that knowledge of achievement is likely to be of little use to educators without knowledge of opportunity to learn.[9]

Summary of Lessons for Administrators

- Resist timetabling that results in periods shorter than 40 minutes, even for special event days (page 35).

- Exercise leadership in encouraging a greater variety of teaching approaches and the use of a greater variety of teaching materials (page 35).

- Ensure that small-group instruction not be used unless it is carefully monitored and evaluated (page 36).

- Encourage teachers to adopt courses of study that include only those topics they can teach intensively so that a majority of students master them (page 38).

- Encourage teachers to introduce new material called for in the guidelines and to make every effort to ensure it is learned in *their* classroom (page 40).

- In the absence of strong evidence to the contrary, avoid ability grouping and attempt to ensure that all students receive instruction in the prescribed curriculum. Officials should reexamine the rationale for separate levels of program in grades 9 to 12 (page 41).

- The amount of learning would likely be increased if teachers had larger, more heterogeneous classes — but fewer of them.

In Japan, teachers have as few as 16 in a five-and-a-half-day
week (page 41).

• Work with department heads to increase the intensity of the
senior mathematics courses (page 43).

• All students who demonstrate by their efforts that they wish
to study advanced mathematics should be given every encouragement to do so (page 44).

• Monitoring of school achievement should include measures
taken at the beginning of significant periods (such as school
years) as well as at the end, and the measures must be linked
at the level of individual students or classroom groups (page 47).

• Knowledge of achievement without knowledge of opportunity to learn will be of little help in improving teaching and learning (page 49).

Notes

1. The author was Research Coordinator of the Ontario study, but the findings and implications reported here have benefited from drafts of the
international reports and from a paper in preparation by Richard Wolfe
(OISE) and Edward Kifer (University of Kentucky), both consultants
to the International Mathematics Committee of SIMS. Their paper is
in part a reaction to a report published in the U.S. (McKnight et al. 1987).

2. A note in passing is that the Japanese conducted their study with
12-year-olds, whereas all other countries followed the international
guideline and included grades in which the majority of students attained
the age of 13 — grade 8 in Ontario and British Columbia. B.C. teaches
more algebra than does Ontario.

3. One reason that the grade 8 level was chosen for inclusion in the study
is that virtually 100 percent of eligible students are still in school in
the countries participating in the study. Algebra is taught and learned
at grade 8 (grade 7 in Japan) in mixed-ability classes all over the world.

4. Their perceptions are rarely based on knowledge of prior student achievement, as the evidence is rarely available in a timely fashion. Few
attempt systematically to gather the evidence themselves, through
careful testing, for example.

5. These lessons are incorporated in the new guidelines for Ontario
academic courses (senior grade 12).

6. Top 1 and 5 percent, that is, on the SIMS achievement items. For this
comparison, the achievement booklets were equated by statistical means
and a score created for analysis, including the mainstream topics of
calculus and functions (Miller and Linn 1985).

7. Good test norms have other uses not discussed here, principally the
opportunity to compare overall levels of achievement with other jurisdictions. Such comparisons have a monitoring function, where the test content is relevant, but they lack the local links to teaching and learning
that are the topic of this section.

8. Students were also asked whether they had been taught the items, and the reports were quite consistent.

9. The large range in OTL is also shown for even more topics in the report on the field trials of OAIP mathematics in grades 7 to 10 (McLean 1982).

References

Cambridge Institute of Education 1985 *New Perspectives on the Mathematics Curriculum: An Independent Appraisal of the Outcomes of APU Mathematics Testing 1978–82*. Department of Education and Science (England and Wales), London

Connelly M, Crocker R, Kass H 1985 *Science Education in Canada*, Vol. 1: *Policies, Practices, Perceptions*. OISE Press, Toronto

Gipps C, Goldstein H 1983 *Monitoring Children: An Evaluation of the Assessment of Performance Unit*. Heinemann Educational Books, London

Joly J-M, Braban M 1985 *Banque d'instruments de mesure de l'Ontario. Le français a l'intermediaire: Administration experimentale de mai 1984*. Ministry of Education, Toronto

McKnight C C, Crosswhite F J, Dossey J A, Kifer E, Swafford J O, Travers K J, Cooney T J 1987 *The Underachieving Curriculum: Assessing U.S. School Mathematics from an International Perspective*. Stipes Publishing, Champaign, Illinois

McLean L 1982 *Report of the 1981 Field Trials in English and Mathematics — Intermediate Division*. Ministry of Education, Toronto

McLean L 1987a *Teaching and Learning Chemistry in Ontario Grade 12 and Grade 13 Classrooms — Teachers, Students, Content, Methods, Attitudes and Achievement*. Ministry of Education, Toronto

McLean L 1987b *Teaching and Learning Physics in Ontario Secondary Schools — Three Classic Wu Li Dances*. Ministry of Education, Toronto

McLean L Pedagogical relevance and large-scale assessment. In: Stake R E (ed.) *Effects of Change in Assessment*. Sage, San Francisco

McLean L, Raphael D, Wahlstrom M 1985 *Intentions and Attainments in the Teaching and Learning of Mathematics: Report on the Second International Mathematics Study in Ontario, Canada*. Ministry of Education, Toronto

McLean L, Wolfe R, Wahlstrom M 1987 *Learning about Teaching from Comparative Studies: Ontario Mathematics in International Perspective*. Ministry of Education, Toronto

Miller M, Linn R 1985 Cross-national achievement with differential retention rates. University of Illinois College of Education, Urbana, Illinois

National Assessment of Educational Progress 1985 *The Reading Report Card: Progress toward Excellence in Our Schools: Trends in Reading over Four National Assessments, 1971–1984*. Educational Testing Service, Princeton, New Jersey

National Assessment of Educational Progress 1986 *The Writing Report Card: Writing Achievement in American Schools*. Educational Testing Service, Princeton, New Jerscy

Orpwood G, Souque J-P 1984 *Science Education in Canadian Schools,* Vol. I: *Introduction and Curriculum Analyses.* Science Council of Canada, Ottawa

Raphael D, Wahlstrom M, McLean L 1986 Debunking the semestering myth: Student mathematics achievement and attitudes in secondary schools. *Canadian Journal of Education* 11(1): 36–52

Schmidt W, Kifer E in press Exploring relationships across countries: A search for patterns. In: Garden R A, Robitaille D F (eds.) *Student Achievement in Twenty-two Countries*, Vol. II. Pergamon Press, Oxford

Science Council of Canada 1984 *Report 36. Science for Every Student — Educating Canadians for Tomorrow's World.* Government Publishing Centre, Ottawa

Stevenson H, Lee S-Y, Stigler J 1986 Mathematics achievement of Chinese, Japanese and American children. *Science* 14: 693–699

Thornton G 1986 *APU Language Testing 1979–1983: An Independent Appraisal of the Findings.* Department of Education and Science (England and Wales), London

Travers K J, Westbury I 1987 *The Second International Mathematics Study,* Vol. I: *Analysis of the International Mathematics Curriculum.* Pergamon Press, Oxford

3/International Lessons for School Effectiveness: The View from the Developing World

Joseph P. Farrell

Farrell argues that some simple strategies which cost little could have major influences in the developing world. In contrast, large-scale, expensive plans in the West are usually doomed to failure. Questions to consider include: Must effective schools be expensive? Why do Westerners emphasize increased or improved human resources so much? Which reforms would be most financially effective in the West?

The Schooling Crisis in the Developing World

One cannot adequately understand or interpret the literature regarding school effectiveness in developing countries without appreciating the state of profound crisis in which the educational systems of most developing nations are enmeshed. Since the great epoch of decolonization in the 1950s and early 1960s, there has been an extraordinary *quantitative* expansion in the availability of formal schooling. From 1960 to 1975 the total number of children in school in developing countries rose by 122 percent. The proportion of age-eligible children who spent at least a few years in primary school increased from 57 percent to 75 percent in the same fifteen years, with corresponding increases at the secondary level (14 percent to 26 percent) and postsecondary level (1.5 percent to 4.4 percent). However, in many nations, particularly many of the largest and poorest nations, total population was growing even more rapidly than the rate of educational expansion. Thus, in the same fifteen-year period the total number of primary-age children not in school grew from 109.2 million to 120.5 million (Farrell 1982 p. 40). Since 1975 these trends have continued, although the annual rates of educational expansion have declined somewhat. Even the most optimistic available enrolment forecasts suggest that by the end of this century no developing region as a whole will have achieved universal primary schooling, although some individual countries, particularly in Latin America, may have come close to providing at least a few years of primary schooling for all of their children. But even these very optimistic projections (far too optimistic in my view) indicate that by the year 2000 there will still be over 100 million 6- to 11-year-old children in the developing world with no exposure at all to formal schooling (Coombs 1985 p. 84). (The term *developing nations* is used here in the loose but conventional sense, referring to the poorer, non-industrial or semi-industrial nations of the world. When statistics are cited, the term refers specifically to those nations classified by the World Bank as "low income" and "middle income.")

This quantitative expansion, even though far from achieving the universal primary schooling which was the dream of many international conferences in the early '60s, has been driven by enormous financial investments by poor nations. For example, some very poor countries spend more than 30 percent of their total national budget on education, and have done so for many years. On average, developing countries spend a higher proportion of their national budgets on education than do rich nations. But in poor nations the total national budget is of course much smaller than in rich nations, which means the total available to education is much less. Moreover, because international financial crises hit poor nations particularly hard, in many such nations the actual national budget, and the educational share, in constant dollars (adjusted for inflation) has been going down. In addition, in rich countries total school enrolments have been declining, while in poor nations, as we have seen, they have been rising significantly. The net effect of all of this is that the educational expenditure *per student* in poor countries, which has always been very low, has been actually declining, while in rich nations it has been rising. The educational expenditure gap between the rich and the poor has been getting worse. During the '70s, the annual per-pupil expenditure in industrialized nations (in constant 1980 US$) increased from $1205 in 1970 to $2343 in 1980. In low income countries the per-pupil expenditure decreased from $109 in 1970 to $75 in 1980 (Fuller 1986 p. 11). A recent survey summarized the situation this way with respect to annual average expenditures per student:

> In 1960 the typical OECD country was able to invest 14 times more per student than did the average poor country; but five years later the gap has risen to 16:1; ten years later it was up to 22:1. Today, 20 years later, it is 50:1. The average (elementary school) student in an OECD country is exposed to 50 times the level of recurrent cost investments as a student at the same grade level in a low-income country. (Heyneman 1985 p. 23)

These comparisons are dramatic enough in themselves, but the consequences in terms of what a North American educational professional would take for granted are even worse. In most poor nations, teachers' salaries (which are themselves very low — in some African nations a village teacher earns the equivalent of US$7.00 per month) and school construction costs absorb most of that minimal per-pupil expenditure, leaving almost nothing for even the most basic instructional materials to support the work of the teacher — chalk, blackboards, books, maps and charts, furniture, and so forth. In 1980, the average expenditure per pupil on instructional materials in industrialized nations was US$92.32. The corresponding figure in low income nations was $1.69. Table 3:1 represents the range in this disparity of instructional resources.

Table 3:1
Annual Per-student Expenditures on Instructional Materials, 1980 — US$

Nation	Per-pupil Expenditure
Bolivia	0.80
Malawi	1.24
Indonesia	2.24
Italy	75.00
Netherlands	220.00
USA	220.00
Sweden	300.00

Source: Heyneman 1985 p. 24

To translate these dollar values into real terms, consider the following. In North America around half of our primary students have at least occasional access to a computer. We take for granted that all students will have complete sets of textbooks for all subjects, plus supplemental instructional materials and well-stocked school libraries. Overhead projectors, slide projectors, tape recorders, television sets (in color no less), and VCRs are common instructional currency. In contrast, in many developing nations thousands of children are in schools where there is not a single textbook, where the teachers themselves have completed but a few years of primary education, where chalk for the blackboard — if there is a blackboard — is in short supply, where even simple furniture is absent. In the Philippines in the late '70s there was an average of one book for every ten children in the primary schools, a figure which through a very large national effort has now been raised to one book for every two students. In one East African country a survey in 1979 found that there was one chair for eight primary students, and only one student in eighty-eight had a desk. Many primary schools in such countries (if there is a school building at all) are lacking in basic safety standards:

> Walls frequently collapse after a rainfall; roofs have holes; wind and storms disrupt classroom activity as a matter of course. The normal classroom is dark and stuffy; students are forced to sit on a bare floor and balance an exercise book on their knees in order to write. (Heyneman 1985 p. 24)

And many students do not even have an exercise book and a pencil; they work with a lump of chalk and a small, hand-held blackboard. Or they learn their letters and numbers by tracing them in the dust with a finger. There may be 50, 60, or more than 80 students in a class with a single, poorly trained teacher. In many developing nations the single most difficult management problem is trying to ensure that teachers actually come to school most days.

One should not conclude that *all* schools in developing nations are as I have just described. But many thousands are, and even more thousands are only minimally better off. And even the "best" schools serving elite populations in capital cities rarely have the kind of instructional materials and equipment, and amenities, which we would consider normal.

We must also bear in mind that even in a rich nation such as Canada there are at least some schools where conditions are little different from much of the developing world. The following advertisement appeared in the Toronto *Globe and Mail*, 16 May 1975.

> TEACHER FOR CHALLENGING AND DIFFICULT POSITION
> The Northwest Territories Department of Education requires one very special teacher for the school year commencing August 18, 1975 for a one-room school in Trout Lake. Trout Lake is a remote isolated community of approximately 55 Slavey Indian people, located one hundred air miles south of Fort Simpson.
> Applicants must be prepared to cope with both extreme personal and professional isolation. Contact with the nearest centre, Fort Simpson, is sporadic at best and limited to unscheduled charter aircraft as weather permits. The community has no utility service whatsoever. Wood for the stove must be hauled approximately 10 miles. The teacher is expected to haul his-her own wood and water. The fifteen children in the school range from a pre-kindergarten to a grade four level. Instruction must necessarily be individualized. The first language of the children is Athabaskan (Slavey dialect). "Furnished" accommodation is provided in a small log cabin heated by a wood stove.

The point to be drawn is that a condition which Canadians regard as most unusual, requiring a "very special teacher," is a perfectly common condition in much of the developing world.

As one might expect, the conditions described above produce levels of learning in developing nations which are typically much lower than in rich nations. There are few systematic cross-national comparisons of student achievement levels, but those which have been undertaken (by the International Association for the Evaluation of Educational Achievement [IEA]) have consistently shown that the scores of children from low- and middle-income countries are lower than those of children of comparable age or grade in industrialized nations. The differences are substantial in some subject areas, small in others, but they are consistent. Moreover, these comparisons involve children at the secondary school level (or, in a few cases, senior primary). In most developing nations students who are neither well-off nor bright do not survive to this level. Most students have long since dropped out of school, often having spent only a year or two in a building called a school.

What all of this means is that when educational officials in a developing nation consider the question that is the theme of this book — "How can we develop policies to make less effective schools more effective?" — they will see it from a perspective very different from that of educational officials in Canada or the U.S. Perhaps most importantly, those educational officials know that they cannot adopt or suggest what is *our* most common approach to improving school effectiveness: throwing money at the schools. If any measure to improve school effectiveness requires additional resources, they will have to be found within the existing educational budget, by spending less on some input or activity which is not clearly related to student learning. A recent review of factors which affect educational achievement in industrialized nations concluded: "If we think of schools as maximizing student achievement, the . . . evidence indicates that schools are *economically* inefficient, because they pay for attributes that are not systematically related to achievement" (Hanushek 1986 p. 1166).

Perhaps because we are rich, we can afford inefficiency, although many are claiming we cannot. However, poor nations cannot possibly afford this level of inefficiency. Thus a kind of discipline is forced upon discussions of school effectiveness in developing nations that is frequently lacking in such discussions in rich nations. Concern must be not simply with effectiveness but with *cost effectiveness* or *efficiency*. This brings me to the meaning I give to "effectiveness" in this chapter.

Toward a Conception of School Effectiveness

The question of what constitutes an "effective" school is subtle and complex. This becomes particularly apparent when one considers the issue in the stark and often desperate context of schooling in the developing world. At the simplest level, student growth or development — learning — is the basic "output" of schooling. The more students "learn" in a given period of time, the more effective is the school.

But the range of learning goals assigned to schools by society is very wide — many of us would say inordinately or impossibly wide. We know how to measure (i.e., "test") only a small portion of the learning goals. For many important learning goals we do not even have an agreed *conceptualization*, which is a necessary precondition to developing a measure of achieved learning. For example, producing "good citizens" is an almost universal goal assigned to schools, and one which is particularly important in many new and fragile nations whose populations are often bitterly divided along class, racial, ethnic, or religious lines. Yet there is little agreement on the meaning of the concept "good citizen," and consequently no effective way to measure it (indeed, the more internally divided a nation, the more difficult it would be to get agreement on the meaning of the concept). Other frequently cited learning goals whose conceptualization is difficult, and whose measurement is therefore problematic, include self-esteem, learning how to learn, advanced thinking skills, problem solving, and decision making. Given the limited range of learning goals which we know effectively how to test, if our schools produced cohorts of effective little test-takers, but did nothing else, or indeed even taught that test taking constitutes learning, would they be judged "effective"? I think not. At least I hope not.

But even if we had testing instruments which accurately and validly assessed student learning on all the multiple goals assigned to schools, we would be faced with another problem in using those test results to evaluate the effectiveness of schools: we would need to assign a kind of agreed social weight to each class of learning outcomes. Is learning to read with comprehension a Hemingway novel more or less important than learning how the digestive system of the human body functions or about the dangers associated with drug use? And how would one fold the learning of civic virtue into this equation?

Finally, even if we were able to solve the problems of conceptualization, measurement, and evaluation noted above, we would still be faced with an even more difficult problem, what economists sometimes refer to as the "value added" problem.

We know that children learn much before they encounter schooling and that children from more privileged backgrounds come to school having learned more (at least of the classes of knowledge valued in schools) than children from less privileged backgrounds. We also know that even while they are undergoing schooling children learn much of pedagogical relevance from their out-of-school experience, and again more privileged children have more school-relevant out-of-school learning resources available to them than do poorer children. The evidence from industrialized nations shows quite clearly that these out-of-school factors (as captured by the socioeconomic status of the student's family) explain more of the variance in students' test scores than do school-related factors themselves. Yet it is to the "value added" to learning by these school-related factors that school effectiveness properly refers, to that portion of learning gains which can reasonably be attributed to the schooling process itself. Within this conception of effectiveness, a school which produces high test scores but deals with learning-privileged children may be less effective than a school which produces lower test scores but serves children with many fewer out-of-school learning resources. The learning gain reasonably attributable to schooling would be less in the former case than in the latter. In a study in which I participated in Chile we found that differences in test scores between elite private schools and the public schools of the nation (which served an economically poorer clientele) were entirely explained by the differences in the students' home backgrounds and that key school-related factors had a greater effect upon the learning of poor primary school children than rich children. In this case the schools serving the poorer children were more "effective" than those serving the most privileged children in the nation, in spite of the higher average test scores in the elite private schools (Schiefelbein and Farrell 1982).

Finally, in poor nations particularly, as I have noted above, one cannot consider the effectiveness of schools, as defined above, in isolation; one must consider the effectiveness of various schooling alternatives in relation to their *cost*. One must be concerned not with school effectiveness per se, but with the *internal efficiency* of schooling, searching for ways to increase the total learning output of the schooling system without increasing total system costs. In the developed world very little work has been done within a cost-effectiveness or internal efficiency framework. With reference to the developing world, because of the educational crisis outlined at the beginning of this chapter, a great deal of attention is being paid to questions of internal efficiency of schooling. A great deal of research has been generated during the past fifteen years that is relevant to the problem. International conferences and seminars have been held within the past year, and more are being planned. The World Bank is preparing a major international policy paper regarding internal efficiency of schooling. It is to the results of this work, and the implications which may be drawn for educational policy and practice, that I now turn.

What the Research Says: The Overall Effect of Schooling in Developing Nations

Starting in the mid-1960s with the now famous "Coleman Report" in the U.S. (Coleman et al. 1966), the Plowden Study in the United Kingdom (Peaker 1971), Jencks's work in the U.S. (Jencks et al. 1972), and the first round of IEA studies, a substantial body of research appeared from developed nations indicating that out-of-school factors had much greater influence on student academic achievements than did school-related variables directly under the control of teachers and educational administrators. While these studies have been criticized on methodological and substantive grounds, the general pattern of results has remained remarkably constant. Indeed, the current concern over school effectiveness can be seen in part as a reaction to these findings.

Beginning in the early 1970s, a series of similar studies began to be reported from developing nations, starting with Chile (Schiefelbein and Farrell 1973), then Uganda (Heyneman 1976), and thereafter many other nations. These results were markedly different from those from rich nations. A survey published in 1982 of the best available set of comparable findings from low- and high-income countries confirmed what some began to conclude in the early 1970s (Heyneman and Loxley 1982). In poor nations, school-related factors are more important than out-of-school factors in explaining differences in student achievement. The relationship is very systematic (indeed, it is one of the most systematic relationships ever uncovered in the comparative study of school systems): the poorer a nation the greater is the influence on academic performance of school quality factors; the richer a nation the greater is the influence of student socioeconomic status.

Several explanations for this consistent pattern have been advanced. I suspect that part of the answer is the move toward a more fully developed, industrial, stratified class system. In poor nations differences in parental occupation or income do not represent differences in language usage in the home, childrearing practices, and provision of out-of-school learning resources to the same degree as in highly stratified industrial societies. I also suspect that in rich nations we are much closer to the limits of perfectibility of the technology of schooling, such that even modest additional gains in achievement require very difficult and costly educational effort. In a nation where most students have no textbooks, the provision of a small set of basic texts for each student (or even a set for every two students) can have dramatic effects upon student achievement. In a nation where schools are already abundantly supplied with books, improvement in learning requires very difficult and costly improvement in the *quality* of the books — even if we knew what kinds of book quality influence student learning. In a nation where most primary teachers have very low levels of formal schooling themselves, and little or no pedagogical training, a modest change or increment in pre-service or in-service training can have significant effects on teacher performance in the classroom and hence on student learning. In a rich nation where almost all primary teachers have university degrees, many have postgraduate degrees, and professional development opportunities are widespread, even small improvements in teacher performance are difficult to achieve and dearly purchased.

There is a double lesson from these comparative data, important and hopeful for educators in both developed and developing nations.

For educators in rich nations the lesson is that when you get near to the best that can be done, without a massive change in the technology and organization of learning producing a system very unlike what we now think of as schooling, even small additional increments in effectiveness of schools will be hard to come by and difficult to identify. In my view this is cause not for despair but for celebration, however frustrating it may be for the educational evaluation or innovation implementation industries.

For educators in the developing world the lesson is that even the very modest improvements in school quality that a poor nation can realistically contemplate have the potential for producing important increases in student learning. For such educators, operating as I have noted within an efficiency rather than an effectiveness framework, the crucial question then becomes: What are the educational "best bets"?

What the Research Says: Factors Which Do and Do Not Influence Achievement

It should first be noted that while the amount of evidence regarding particular schooling characteristics that affect educational achievement in developing countries has been increasing rapidly in recent years, the total amount available is far less than in developed nations. On questions about which there may be hundreds of studies in North America, there may be none, or only a few, from the entire developing world. It is also clear now that research findings from developed nations cannot be automatically transferred to developing nations. But poor nations, being poor, have little money to spend on research. Of the evidence available, some has been financed by local governments but most has been funded by international aid agencies. The available evidence is also spotty. Some questions have received much attention, others little. Some regions and individual nations have produced much more educational research than others. Much of the research that has been produced is not readily accessible. Moreover, the investigations themselves are of several different types. Some are large-scale correlational exercises where tens if not hundreds of separate factors have been thrown into the statistical hopper to see which ones relate best to student achievement. Others are small, carefully controlled experiments. Still others are large-scale evaluations of a particular program or policy within a given nation. Finally, just as we cannot assume that research results from developed nations will apply to developing nations, we also cannot assume that findings from one part of the developing world are generalizable to other parts. The anthropological evidence is now clear that children from different cultures "learn to learn" differently (something which educators in the increasingly heterogeneous and multicultural industrial West should bear in mind, but that's another story). What will "work" educationally for children in Latin America will not necessarily be effective among East African or Chinese children (Farrell in press). What all of this suggests is that any conclusions drawn from the available evidence must be cautious and tentative. As is always the case, however, practitioners and policymakers must make their decisions on the basis of such information as is available, even if it is less than perfect.

With these caveats in mind, Table 3:2 is a summary of the evidence from the best available review of studies which have related one or more schooling factors to student achievement. All of the studies included have attempted to control in one way or another the effect of student socioeconomic status so as to get estimates of the independent effect of the schooling variables. For each "school indicator" we first have the expected direction of the relationship with achievement, either positive or negative. Next, we have the total number of studies in which the particular indicator has been included. The last three columns indicate the number of analyses in which the results were in the "expected" direction, the number in which they were not, and the "confirmation rate," which is the percentage of all analyses in which the results were in the expected direction.

The table does not include information regarding the strength of a particular indicator's association with achievement. This is a very important consideration, obviously, but it is very difficult to produce a meaningful summary measure from studies employing different methodologies and statistical techniques. However, the discussion below will be informed by my own understanding of the strength of association reported in the underlying studies. One may also note that there is almost nothing in this table regarding classroom process or teaching practice. Little work on this key aspect of schooling has been done in developing nations, and what is available is not amenable to this kind of cross-national aggregation. This may be just as well. Given that children in different cultures learn differently, as noted above, any summary indicator of effective teaching practice taken from a few studies in several different cultures could be quite misleading.

At first glance the array of results portrayed in Table 3:2 may be rather confusing. Some clarity may be gained by identifying three clusters of factors: (1) those where we have a relatively large number of studies and a high confirmation rate; (2) those where we have a relatively large number of studies and a low confirmation rate; and (3) those where we have few studies but the confirmation rate is very high. The "best bets" for improving school effectiveness are in the first cluster. The probability is reasonably high that improvement on these dimensions will increase student learning. The second cluster contains "worst bets." The probability is low that investing in these areas will increase school effectiveness. They may represent areas where money could be saved to redirect to the first cluster. The third cluster constitutes promising possibilities, many with a high degree of intuitive appeal even if the research base is narrow.

"Best Bets"

In this cluster, two variables stand out: "tests and reading materials" and "library size and activity." It should not surprise us that children who have access to textbooks and other reading material learn more than those who do not and that the more books they have the more they learn. One particularly impressive thing about the research results regarding reading material is that the reported positive associations with achievement tend to be strong, particularly in carefully controlled large-scale experiments. In the Philippines, for example, a large experiment found that providing one book for every two primary students, as opposed to one for every ten, produced the following achievement gains among first grade pupils: .51 of a standard deviation in science; .30 in mathematics; and .32 in Filipino. These results reinforced the determination to mount a national textbook provision scheme. From an efficiency point of view it is worth noting that the cost of the national textbook program represents 1 percent of the annual educational budget. As one observer of the Philippine program has noted: "This improvement [in achievement scores] is twice the impact of what would be gained by lowering class size from 40 to 10" (Fuller 1986 p. 40), which would involve an enormous cost increase. There is also strong evidence that provision of texts and other reading material has the greatest impact upon the achievement of poor children (Heyneman, Farrell and Sepulveda 1978). Thus, from the "value added" perspective outlined above, the impact of reading material on school effectiveness is particularly great. Moreover, several poor countries have demonstrated that by charging a small fee for textbooks (small enough that even very poor families can bear the cost) a national textbook provision program can be sustained with *no* additional cost to the national budget. Lesotho, for example, has a very effective program of this sort (Overton and Aime 1985). China produces about two billion school texts a year and recovers most of the cost by charging a small fee for the books.

There is also some indication that the availability of books allows teachers to assign homework, one of the "promising possibilities" in Table 3:2. Beyond this, there is some observational evidence that the presence of textbooks in the classroom allows teachers to diversify their teaching repertoire and to work with small groups and individual students. In a classroom with no books, about the only teaching-learning style possible is teacher lecture and group recitation and rote memorization. Books allow other options. Finally, there is some indication from various countries that a well-designed teachers' manual accompanying a textbook set is a very effective form of in-service training for poorly trained teachers. All in all, textbooks appear to be the best available investment a poor nation

Table 3:2
Influence of School Quality Elements on Student Achievement

School Indicator	Expected Direction of Relationship	Total Number of Analyses	Number of Analyses Confirming Effect	Number of Analyses Reporting No or Negative Effect	Confirmation Rate
School Expenditures					
1. Expenditures per pupil	+	11	6	6	54%
2. Total school expenditures	+	5	2	3	40%
Specific Material Inputs					
3. Class size	−	21	5	16	24%
4. School size	+	9	4	5	44%
5. Instructional materials					
Texts and reading materials	+	22	14	8	64%
Desks	+	3	3	0	100%
6. Instructional media (radio)	+	3	3	0	100%
7. School building quality	+	2	2	0	100%
8. Library size and activity	+	18	15	3	83%
9. Science laboratories	+	11	4	7	36%
10. Nutrition and feeding programs	+	5	5	0	100%
Teacher Quality					
11. Teachers' length of schooling					
Total years of schooling	+	25	11	14	44%
Years tertiary & teacher training	+	30	21	9	70%
12. In-service teacher training	+	5	4	1	80%
13. Teachers' length of experience	+	23	10	13	43%

14. Teachers' verbal proficiency	+	2	2	0	100%
15. Teachers' salary level	+	13	4	9	31%
16. Teachers' social class background	+	10	7	3	70%
17. School's percent of full-time teachers	+	2	1	1	50%
18. Teachers' punctuality and (low) absenteeism	+	2	0	2	0%
Teaching Practices/Classroom Organization					
19. Length of instructional program	+	13	11	2	85%
20. Homework frequency	+	7	5	0	71%
21. Active learning by students	+	2	0	2	0%
22. Teachers' expectations of pupil performance	+	3	3	0	100%
23. Teachers' time spent on class preparation	+	5	4	1	80%
School Management					
24. Quality of principal	+	7	4	3	57%
25. Multiple shifts of classes each day	−	3	1	2	33%
26. Student boarding	+	4	3	1	75%
27. Student repetition of grade	+	5	1	4	20%

Source: Fuller 1986 p. 20

can make from an educational efficiency point of view (see Farrell and Heyneman forthcoming).

"Years of tertiary and teacher training" is another variable in this first cluster. It is particularly interesting to consider this variable in relation to "total years of teachers' schooling," which is in the second cluster, and to "in-service teacher training," which is in the third cluster. When one considers all the evidence regarding these three variables, taking into account the quality of the various studies and the strength of association with achievement, plus observational and ethnographic evidence which is not summarized in Table 3:2, three conclusions appear well supported. First, it is important for teachers to have achieved a level of formal schooling at least just above that of the students they are teaching. That is, primary teachers should themselves have junior secondary; junior secondary teachers should have a university degree. However, providing or requiring more formal education than these minima can be a very bad investment. Some poor nations provide university education for primary teachers. The payoff for this additional formal education in terms of student achievement appears to be minimal or nil. Yet the cost is very great, with respect to the university education itself and the additional lifetime salary of the university-educated teacher (most salary scales reward years of formal schooling). Thus one has a high cost/low payoff item, which is most unfortunate from an efficiency point of view. Second, pre-service teacher training is important, but not as strongly associated with achievement as textbook provision. The available data do not speak clearly to this point, but there are some hints (backed by much anecdotal evidence) that the most cost-effective combination would be a relatively brief pre-service teacher training experience followed by systematic provision of in-service training, especially during the early years of training. Third, in-service training appears to be very important. The solid studies are few but the results seem strong. There is some evidence that the effect of in-service training is strongest when it is relatively participatory and responds to needs teachers themselves have identified and weakest when it consists of "experts" telling teachers what "they ought to know" (Shaeffer 1986).

Although there is no clear and direct evidence on this point, I suspect that the points noted above help explain the rather puzzling lack of strong and consistent association between "teachers' length of experience" and student achievement (particularly puzzling because most teaching salary scales reward years of experience, implying a strong positive relationship with student achievement). It is probable that teachers with very low levels of formal schooling and little or no pre-service or in-service training are not equipped to learn from their experience. They simply repeat year after year the same ineffective teaching patterns. Put another way, investments in pre-service and in-service training may have a kind of "multiplier effect" by enabling teachers to become more effective with the years of experience that most salary grids pay for.

The final variable in the first cluster is "length of instructional program." It is hardly surprising to discover that children who spend more time studying something learn more of it on average than those who spend less time, all else equal. But there are some caveats or problems here. First, the relationships discovered between achievement levels and total class time (e.g., length of school day or length of school year) are generally very moderate. Clearly, what is important is not so much the amount of total time available but how the time is used (i.e., the underlying issue is one of teaching strategy or classroom management, which refers back to the teacher training issues discussed above). If ineffective classroom management practices are not changed, lengthening the school day or year will simply add to the time students waste in ineffective schools. Second, results in this area are strongest when they relate time spent on a particular subject (e.g., science) to achievement in that subject. But this runs one up against the fact that in all societies school time is limited and fixed. The scarcest curricular resource is time, and the more time devoted to any one subject, however effectively or ineffectively it is used, the less time there is available for everything else. This is a truism which primary teachers facing a hopelessly overloaded curriculum know in their bones. Third, it is this latter phenomenon which makes the presence of testing programs which do not adequately cover the entire intended curriculum (including both cognitive and affective domains) potentially dangerous, for they inevitably drive teachers to devote most of the available instructional time to those curriculum areas which are included in the tests. The international evidence regarding this "backwash" effect of testing is overwhelming.

"Worst Bets"

Beyond the "teacher schooling" and "teacher experience" variables discussed above, three other variables in this cluster stand out: "class size," "science laboratories," and "teachers' salary level." All three represent areas of high educational cost and none has been found to be consistently and powerfully related to school effectiveness. They all are areas in which significant cost savings could be realized without important effects on student achievement, which would free funds to be invested in the areas discussed above. A study carried out in Chile more than a decade ago indicated that even very modest increases in average class size and reduction of the teacher wage bill (by hiring more primary teachers with secondary-level normal school training rather than university training) would free up enough funds to fully finance a national textbook provision program at the primary level and to provide resources for other programs discussed below under "promising possibilities." It was concluded that such a rearrangement of investments would significantly increase school effectiveness without increasing total system costs (Schiefelbein and Farrell 1973). To the North American educator, accustomed to a relative abundance of educational resources, this may seem to be a rather brutal approach. In the poor nations of the world there is no other reasonable recourse. The educators of the poor must make the hard choices which we, with our bounty, have been cheerfully able to avoid.

"Promising Possibilities"

In this cluster there are several variables which seem obviously promising, even though the hard research base regarding them is small: "desks," "instructional media (radio)," "school building quality," and "nutrition and feeding programs." The provision of desks and adequate buildings is a minimal condition for almost any kind of effective teaching. Children who come to school day after day with insufficient nourishment will not learn well, nor will they live well. For such children, numbering in the hundreds of thousands in the developing world, using schools as feeding stations can have significant effects upon their ability to learn, and with careful planning and administration it can be done very inexpensively.

The evidence regarding the use of radio as an instructional medium, which is very impressive in the few cases where it has been seriously tried and carefully evaluated, introduces a new theme. What is important about some of these experiments with instructional radio is that they do not involve simply adding a radio program to a standard traditional classroom. The radio is used rather as a substitute for a fully trained teacher. It represents a *reorganization* of the standard technology of schooling. Throughout the developing world one finds small and large attempts to alter fundamentally the traditional technology of schooling, using combinations of fully trained teachers, partially trained teachers, para-teachers, radio, correspondence lessons, cross-age peer tutoring, and so forth to deliver learning opportunities in fundamentally new ways. It is too soon to tell, but the early results seem to me to be promising, and there is much discussion at national and international policy levels about ways to break out of the traditional image of "schooling" so as to deliver learning opportunities to more children more effectively and more efficiently.

Conclusion

Early in this paper I suggested that in North America we are reaching the "limits of the possible" with the technology of schooling as we normally have conceived it. If in very poor societies fundamental changes in that technology are being talked about and experimented with, what might we do in our resource-abundant societies if we put our imaginations to work? This is not an argument for some simple-minded sort of "de-schooling" as was occasionally promoted in the '60s. Nor is it an argument for introducing into standard classrooms the oddments and detritus of modern communications technologies: films in the '50s, television in the '60s, computers and VCRs in the '80s. Rather, the argument is that if we are going to achieve any significant increases in what our young people learn we will probably have to radically rethink how we deliver opportunities to learn. So long as we maintain the image that schooling involves compulsorily delivering several hundred kids to a single building for five to six hours a day, where they are divided into groups of 20 to 40 to work with a single adult in a single small room for discrete periods of 40 to 60 minutes, each devoted to a separate "subject," there is very little that the innovation implementors or school effectiveness promoters can do for us. The most one can hope for is modest improvement at maximal cost. Perhaps that is a luxury we can afford because we are rich. It is a luxury most of the educators in the world cannot afford.

I have described typical conditions in schools in the developing world. I have outlined the effectiveness-efficiency crisis being faced there and the ways in which much thinking and some practice is being reoriented to try to deal with that crisis. It is in some respects a grim and desperate picture. But I would like to close on a somewhat more optimistic note. For all the difficulties they face, there is still a great deal of good teaching and effective learning occurring in poor countries. I have seen students and teachers in very poor circumstances accomplish quite remarkable things. In middle-income nations there are many schools where the learning achieved is the equivalent of that in our own best schools. Clearly, most children in poor nations do not have the opportunity or good luck to attend such schools, but some do.

Returning to my original conception of school effectiveness, I would claim that from a "value added" perspective many schools in the developing world are doing better than schools in the developed world. They are accomplishing greater learning gains with far fewer resources. They are doing *more* with *less*. Why should that be so? That is the question, and the challenge, that I present on behalf of the besieged educators of the developing world.

References

Coleman J S et al. 1966 *Equality of Educational Opportunity.* U.S. Government Printing Office, Washington, DC

Coombs P H 1985 *The World Crisis in Education: The View from the Eighties.* Oxford, New York

Farrell J P 1982 Educational expansion and the drive for social equality. In: Altbach P G, Arnove R F, Kelly G P (eds.) *Comparative Education.* Macmillan, New York

Farrell J P in press Cultural differences and curriculum inquiry. *Curriculum Inquiry*

Farrell J P, Heyneman S P (eds.) forthcoming *Economic and Pedagogical Choices in the Production and Distribution of Textbooks*

Fuller B 1986 *Raising School Quality in Developing Countries: What Investments Boost Learning?* The World Bank, Washington, DC

Hanushek E 1986 The economics of schooling: Production and efficiency in public schools. *Journal of Economic Literature* 24(2): 1141–1177

Heyneman S P 1976 Influences on academic achievement: A comparison of results from Uganda and more industrialized societies. *Sociology of Education* 49(2): 200–211

Heyneman S P 1985 Research on education in developing countries. *International Journal of Educational Development* 8(2): 41–56

Heyneman S P, Farrell J P, Sepulveda M 1978 *Textbooks and Achievement: What We Know.* The World Bank, Washington, DC

Heyneman S P, Loxley W A 1982 Influences on academic achievement across high and low income countries: A re-analysis of IEA data. *Sociology of Education* 55(1): 13–21

Jencks C et al. 1972 *Inequality: A Reassessment of Family and Schooling in America.* Basic Books, New York

Overton J, Aime A 1985 Textbook program in Lesotho. Paper presented at a World Bank seminar on economic choices in the production and distribution of textbooks, Washington, DC

Peaker G F 1971 *The Plowden Children Four Years Later.* National Foundation for Educational Research, London

Shaeffer S 1986 Participatory approaches to teacher training. Paper presented at the IMTEC conference on improving the quality of teachers and teaching in the lesser developed world, Denpasar, Indonesia

Schiefelbein E, Farrell J P 1973 Expanding the scope of educational planning: The experience of Chile. *Interchange* 2(1): 18–30

Schiefelbein E, Farrell J P 1982 *Eight Years of Their Lives: Through Schooling to the Labour Market in Chile.* International Development Research Centre, Ottawa

Part Two

SCHOOL-LEVEL POLICY ISSUES

4/School System Policies for Effective School Administration

Kenneth A. Leithwood

Leithwood suggests that administrative in-service is generally inadequate and unfocussed. He goes on to argue that a comprehensive program for the development of growth in school administrators is the best bet for district improvement. Questions to consider include: Do we really know that school administrators are the key to effective schools? What kind of leadership do we really want? Is one set of skills appropriate for the ideal administrator in all circumstances?

As part of a recent review of research about the effects of class size on achievement of elementary school children, Robinson and Wittebols (1986) concluded that the following variables are the most to the least cost effective: improving the training of school principals; improving the training of teachers; reducing class size. This conclusion takes us beyond the now extensively documented claim that school administrators have significant effects on the quality of education in their schools. We are reminded that school system policy choices have a significant bearing on the size and direction of those effects. I address some of these policy choices in this paper by reflecting primarily on implications of a loosely related set of studies undertaken over the past several years by my students, colleagues, and myself. These studies are used in support of an argument, the broad outline of which follows.

Schools are usually members of a larger organizational structure (a board or district) and judgments about their effectiveness depend, in part, on their contribution to the effectiveness of that larger organizational structure. Arguably, the most fundamental basis for judging the effectiveness of schools and school systems is the "coherence" of their designs, reflected most obviously in the policies which establish, maintain, and change those designs.[1] Such coherence should be developed across policies addressing different elements of the organization's design and within policies focussed on the same design element.

Personnel policies concerning school administrators are a major source of incoherence in the design of many school systems at the present time. As a consequence, they warrant serious attention by those responsible for organizational design (at the least, by elected officials, chief executive officers, and senior administrative staff). These policies can be classified as pre-service preparation, in-service development, selection, and appraisal. We now possess enough knowledge about organizational design and about each of these policy areas to significantly increase their contribution to organizational effectiveness.

Importance of Internally Coherent Policies

The argument I have sketched out emerges from a particular perspective on schools and school systems and on the criteria for judging their effectiveness. It is a perspective a colleague and I adopted in a recent fourteen-year retrospective case study of curriculum change in a medium-sized school system in Ontario (Jones and Leithwood 1987). This perspective, adapted from Galbraith (1977), suggests that achievement of goals collectively valued by organization members depends on choices made within four sets of variables or elements of the organization's design. These design elements include: the tasks carried out by organization members and their level of performance; administrative structures or modes of organizing; personnel policies; and information and decision-making processes. Interventions affecting the implementation of curriculum change in the case study school system were readily accommodated by these categories. Furthermore, "coherence," the degree to which conditions created in one design element supported or conflicted with the effects of conditions in other design elements, explained much of the success or failure of changes in design. This included coherence between officially espoused organizational goals and the goals of individual members. As well, it included coherence between tasks and goals and among tasks, organizing modes, personnel policies, and information and decision-making processes.

Gradual development of coherence in the design of the school system was the product of what we termed "persistent, reflective problem solving." This problem solving led the system through three phases of development. The first phase emphasized climate development and decentralized decision making. The second phase was preoccupied with improving processes for solving technical, curriculum management problems. Integrating personnel and program policies was the predominant thrust in the third phase. We do not believe the order of these phases to be a crucial matter. However, it was not until serious efforts were made to integrate program and personnel policies that the curriculum changes advocated by the school system became a routine part of the lives of those in schools. Support for the claim that such integration is a prerequisite for the institutionalization of change, more generally, can also be found in Miles et al. (1984) and Leithwood (1985).

Basis for Coherence in Personnel Policies for School Administrators

High levels of coherence in personnel policies for school administrators depend on the presence of a widely shared, explicit conception of growth in the effectiveness of school administrative practices within a school system. There are three sources of information from which to develop such a conception. One source is to be found in the school system context, in the decisions made concerning the other elements of the school system's design. Personnel policies for school administrators should foster practices that support decisions made about other design elements. So, for example, if decentralized decision making about program is part of the organizational design, training programs for school administrators should develop skills in that area and appraisal practices should reward growth in the performance of those skills.

A second source of information is the school context. While schools are part of a larger system and so share some common purposes and practices, each is unique in some ways. This uniqueness may be reflected, for example, in the character of the student population, the expectations of the community, the nature of the school's resources, or the values, interests, and special skills of the staff. Failure to address these sources of uniqueness erode the chances of achieving agreed-upon school system goals within that school site, as well as goals particular to that site. Personnel policies for school administrators should foster administrators' ability and willingness to respond to such uniqueness in ways that promote rather than detract from the goals of the school system, as a whole (e.g., the ability to accurately assess program weaknesses, community preferences, etc.).

The final source of information from which to develop a conception of growth in school administrators' practices lies outside either the school or school system context in which the administrator works. It is what we know about effective practice that seems to be important, independent of context. Recent research on the principalship is an obvious repository of some of this knowledge (e.g., Dwyer et al. 1984; Leithwood and Montgomery 1982; Morris et al. 1984), especially research which identifies stages of growth in effectiveness (e.g., Leithwood and Montgomery 1986; Rutherford et al. 1983). Although a detailed treatment of the results of this research cannot be undertaken in this paper, a brief sketch is useful for subsequent discussion. Underlying the discussion is the assumption that judgments about the effectiveness of a principal's practices depend on the goals one values for students. A principal's practices are more or less effective to the extent that they contribute directly or indirectly to the realization of such goals. Adopting a relatively narrow set of valued goals for students — say, basic math and language skills, as is the case with much of the effective schools research — narrows the focus of attention to the principal's practices influencing growth in such goals. My colleagues and I have adopted an extremely ambitious set of goals for students as the basis for judging the effectiveness of principals. These goals are consistent with officially espoused goals of educators in most Canadian provinces. Emerging from an image of the educated person as a self-directed problem solver, these goals encompass the acquisition of a broad range of knowledge, complex as well as simple; intellectual skills development; such social goals as esteem for the culture and customs of others; and personal, affective goals such as the development of self-concept.[2] This relatively complex set of valued goals for students helps account for a comparatively complex conception of what is involved in effective school administration.[3]

Direct observations of principals at work have revealed a pattern of activity that is hectic, distributed across many different tasks over the course of a day, and somewhat unpredictable and spontaneous (e.g., Martin and Willower 1981; Morris et al. 1982; Wolcott 1978). Principals, it also appears, are primarily engaged in solving problems which, considered individually, seem relatively trivial. Because this description of principals' work seems to apply to virtually all those in the role, it is important to distinguish the characteristics of the work of the highly effective principal. A crucial part of the distinguishing characteristics is coherence or "consistency," the ability to accumulate the effects of many seemingly trivial decisions so that they move the school in the directions valued by the school system, the community, the staff, and the principal. Principals are effective in improving their schools to the extent that they have a well-defined set of legitimate purposes as well as the skill and the knowledge to use even apparently unrelated opportunities to move the school toward achieving those purposes. Effective principals are, in this sense, the glue holding the many different parts of the school together in some coherent framework; a significant part of their role is to help others in the school meaningfully interpret school life in terms of such an overriding sense of purpose.

Our initial efforts to describe growth in principal effectiveness (Leithwood and Montgomery 1986) suggested substantial differences among principals both in the goals that they strive to accomplish and in the factors in the classroom and the school that they try to influence. Substantial differences were also observed in the strategies principals use to influence the factors and in the nature of their decision making about goals, factors, and strategies. As principals increase in effectiveness, their goals are clearer and more student oriented and they form the basis for most of the principals' decision making. Principals' knowledge about factors influencing student learning increases, as does the clarity of their expectations for staff in relation to these factors. Principals become increasingly skilled in the use of a wider repertoire of strategies. They are better able to select strategies appropriate to the task and they more frequently employ strategies requiring special technical knowledge, for example, program evaluation, staff supervision, curriculum development. Finally, improvement in effective decision making by principals seems to be characterized by a growing commitment to the collection and use of relevant information and to a fostering of conditions in the school conducive to more staff participation in decision making. The principal's sensitivity to the need to adjust decision-making forms and procedures to fit is also associated with increases in administrative effectiveness.

How can these differences in principals' practices be explained? Research now underway (Leithwood and Stager 1986) seeks such explanation in principals' thought processes and problem-solving strategies. We are beginning to discover that underlying the differences in principals' practices are, first, important differences in how principals *classify* and *manage* their problems. For example, highly effective, as compared with moderately effective, principals:

- assign more weight to problems likely to be solved through the involvement of greater rather than lesser numbers of people; these problems seem likely to be complex and time consuming;
- use a much more deliberate and explicit sorting process; this is symptomatic of a generally more reflective posture toward problem solving as a process in its own right;
- give greater priority to problems affecting school programs, overall school direction, and staff as a whole than to problems with much narrower impact;
- systematically use more explicit daily routines for managing time and predicting potential future problems, thus preventing them from becoming time-consuming crises; these techniques create the opportunity for principals to devote attention to high-priority problems;
- focus on the availability of clear problem-solving procedures, where knowledge permits, and recognize those aspects of problems that are truly novel and should be treated as such.

Second, there are important differences in the problem-solving *strategies* of principals; those of highly effective principals can be summarized as:

- having an overall style which provides a more central role for others (consultative, collaborative, shared problem solving);
- devoting greater effort to systematically collecting information relevant to the problem;
- exhibiting a greater tendency to risk defining large, signifi-

cant problems and also a tendency to solve those problems through a very methodical, riskless process (i.e., "front-end" risk-takers);

• guided by a more explicit, conscious model of the problem-solving process, one which includes an optimal sequencing of steps;

• giving greater attention and time to initial problem clarification;

• establishing more formal structures to facilitate the problem solving of staff in both the short and long term;

• assuming that a major reason for staff involvement is to produce better solutions;

• drawing on larger amounts of knowledge from more sources external to the school and school system.

And, finally, our data concerning *influences* on problem-solving processes suggest that highly effective principals:

• with administrative experience, become more reflective about their own processes and refine these processes over time;

• although similar to moderately effective principals in general moral values and in personal values, are more influenced by their beliefs concerning principals' roles and responsibilities and are more able to specify day-to-day consequences of such beliefs;

• are more aware of school system needs and requirements and try harder to take them into account in school-level problem solving;

• derive more personal enjoyment from problem solving and, partly as a consequence of this, are more proactive in dealing with school problems.

Developing a coherent conception of growth in school administrators' practices using information from the school and school system contexts as well as research-based information is a demanding task. Carrying out this task adequately will probably require resources from within and without the school system, most likely people working together through a deliberative process.

Categories of policies examined in the remainder of the chapter are pre-service and in-service education and selection and appraisal policies. The goals such policies ought to achieve are specified, current practices are judged in relation to such goals, and implications for new policy are identified.

Pre-service and In-service Opportunities

Prior to selection for the role of school principal, the major sources of preparation include on-the-job experiences and formal education programs. In the latter category are university credit programs, board-sponsored leadership programs, and provincial certification programs. There are at least seven plausible objectives to be met by school system policies governing these sources of preparation, which should:

1. Be available to all those in the role and to all those aspiring to the role who are considered by their school systems as having potential for the role (Access);

2. Develop capabilities directly related to effective school administration practices (Relevance);

3. Assist participants in the application of such capabilities to typical administrative problems in actual school contexts (Utility);

4. Encompass the full array of capabilities required for initial and continuing competence in the role (Comprehensiveness);

5. Incorporate methods that are effective in developing not only knowledge but skills, attitudes, and values as well (Effective Delivery Methods);

6. Provide feedback helpful in guiding short-term decision making about areas of strength and areas of needed growth (Short-term Feedback);

7. Provide guidance in long-term career planning (Long-term Planning).

Table 4:1 summarizes my assessment of how well typical current practices meet each of these seven school system policy objectives.[4] What are the grounds for this assessment?

On-the-job Experience
A recent review of evidence about policies governing the pre-service preparation of principals in Canada (Leithwood and Begley 1986) suggested that the typical career path for principals is quite direct — from teacher to vice-principal to principal. Secondary principals sometimes move through department headships or act as guidance counsellors, but this latter route appears to be less typical than might be expected, as Seger, Miklos, and Nixon (1981) found in Alberta. The typical career path for principals offers a narrow range of work experience in comparison with expectations held for the principal's role. Very few principals have had the school system program and instructional development experience that would be provided in the role of curriculum consultant, for example. Prior to their assumption of the vice-principalship, the work experience of principals seems largely confined to teaching in their own classrooms.

Nor does it seem that the vice-principalship, as experienced by most who have moved through the role, offers an experience as useful as it might be in preparation for the principalship. Wiles's (1983)

Table 4:1

An Assessment of "Typical" Pre-service and In-service Preparation Opportunities for School Administrators

SCHOOL SYSTEM POLICY OBJECTIVES	PRE-SERVICE PREPARATION OPPORTUNITIES				IN-SERVICE OPPORTUNITIES
	On-the-job Experience	University Credit Programs	Board Leadership Programs	Provincial Certification Programs	Professional Development
1. Access	medium	low	high	medium	low
2. Relevance	low	high	high	high	high
3. Utility	high	low	high	medium	medium
4. Comprehensiveness	low	low	low	high	low
5. Effective Delivery Methods	high	low	medium	medium	medium
6. Short-term Feedback	low	low	high	high	medium
7. Long-term Planning	low	low	low	low	low

survey of vice-principals in Ontario provides convincing support for this point. For example, the 661 elementary vice-principals in his study reported carrying out some 43 functions in the school. Of these, the ten most frequently demanded functions focussed primarily on routine building administration (i.e., listening to concerns, disciplining students, attending to duty schedules and emergency procedures). Some educational leadership functions emerged in the next ten most frequently demanded activities (namely, developing school goals, supervising staff, acting as educational resource person). But not mentioned anywhere in the twenty most frequently demanded functions were core tasks typically associated with prescriptions for educational leadership (i.e., staff development, staff evaluation, program innovation, curriculum development, program evaluation). Given these Ontario data, similar to data collected in other parts of Canada and the U.S., it appears that most vice-principals find themselves primarily responsible for routine, school maintenance tasks, tasks which need to be mastered but which are only remotely linked to those school improvement responsibilities central to our emerging image of the effective principal.

As compared with formal training, however, on-the-job experience prior to assuming the principalship offers enormous potential for shaping the principal's image of the role, fostering well-developed theories of administrative action, and refining administrative skill. On-the-job experience is intense, prolonged, and practical, characteristics which formal training can approximate only modestly. Experiences while a vice-principal seem especially crucial. Most vice-principals view themselves as preparing for the principalship (79 percent in Wiles's [1983] study) and almost all principals in larger school systems are promoted from the vice-principalship. It is the job which, potentially, most closely simulates the conditions of the principalship, and so provides an ideal context for professional development.

In order to more fully realize the policy objectives for pre-service preparation of principals summarized in Table 4:1, three types of school system policies seem likely to be helpful:

- policies requiring experience in an out-of-school position, preferably in support roles for schools in areas of curriculum and instruction; such policies imply the provision of adequate opportunities by the school system for aspiring principals to play these roles;
- policies concerning the duties of the vice-principal; these duties should extend beyond routine school administration and include responsibility for school improvement initiatives as well;
- policies concerning the role of principals in identifying staff members with future administrative potential and in assisting them (e.g., monitoring) to acquire suitable on-the-job experiences and to make long-term career decisions.

Formal Pre-service Preparation Programs

Universities, school systems, and provincial agencies offer formal programs of preparation to aspiring principals. The availability, nature, and quality of these programs varies widely, however, depending upon the geographical region and sponsoring institution.

Universities. Depending on the province, one-third (e.g., B.C., Alberta) to two-thirds (Ontario) of Canadian principals are estimated to hold master's degrees (Leithwood and Begley 1986). Such preparation is becoming an increasingly common expectation for entry into the principalship. For example, 50 percent completion of a master's degree or its equivalent is now a prerequisite for entry into Ontario's pre-service principal certification courses. The outcomes of such preparation, however, bear a highly unpredictable relationship to the needs of the beginning principal for several reasons. Universities typically assume little sense of obligation for the development of practical administrative skill, in sharp contrast to their stance toward teacher preparation. The complement of courses selected by a student is likely to be highly individualized and remotely connected, at best, to the practice of school administration. Students wishing to use their masters programs as direct preparation for school administration are often misled by the departmental nomenclature of some universities. For example, a degree at OISE composed exclusively of courses from the Department of Educational

Administration would address a very small proportion of the knowledge required for effective school administration and virtually none of the skills required for the administrative role as I have outlined it.

At best, university programs provide students with some fundamental conceptual tools and the disposition to adopt a more reflective posture toward their own administrative practices and those of others. These are undeniably important cornerstones for effective administration, but they represent only a modest proportion of the total professional armament required for such administration.

School systems. Pre-service programs sponsored by school systems have substantial potential advantage over other types of pre-service programs. Access is controlled by those criteria school systems judge relevant. Many school systems have sufficient resources to design high-quality programs and implement them over the extended time periods required to produce significant growth. Only school system programs are able to reflect school and school system sources as well as context-independent sources of information about administrative effectiveness.

There is little systematically collected information available about pre-service programs offered by Canadian school systems, however. A few such programs have been described in the literature, for example, by Bruce (1976) in British Columbia and by Musella and Jones (1982) in Ontario. Personal contact with a number of programs and inferences from data concerning board in-service programs are the bases for the impressionistic judgments reflected in Table 4:1. These impressions suggest that the majority of school systems have no pre-service programs. Where such programs do exist their relevance and utility tend to be limited by their narrow focus on short-term problems and policies and by the absence of a coherent conception of growth in administrative effectiveness. There is also a tendency for them to be restricted in duration (a few days to a week) and offered to anyone interested in "leadership." These programs often make little contribution to the long-term career planning needs of aspiring school administrators.

Provincial programs. A cross-Canada survey by Goldsborough (1977) indicated that about half of the 63 boards sampled formally required no special pre-service courses or programs prior to appointment as a school administrator. This seems likely to have changed in the past decade. Nevertheless, Ontario, New Brunswick, and Nova Scotia appear to be the only provinces now requiring such background as part of provincial policy. As in the case of board-sponsored programs, information about provincial programs is hard to come by and judgments in Table 4:1 are based exclusively on recently implemented Ontario programs. Ontario requires the successful completion of a two-course plus practicum program spanning some 375 hours for eligibility for selection as a vice-principal or principal. For the past three years, alternative versions of this program have been offered by faculties of education, OISE, and the Ministry in regions throughout the province. Guided by a common policy, these programs are significant improvements on most of their predecessors in meeting all the policy objectives in Table 4:1. An accumulation of systematically collected evidence now supports their significant impact on candidates and contributes to their ongoing refinement; one of these program alternatives has been described by Leithwood, Kelly, and Armstrong (in press). Even the best of these programs, however, make limited contributions to the development of administrative skill and long-term career planning. Furthermore, access to these programs and hence to positions of school administration is normally restricted to those with postgraduate degrees and teaching qualifications across three of the four levels of schooling in Ontario (primary, junior, intermediate, senior).

What are the implications of this assessment of formal pre-service preparation programs for school system policy development?

• School systems without their own pre-service programs should initiate such programs. These programs may be carried out in collaboration with adjacent school systems when resources are scarce.

• School system programs should be designed to integrate with other pre-service experiences candidates are likely to have.

• School systems, in deliberation with local faculties, may identify several courses or categories of courses recommended to aspiring school administrators as part of their graduate university programs.

• School systems should consider making greater and more integrated use of external agencies and expertise in their own programs as a way of increasing the comprehensiveness of these programs.

In-service Professional Development Programs

Once in the position of school administrator, the individual encounters a wide array of continuing professional development options. Perhaps the most visible option, and one over which the school system has control, is in-service programs offered by school systems. Table 4:1 summarizes the adequacy of this area of practice in relation to the same set of policy objectives considered appropriate in assessing pre-service preparation opportunities.

School systems are an important source of potential principal in-service education. On the one hand, school systems carry the bulk of responsibility for ensuring implementation of programs and practices to meet the changing and increasingly complex needs of their students. On the other, they appear to be uniquely well positioned to provide the kind of sustained, coordinated, long-term professional development that principals will require if they are to optimally contribute to these student needs. A principal's school and school system provide the problems against which the value of new ideas are judged and the context for assessing the practicality of innovative procedures. The principal's school system is also the most likely source of role models, colleagues, advisors, and ongoing professional coaching; it is certainly the central source of a principal's intrinsic and extrinsic professional rewards, over which it exercises considerable control. And, finally, although this assertion is no doubt contentious, locally controlled school systems are likely able to create more resources for principal development, at the margins of their budgets if need be, than are available to other agencies more traditionally considered responsible for such development.

There is little descriptive information available concerning in-service education for Canadian principals provided by school districts. The assessment provided in Table 4:1 is based on data from a recent survey of 129 school systems across Canada (Leithwood and Avery 1986). Based on a model of in-service education developed by Sparks (1983), this survey asked questions about the context, instructional processes, goals, and content of in-service programs. Responses provide some evidence directly or indirectly related to the seven criteria in Table 4:1.

The low rating given to in-service programs on the "access" criterion is based on the time provided for such in-service. Over the course of a year, school systems appear to be devoting from about two days (46 percent of school systems) to five days (33 percent) to this in-service. Standing alone, this amount of time is relatively meaningless. However, systems examined in the small number of studies reporting significant in-service effects (Gerald and Sloan 1984; Sadler 1984; Silver and Moyle 1984) used two to four times the amount of time reported by most Canadian school systems. Only 14 percent of Canadian school systems reported devoting more than a week per year to school administrator in-service.

Canadian in-service programs were given high marks for "relevance." This assessment is based on two pieces of information: first, 71 percent of systems claimed to be basing their programs on a concept of the principal as instructional leader; second, more than 90 percent of systems reported the involvement of principals (49 percent) and senior administrators (44 percent) in determining the objectives for in-service. Of course, the assessment can be challenged on the grounds, for example, that the concept of instructional leader was not sufficiently well understood to have much practical consequence.

Judgments about utility depend on the extent to which in-service participants are assisted in applying what they learn to typical administrative problems. Evidence about the utility of typical in-service programs is to be found in the frequency with which those instructional techniques which permit such application (case studies, in-basket techniques, simulations, practice with feedback) are used. Fewer than a third of responding school systems reported using most of these techniques. These data are also relevant to judgments about the extent to which participants receive short-term feedback (moderately, through peer interaction most likely) and are assisted in long-term planning (probably not at all as part of in-service experiences). Evidence concerning how evaluations are conducted is also relevant to judgments concerning long-term planning. Such evaluation seems restricted to judgments about the program, as distinct from the participants, and is done in a superficial manner. The most frequently reported instructional techniques were lectures (80.6 percent) and small-group work (89.1 percent). Studies of effective instructional techniques for school administrators support the use of highly interactive, experience-based strategies, as mentioned above. Hence the judgment about typical delivery methods contained in Table 4:1 is premised on the view that excessive lecturing is typical, as is the use of an unnecessarily restricted set of interactive methods.

In order to enhance the value of in-service programs offered locally, school board policies should:

- significantly increase the time available for the formal in-service education of school administrators; a realistic goal to work toward would be ten to twelve days per year;
- be based on a clear, comprehensive conception of growth in effective school administrator practices;
- recommend instructional techniques which actively involve participants and allow them to draw extensively on their own experiences;
- foster the development of more rigorous, ongoing evaluation processes;
- encourage collaboration with external in-service agencies in the planning, delivery, and evaluation of in-service programs.

Selection and Appraisal Procedures

Objectives to work toward in relation to school administrator selection and appraisal procedures are similar in many but not all respects to objectives for pre-service and in-service education opportunities. Under typical circumstances, selection and appraisal procedures should:

1. Be based on criteria relevant to the prediction or description of actual job performance (Relevance);

2. Be based on a comprehensive set of relevant criteria; criteria should extend beyond the requirements of the immediate school placement, for example, since principals and vice-principals will

usually administer many schools during their careers (Comprehensiveness);

3. Employ data collection procedures which yield reliable, valid information (Quality of Information);

4. Incorporate decision-making processes which are publicly known, fair, and perceived to be fair by as many people as possible; as Baltzell and Dentler (1983) found, impressions of such fairness influence the trust and confidence school system personnel have of senior administrators; the selection of a principal through procedures judged by school staffs as unfair may also foster initial pessimism among staff about the quality of the principal's leadership (Fairness);

5. Provide information to all applicants or appraisers helpful in guiding short-term and long-term decision making about areas of strength and areas of needed growth (Feedback);

6. Be cost-effective, that is, the procedure should require as little time as possible of selectors or appraisers while still resulting in valid appraisals and the selection of the best applicants (Efficiency).

Selection Procedures

Table 4:2 includes a "report card" on typical practices for selecting school administrators in Canada. This report card does not reflect, however, what may be considerable variation both within and across provinces. The extent of such variation cannot be estimated with the evidence at hand. This evidence consists of Goldsborough's survey in 1977 of practices in 63 school boards across the country; a description of practices in British Columbia published by Kelsey and Leullier in 1978; and a recently completed survey in Ontario conducted by Musella and Lawton (1986).

Table 4:2
An Assessment of "Typical" School Administrator Selection and Appraisal Procedures

SCHOOL SYSTEM POLICY OBJECTIVES	Selection Procedures	Appraisal Procedures
1. Candidate Pool	medium	not appropriate
2. Relevance	medium	high
3. Comprehensiveness	medium	low
4. Quality of Information	medium	medium
5. Fairness	medium	low
6. Feedback	low	medium
7. Efficiency	medium	not appropriate

In general, Canadian selection practices appear to be of much higher quality than practices reported in either the U.S. (Baltzell and Dentler 1983; Cornett 1983) or the U.K. (Moran, Hall and Mackay 1983). Further, Ontario practices appear to be of higher quality than those in other provinces where data are available. However, this apparent edge in quality for Ontario may be a function of time, the Ontario data being considerably more recent than the rest. It is plausible to suppose improvement in selection practices over the past five to ten years. For this reason, the Ontario data will be used as a best estimate (possibly skewed in a positive direction) of current practice.

Musella and Lawton's (1986) study was based on the survey responses of 534 public and separate school vice-principals and principals in 28 school boards across different regions in Ontario (a 63 percent response rate); responses of the two groups were similar on most issues. These responses are quite helpful in assessing selection practices on all but two of the criteria in Table 4:2 (although a medium rating has been assigned). About 95 percent of respondents reported being notified by letter or memo about the opportunity to apply. Personal contacts of one sort or another were reported in about a quarter of the cases. One's judgment about how well the application process captured the attention of qualified candidates depends on one's assumptions about how wide and careful was the distribution of letters announcing the application opportunity. We do not have information about this, but we do know personal contacts were not common. Further, Musella and Lawton's (1986) data do not say much about the efficiency of procedures. However, neither principal nor vice-principal applicants (nor their selectors) indicated a need for change that was related to reduced time requirements or other elements of efficiency.

The overall assessment of selection practices warranted by the data is a rating of "moderate" quality. Of the 28 boards surveyed, 24 percent had either no policy or one not complete. While a well-developed policy provides no guarantees of good practice, the absence of policy permits wider variation in the quality of selection practices. In addition, about 60 percent of respondents saw the need for some change in policies, where such policies existed.

Objectives in Table 4:2 concerning relevance and comprehensiveness address the nature of the criteria used in selection. About 18 percent of respondents believed the criteria to be largely unrelated to performance in the role; about a third believed the criteria to be based largely on merit in performance. These same respondents attributed much more importance to interpersonal, managerial, and decision-making skills as criteria than to curriculum change skills. In addition, they believed even more emphasis should be placed on these criteria than the substantial importance already awarded them. These data suggest that there is some inconsistency between criteria judged relevant at least by current research and criteria presently in use and regarded as important. The data are less clear about the comprehensiveness of criteria used, but it seems unlikely, from what evidence there is, that current procedures have more than moderately achieved this objective.

Do current selection procedures use data collection methods likely to yield reliable and valid information? From the applicant's point of view this objective has only been moderately achieved. Approximately a quarter of respondents reported the haphazard collection of information from only single sources. Collection of data from multiple sources was reported by a third of the respondents; only 10 percent believed the information collection process to be extremely rigorous.

The judgment about fairness of selection procedures was based on several pieces of data:

- 56 percent of respondents reported either no or inadequate opportunities provided by the board to prepare them for the process;
- 24 percent explicitly noted that greater effort was needed to ensure fairness;
- 50 percent of principal respondents indicated that board selection policies were not followed in practice;
- only about 40 percent of boards were reported to explicitly state their standards for selection in policy; in the remainder of cases the selectors set the standards one way or another.

On the basis of these data a judgment of moderate achievement of the objective of fairness seems generous.

The final objective concerns the provision of information to applicants helpful in guiding decisions about areas of weakness and strength. This objective is not being achieved at all in most cases, it appears. In the case of vice-principals, only 22 percent reported having an opportunity to be debriefed after going through the selection procedure; only 35 percent of this group took advantage of that opportunity. About a third of the principals were debriefed.

Performance Appraisal

The assessment of practices for appraising school administrators reflected in Table 4:2 depends on evidence reported recently by Lawton, Hickcox, Leithwood, and Musella (1986). This evidence is based on responses to a survey study by 879 principals from a stratified random sample of 30 Ontario public and separate school systems. Directors and superintendents also provided relevant information. In general, the data suggest that appraisal of school administrators, while taken seriously enough, mostly generates reinforcement for current practices and provides little concrete direction for improvement. More specifically, the data indicate that

- The criteria on which evaluations were based reflected a broad range of responsibilities and functions clearly part of the principals' role (Relevance);

• Criteria emphasized the overt actions taken by the principals and paid no attention to their goals, the factors they tried to influence in the classroom and school, and their decision-making processes (Comprehensiveness);

• Usually, sources of information were restricted to the appraiser and appraisee and information was collected hastily (Quality of Information);

• Standards for appraisal were quite often considered to be negotiable or were not available for scrutiny (Fairness);

• Reporting of data to the appraisee generally seemed to be done thoroughly and to the satisfaction of most; however, long-term plans for follow-up were developed in fewer than a third of the cases (Feedback);

• It was not possible to estimate "efficiency" of procedures from the data.

What are the implications of this assessment of existing selection and assessment procedures for school system policy development?

• School systems without formal selection and appraisal policies for school administrators should develop them. While their existence does not ensure their use, they will at least foster uniform practices and, hence, fairness.

• Selection and appraisal policies should be based on the same conception of growth in relevant and comprehensive practices as are pre-service preparation and in-service education opportunities.

• Information should be collected from multiple sources and be requested in relation to detailed, specific aspects of practice. Dependence on information derived from typical applicant interviews, in the case of selection procedures, should be reduced because of its questionable validity.

• Careful preparation of selectors and appraisers is warranted in collecting and interpreting information.

• Policies should give more emphasis to the importance of feedback concerning strengths, weaknesses, and future career plans. Such feedback ought to be a starting point for the improvement of practice.

Conclusion

Senior school system administrators might do well to view themselves as organizational designers. From this perspective, their job is to assist members of the school system organization to clarify the legitimate purposes to be pursued through the organization. With such goals in mind, the design process then involves helping organization members bring coherence to the different elements of the organization, including policies shaping the character of those elements.

Principals and vice-principals appear to be especially crucial in efforts to achieve the purposes of the school system organization. As a consequence, policies governing their roles deserve careful scrutiny by organizational designers. To be most effective, such policies should be based on a comprehensive conception of growth in the effectiveness of school administrators in accomplishing the purposes of the school and the school system. They should also include other features known to be characteristic of effective policies. Available evidence about relevant current policies and practices in Canadian school systems suggests room for improvement. This paper has offered a number of suggestions for how such improvements might be made through policies governing the pre-service, selection, in-service, and appraisal of school administrators. Such improvements are a promising strategy for enhancing school effectiveness.

Notes

1. Of course, such policies may or may not be well reflected in the practices of school and school system staff, but I will not address that problem in this paper.

2. For a more explicit statement of such goals see *Issues and Directions* (Ministry of Education 1980).

3. One of the major impediments to adopting such a complex set of goals as criteria for judging the effectiveness of schools and school administrators is the lack of appropriate instruments for assessing growth in such goals. Test developers have focussed their efforts on "the traditional basics" and have been driven toward test items that are readily scored (preferably by machine). This should not be interpreted as a claim that measures of more complex goals are not possible, however. Such measures seem likely to emerge from recent concerns for theory-driven tests (e.g., Haertl 1985) which reflect prior analyses of the substantive abilities, traits, and the like of interest. Further, goals concerned with such affective traits as self-worth have been assessed by researchers for many years; see Ross and Nagy (1987) for a review of instruments used in assessing esteem for the culture and customs of others. The work of Robinson, Ross, and White (1986) illustrates the feasibility of using such assessments. Although instruments and procedures such as these undoubtedly could be refined, they undermine the claim that since measurement of such non-traditional goals is not possible, we should not strive toward their achievement.

4. The second and fourth of these objectives (relevance and comprehensiveness) are features of a defensible conception of growth in administrator effectiveness, the importance of which was discussed previously.

References

Baltzell D C, Dentler R A 1983 *Selecting American School Principals.* ABT Associates, Washington, DC

Bruce C A 1976 A program for preparing principals. *Education Canada* 16(1): 35–37

Cornett L M 1983 *The Preparation and Selection of School Principals.* Southern Regional Education Board, Atlanta, Georgia

Dwyer D C, Lee G V, Barnett B G, Filby N N, Rowan B 1984 *Instructional Management Program.* Far West Laboratory for Educational Research and Development, San Francisco

Galbraith J R 1977 *Organization Design.* Addison Wesley, Reading, Massachusetts

Gerald V W, Sloan C A 1984 Inservice education program for principals promotes effective change. *Catalyst* 13(3): 12–14

Goldsborough H 1977 *Hiring and Promotion Practices.* Canadian Education Association, Toronto

Haertl E 1985 Construct validity and criterion-referenced tests. *Review of Educational Research* 55(1): 23–46

Jones L, Leithwood K A 1987 Draining the swamp: A case study in organizational design. Ontario Institute for Studies in Education, Toronto

Kelsey J G T, Leullier B 1978 School district policies for the identification, selection and training of principals. *The Canadian Administrator* 17(5): 1–6

Lawton S, Hickcox E, Leithwood K, Musella D 1986 *The Development and Use of Performance Appraisal of Certificated Education Staff in Ontario School Boards: Technical Report,* Vol. 2. Ministry of Education, Toronto

Leithwood K A 1985 Implementing core curriculum. In: Gonter R J (ed.) *Views on Core Curriculum.* National Institute for Curriculum Development, Enschede, Netherlands

Leithwood K A, Avery C 1986 In-service education for principals in Canada. In: Leithwood K, Rutherford W, VanderVegt R (eds.) *Preparing Principals for School Improvement.* Croom Helm, London

Leithwood K A, Begley P 1986 School management in Canada. In: Bloom R et al. (eds.) *The School Leader and School Improvement.* ACCO Press, Leuven, Netherlands

Leithwood K A, Kelly F, Armstrong M in press The pre-service preparation of school administrators in Ontario. In: Bloom R et al. (eds.) *Training School Leaders for School Improvement.* ACCO Press, Leuven, Netherlands

Leithwood K A, Montgomery D J 1982 The role of the elementary school principal in program improvement. *Review of Educational Research* 52(3): 309–339

Leithwood K A, Montgomery D J 1986 *Improving Principal Effectiveness: The Principal Profile.* OISE Press, Toronto

Leithwood K A, Stager M 1986 Differences in problem solving processes used by moderately and highly effective principals. Paper presented at the annual meeting of the American Educational Research Association, San Francisco

Martin W J, Willower D J 1981 The managerial behavior of high school principals. *Educational Administration Quarterly* 17(1): 69–90

Miles M B et al. 1984 Unravelling the mysteries of institutionalization. *Educational Leadership* 41(3): 14–23

Ministry of Education 1980 *Issues and Directions.* Ministry of Education, Toronto

Morgan C, Hall V, Mackay H 1983 *The Selection of Secondary School Headteachers.* Open University Press, Milton Keynes, England

Morris V C, Crowson R L, Hurwitz E, Porter-Gehrie C 1982 The urban principal: Middle manager in the educational bureaucracy. *Phi Delta Kappan* June: 689–692

Morris V C, Crowson R L, Porter-Gehrie C, Hurwitz E 1984 *Principals in Action.* C. E. Merrill, Columbus, Ohio

Musella D, Jones H 1982 Training for promotion. *The Canadian School Executive* December: 10–12

Musella D, Lawton S 1986 *Selection and Promotion Procedures in Ontario School Boards,* Vol 1: *Technical Report.* OISE Press, Toronto

Robinson F G, Ross J, White F 1986 *Curriculum Development for Effective Instruction.* OISE Press, Toronto

Robinson G, Wittebols J 1986 *Class-size Research: A Related Cluster Analysis for Decision Making.* Educational Research Services Inc., Arlington, Virginia

Ross J, Nagy P 1987 Esteem for the customs, cultures and beliefs of a wide variety of cultural groups. *Interchange* 18(3): 1–21

Rutherford W E, Hord S M, Huling L L, Hall G E 1983 *Change Facilitators: In Search of Understanding Their Role.* Research and Development Center for Teacher Education, Austin, Texas

Sadler D R 1984 Follow-up evaluation of an inservice programme based on action research: Some methodological issues. *Journal of Education for Teaching* 10(3): 209–218

Seger J E, Miklos E, Nixon M 1981 Administrative services and resources in education: Practices and issues. Department of Educational Administration, University of Alberta, Edmonton, Alberta

Silver P F, Moyle C R J 1984 The impact of intensive inservice programs on educational leaders and their organizations. *Planning & Changing* 15(1): 18–34

Sparks, G M 1983 Synthesis of research on staff development for effective teaching. *Educational Leadership* November: 65–72

Wiles D A 1983 *The Vice-Principal: A Forgotten Leader?* The Ontario Public School Teachers' Federation, Toronto

Wolcott H F 1978 *The Man in the Principal's Office.* Holt, Rinehart and Associates, New York

5/Problems in Policy Implementation

Donald F. Musella

Musella uses an anecdote to illustrate the perils of unplanned implementation. He goes on to lay out a plan for coherent implementation. Some questions to consider: Do implementation plans take sufficient notice of the worth of what is being implemented, in the values and beliefs of the people being changed? Will a single plan fit a variety of circumstances?

The focus in this chapter is on problems in policy implementation. One of the assumptions that can be made when addressing either policy development or policy implementation is that practically all school system policies have as their intention some form of school improvement. The intent here is to deal specifically with policies that directly relate to the teaching-learning environment. The major topics covered include policy development, policy implementation, and policy evaluation. Although it is not possible in practice to separate development completely from implementation, it is useful to discuss these as distinct sets of activities. Before beginning the review of policy-related problems and solutions, I present a case study of an attempt at program change in order to set the stage. The case study selected could have happened anywhere in North America. It exemplifies the reality of a multitude of similar events.

A Case Study
Upon the recommendation of the senior administrators, the board of education of a rather large school district (twenty-five schools) had passed a policy stating that all classroom teachers were to implement changes consistent with the government guidelines recommending language teaching in all subjects. In other words, the practice of "language across the curriculum" was to be implemented in

all schools by the end of the school year. The senior administrator responsible for program development, implementation, and evaluation, with the support of the chief education officer of the board, decided to hold a one-day in-service session for all twenty-five principals and the four senior administrators; the in-service program was to be conducted by the two language consultants.

The purposes of the day-long session were to review the objectives of the changes, to discuss implementation strategies, and to clarify any questions or concerns that the principals responsible for implementation would have. Each principal was to hold a staff meeting after school the following day and inform the teachers of the new policy and expectations for change. I was asked by the senior administrator responsible for programs to attend the in-service program as an observer and, at the end of the day, to present a summary of my impressions, providing an evaluation of the in-service and offering recommendations to assist the principals and other participants in the implementation process.

The session began with a presentation of the day's objectives by the senior administrator responsible for program development and implementation. It was followed by a presentation of the government guidelines on "language across the curriculum" by one of the two language consultants employed by the board. The principals were asked to seat themselves in groups of seven or eight in order to discuss the presentations and to work on implementation strategies. The consultants were available for assistance as requested by each group. My role was essentially one of observer; I moved from group to group and listened to the discussions. This activity extended throughout most of the day.

Given the brief explanation of the intent of the new program and the procedures for implementation, the concerns and questions increased both in number and in severity as the implications of what was being asked of the principals became evident. Some of the concerns I heard discussed were: the lack of clarity in outlining the problem and the goals; the lack of specific guidelines and procedures for implementing the changes; the lack of adequate resources, including time to work with teachers; a feeling of inadequacy about undertaking this initiative at this time; and a feeling of frustration with the manner in which this change was being "put on them." There was not general open disagreement with the intent of the program change, although a few of the principals did question the program's value. In fact, it was alleged that there were many principals and teachers who believed language teaching to be the responsibility of language teachers. However, given the fact that both board policy and senior administrative commitment were firm, the question of the value of the change was not given a serious consideration. The focus was on how to implement the change.

As the day went on, it became clear to me that no one (not even the consultants) knew what they were going to do in the schools as follow-up to the day's activities. The questions and concerns were directed to "why it can't be done" rather than to the task of developing implementation strategies. Further, although the principals were "polite" and willing to "follow the leader," their frustration about the lack of preparation for the change was evident. Given the severity of the situation, I decided this was not the time to offer congratulations for initiating a worthwhile program change.

I began my remarks with some observations by researchers on program implementation, commenting first on the list of reasons for resistance to change presented by Zander (1962):

1. The purpose is not made clear.

2. Those responsible for changing are not involved in the planning.

3. An appeal is based on personal reasons.

4. The social patterns of the work group are ignored.

5. There is poor communication regarding a change.

6. There is a fear of failure.

7. Excessive work pressure is involved.

8. The "cost" is too high, or the reward for making the change is seen as inadequate.

9. The current situation seems satisfactory.

10. There is a lack of respect for and trust in the change initiator.

Although I did not say so directly, I implied that the board did not know what it was doing. My recommendation was to spend one year studying the situation, developing a long-term plan with realistic goals, acquiring sufficient resources for in-service and implementation, and providing extensive in-service for all participants. The response from the principals was enthusiastic endorsement. From the chief education officer I received a letter indicating that I had set back curriculum change in that board by three years; however, six months later I received another letter from the senior administrator responsible for program saying that I was right in stating what I did at the time. She indicated that they were still studying the situation and were in the midst of developing a plan.

An examination of the nature of the changes required by this board's teaching staff and of the process the board used to prepare for implementation reveals obvious obstacles to change. The content of the changes intended by the policy included changes in curriculum content and methodology in most of the subjects, changes in the style of teaching by most of the teachers, and changes in student activities and expectations. Most of the constraints on successful implementation were present and ignored:

1. Teachers were not involved in the planning or goal-setting process.

2. The problems the changes were to solve were not clearly articulated, and there was no acknowledgement of there being a problem to begin with.

3. Information about the nature of the change was neither consistent nor clearly understood by those responsible for facilitating and implementing the change.

4. The resources available to assist in the implementation process were inadequate.

5. It was not clear what specific changes were expected, hence there was no way of knowing if the changes could be implemented.

6. What were presented as minor changes were, in fact, major changes in teacher role.

7. The timeline set for implementation was far from realistic.

It was obvious that any attempt to implement the policy would lead to frustration on the part of principals, who were responsible for implementation in their schools, and anger on the part of teachers, who were already burdened with other curricular changes. At best, the effect would be token acknowledgment of and adherence to board policy by the principals, without real change.

Framework

Several assumptions underlie the conceptualization of policy implementation. One assumption I am making is that there is *more than one way* to conceptualize policy implementation. Three ways are summarized by LaRocque (1983) in her review of the work of Berman (1981), House (1981), and Wildavsky (1979). They are the classical or technological model, the political model, and the cultural or evolutionary model.

In the classical or technological model the relationship between policymakers and policy implementors is assumed to be hierarchical, that of superordinate to subordinate. Thus it is assumed that policy decisions at the superordinate level will be followed by implementation at the subordinate level. The role of the administrator is one of ensuring that policy change orders are carried out. If applied to all policies, then we can expect that board policy, along with administrative and supervisory direction, leads directly to the implementation of changes. Consider a specific example. If the policy change is directed to changing how teachers teach, then the assumption that change will simply follow policy determination and administrative direction is almost certainly invalid. If, however, the policy mandates changes in bus routes, then one can predict, with considerable assurance, that the changes in bus routes will take place. The assumption made in this chapter is that the classical model can be applied to certain policy changes and not to others.

In the political model, the policy process is seen as a system of three environments, each with a specific function — policy formation, policy implementation, policy evaluation. The relationship between policymakers and policy implementors is assumed to be based on a balance of power, with each group having different resources under its control. Hence cooperation between implementors and policymakers must be negotiated. Using the example above, changes in how teachers teach must be negotiated between teachers and policymakers. In this example, one must question whether the supervisor and administrator are considered policymakers, enforcers, or facilitators (or a combination of all three). However, in the example of the changes in bus routes, or, to add another example, the addition of French immersion classes, there may be little need or opportunity for negotiation. It depends on the characteristics of the specific policy changes. Some decisions made by policymakers simply are not negotiable. The assumption here is that the political model cannot be applied to all policy changes.

In the cultural or evolutionary model, policy is assumed to be a set of multiple dispositions to act, the realization of which depends both on the intrinsic qualities of the policy and on the characteristics of the setting for implementation. In this model, the administrator and supervisor must understand the environment and the "fit" of the specific change to the environment at the time in question. This model can be applied to most policy changes, if one assumes that the process leading to the policy change is just as important as the process that follows the policy change. The actual policy statement, as legitimated by vote of the school district's elected officials, is not the start of policy implementation. The process leading to the vote and the process following the vote are *both* integral parts of the implementation process. Once again, the type of policy (type referring to a host of variables such as extent of effect on influential others, extent of and availability of required resources, and extent of change in preparing staff) is crucial to the usefulness of this model for increasing understanding of the implementation of policy changes. Some types of change in policy (for example, changes in the legal length of the school day and school year) receive widespread adherence irrespective of the "characteristics of the implementation setting."

Thus, *none* of the models apply to all changes in policy. What is needed is a framework which considers the types of policy change and which differentiates the corresponding role of the administrator and supervisor in each of the types. Table 5:1 illustrates a framework within which three sets of interacting variables constitute the model. The variable in the first line refers to the type of policy change implied in the conceptualization of each of the classical, political, and cultural models. The second variable refers to the state of readiness for change as indicated by a host of factors unique to the particular setting at a specific time with a given set of actors. The third variable takes into account the varying roles of the administrator and supervisor as required by the three possible conceptualizations of policy implementation identified above.

Table 5:1
Conceptualization of Policy Implementation

Type of Change	Mandated	Negotiable	Situational
Setting	Not Ready	Limited Readiness	Ready
Role of Administrators	Enforcers	Negotiators	Facilitators

Although much of what follows in this paper refers to program and curriculum change and hence emphasizes the interaction of only a few of the aspects of the model, the complexity of the change process necessitates a model that encompasses a greater variety of change characteristics than is found in any one type of policy change. In other words, the scope of the model exceeds that required for the implementation of any one set of policy changes.

Developing Realistic Policies

The American National School Boards Association (NSBA) offers assistance to school boards wanting help with policy development. It warns board members what can happen when boards fail to take policy development seriously. In a NSBA publication, *Board Policies on Policy Development* (1972 p. 3), some practices to avoid are pointed out:

1. *Instant policymaking.* That happens when the school board makes a decision hastily, without benefit of research, study, cool deliberation, due notice or professional opinion.

2. *Dictatorial policymaking.* That happens when the school board makes policy unilaterally, without seeking the counsel or advice of those who are to be affected.

3. *Illegal policymaking.* That happens when the school board fails to consult its attorney on matters where case law is still being written.

4. *Sloppy policymaking.* That happens when the board fails to assign the drafting of policy statements to a competent writer.

5. *Contradictory policymaking.* That happens when the board has no mechanism for the immediate retrieval of all past policy decisions which exist only as historical items buried in the books of minutes.

Not all of these poor practices apply equally well to problems of policy development and of implementation. The first, second, and fourth types are most directly related to the research on implementation. The research suggests that sometimes the difficulties experienced with, or the failure of, the implementation of change have less to do with the legalistic or contradictory nature of the actual policies than with a lack of involvement, the inappropriateness of the time and time limitations (Bernstein 1956; Downs 1972), a lack of commitment by those responsible for the actual implementation, and a lack of clarity and understanding of the problem and of the goals and procedures (Ingram and Mann 1980). Lay members of boards of education and administrators making recommendations to boards might be better off if they were more concerned with *how policy is set* — not just with what it says.

The research on policy development and the implications for implementation clearly emphasize the interrelatedness of development and implementation. The message for policy decision-makers is clear: implementation must be considered prior to the decision to legislate policy. Kritek (1976) points this out in a summary of the research identifying what policymakers and program planners need to do to reduce the problems that impede implementation:

1. Avoid abstract or overly ambitious objectives.

2. Incorporate user input into goal reformulation.

3. Avoid the tendency to underplan.

4. Consider the complexities of implementation.

5. Provide enough resources to deal with unanticipated problems which normally arise during implementation.

6. Consider the role change required of participants.

7. Prepare program managers to take an active role in assisting their staffs to deal with the problems of implementation, in creating conditions that foster motivation, and in monitoring and providing feedback in order to counter negative, unanticipated consequences and to capitalize on positive ones.

A comprehensive summary of the factors believed to affect implementation is provided by Fullan (1982). He contends that "twelve years of research has produced enough evidence for us to be fairly confident about what factors have the most influence" (p. 57). He categorizes the factors as (1) characteristics of the change, (2) characteristics at the school district level, (3) characteristics at the school level, and (4) characteristics external to the local system.

If we are to follow his advice in reducing the impediments to the successful implementation of program policies leading to school improvement, policy developers and decision-makers should do the following: (1) ensure there is a perceived need for change; (2) clarify the goals and means of the change; (3) assess the complexity of the change, that is, the degree of difficulty and extent of change required — high complexity might require the differentiation of activities into an array of components (Rosenblum and Louis 1979); and (4) use well-developed and high quality practical program materials. Although Fullan does not refer to the possibility that the perceived need is not necessarily a "real" need, that is, one supported by some significant others and/or by a factual rationale, policy developers ought to be assured that the reality of significant others (accompanied by substantiated evidence) coincides with the perception of those involved in the change.

For many practising educators and school board members, the research on effective schools has provided the impetus needed to recast their image of the school system into that of an entity that can improve schooling simply by changes in policy. Consequently, we have seen school district policies on goals, five-year plans, revised curricula, revised organizational structures, new program and student evaluation procedures, increased monitoring of systemwide progress, and revised procedures for the evaluation of teachers, consultants, and administrators. All these changes or additions in policy, obviously, are directed at improving schooling, which in many cases means improved test scores (Cuban 1984).

The policy changes are based on the belief that the connection between board decisions and classroom practices is direct, that is, that the structure of the school system is such that the line officers (superintendent, principal) can deliver the changes and hence assure the desired outcomes. Although this belief does not coincide with the evidence, it still remains in the minds of many of those responsible for policy development and decision making. Consequently, less attention has been paid to the implementation of policies. While the issues surrounding implementation are often less complex than those arising when policies are decided upon, implementation issues are much less easily resolved than policy development issues — the politics of implementation are more volatile because there are more people involved. As well, it is not easy (and sometimes impossible) to identify which implementation practices will lead to the desired outcomes and what unintended, and undesired, outcomes will emerge.

In an example of a board policy that was handled badly, Splitt provides a useful analysis of the problems arising after a board policy decision "to promote only those students who satisfactorily complete all course requirements each year. The practice of social promotion

is prohibited" (1981 p. 2). The stated causes of the problems that
followed were:

- the board acted too fast;
- there was no administrative analysis of the policy or of the
problems which might arise in trying to implement the policy;
- there was no detailed implementation plan for school
administrators;
- there was insufficient public awareness of the policy and no
opportunity for interested parents to become involved in the
policy-making process;
- there was no forum for give-and-take among the various participants in the policy-making process.

Policy Implementation

The Principal

Assuming that the principal is one of the key actors in policy implementation at the school level, Trider (1985) identified in a
literature search the factors claimed to influence the implementation behavior of principals. He categorized the factors into policy
specifications and context factors, as shown in Table 5:2.

Trider's own study of the factors influencing the policy implementation behavior of principals supported, in general, the results of
the studies he reviewed. In addition, based on the perceptions of those
surveyed, he was able to single out those factors that had the most
influence:

- principals' beliefs about what is best for students;
- principals' professional experiences;
- principals' agreement with the goals of the policy;
- principals' knowledge of the content of the specific change
being implemented;
- support of the central office administrators;
- extent of the planning undertaken by central office
administrators;
- value of the assistance provided by support personnel;
- working relationships among all levels of the professional
staff;
- the amount of direction the teaching staff was willing to accept
from the principal.

"All major research on innovation and school effectiveness shows
that the principal strongly influences the likelihood of change,"
(Fullan 1982 p. 71). The implications of this research for policymakers at the board and senior administrative levels extend to the
selection, promotion, and professional development of principals and
those who aspire to this position. Research also indicates the importance of the quality of working relationships among those who

Table 5:2
Research Conclusions Concerning the Implementation Behavior of Principals

---

POLICY SPECIFICATIONS
1. **Clearly Articulated Program Objectives**
    1.1   Objectives are easily understood by others
    1.2   Objectives are easily translated into appropriate behavior patterns
    1.3   The purpose of the project is clearly defined
    1.4   The impact on the "basic mission" of the institution
2. **Implementation Strategy**
    2.1   The implementation strategy is stated within the policy document
    2.2   The implementation strategy is easily understood
    2.3   Managing and monitoring procedures are stated in order to assure implementation
    2.4   Provision is made for appropriate local choices in the implementation process
    2.5   Strategy allows the teacher easy access to needed materials
    2.6   Strategy is compatible with differing styles of leadership
    2.7   The language of the written policy is motivational
3. **Complexity of the Innovation**
    3.1   The innovation as specified is easy to administer
    3.2   The policy specifications allow for teacher direction more so than administrative direction
4. **Structural Changes**
    4.1   Structural changes accompany the policy
    4.2   Structural changes delineate responsibilities for staff
    4.3   Policy contains specific job descriptions for key actors
    4.4   Policy provides a temporary structure compatible with the present administrative structure
    4.5   The necessary specialist assistance is made available by the policy

CONTEXT
1. **Personal Factors**
    1.1   Stage of concern of the change facilitator (principal)
    1.2   Assumptions pertaining to the teachers' training and ability to engage in the implementation process
    1.3   Principal's perception of his/her role
    1.4   Adopter's definition of the problem
2. **Organizational Factors**
    2.1   Resources—funding, time, personnel
    2.2   Planning—cooperative, on-line
    2.3   Adequately trained personnel
    2.4   A reward system consisting of morale, work, achievement and satisfaction
    2.5   Managing and monitoring procedures are initiated; management control will prevent distortion of goals
3. **Political Factors**
    3.1   Support of local administration
    3.2   Central office climate regarding innovation
    3.3   Technology level of the school district
    3.4   Demographic factors of the school
    3.5   Complexity of the organization
    3.6   Relationship between structure and environment
    3.7   Lack of awareness of the impact of the change on the "basic mission" of the organization
    3.8   Conflict over the relative importance of the goals
    3.9   Adoption based upon the principal's context
    3.10   Teachers' zone of acceptance and administration
    3.11   Understanding people, communities and cultures

Source: Trider 1985 pp. 29–32

must implement the change (Berman and McLaughlin 1978; Miles et al. 1978; Rosenblum and Louis 1979). These conclusions are justified in terms of experience and observation, but conclusive, empirical research results are still lacking.

The School

Leaving aside the crucial role of the principal (and the principal's relations with the central office) in the implementation of change, let us review what else we know about schools that relates to implementation of change. Consider some of the characteristics of the school as an organization, characteristics that can affect how school personnel deal with change.

First, school goals are diffuse. The school's mission is usually stated in abstract terms, making the measurement of overall outcomes extremely difficult to assess. In fact, some unintended outcomes of change are not known until long after the interventions are made (Miles and Schmuck 1971). Second, technical capability is often below what is needed. The knowledge base underlying educational practice is relatively weak and not well transmitted to teachers and principals. The skills needed to bring about change are sometimes below the level needed to achieve success in implementation (Fullan et al. 1986). Third, there are typically problems of horizontal coordination and vertical articulation both within schools and between them and other sectors of the school system. Also, if we accept the position that schools and school districts tend to be low-interdependent, "loosely coupled" systems (Weick 1976), then we can assume that goals and means often do not connect well and that accountability will be low and autonomy high. Fourth, schools have "thin walls"; they are relatively open to influence from pressures emanating from sources outside of the school itself. Schools, in fact, are "owned" by their environments and are non-competitive for resources. Consequently, since their survival is guaranteed, it follows that the incentives for change are sometimes rather feeble (Pincus 1974). Schools are constrained and decentralized. Although there is often considerable decentralization within the school and the school district, government directives and incentives do lead to norms and regulations which effectively limit autonomy within the school district (Miles 1977).

Three school-level factors summarize the influence of the school on implementation: the role of the principal, peer relationships, and teacher orientation (referring specifically to the extent to which teachers expect the students to reach appropriate levels of achievement).

The District

Characteristics at the level of the school district need to be considered as a factor in implementation. We should (1) be knowledgeable of the immediate past history of the individuals' and groups' experience with change; (2) make every attempt to ensure implementation-level participation in decisions about the change, which will tend to produce a higher quality planning process; (3) ensure that districtwide changes have the support of central administrators; (4) include ongoing staff development programs, with participant input into program decisions; and (5) adhere to a timeline that takes into consideration the slow development of the meaning of change at the individual level (Fullan 1982).

Empirical research studies have confirmed the importance and skill of district-level personnel in implementing innovations (Corbett et al. 1984; Cox 1983; Gerstein et al. 1986; Huberman and Miles 1984; Odden et al. 1986). All these studies point to the critical role of ongoing assistance, support, and pressure from district consultants and/or district administrators in implementing change.

In four case studies of curriculum implementation, Fullan et al. (1986) arrived at some major "thematic" conclusions that exemplify what was happening in the four school districts examined:

• a shift in the focus of concern away from implementation of specific innovations toward organizational or system approaches to program improvements;
• the integration of curriculum and professional development;
• the integration of authority and support;
• school-level and district-level co-development;
• greater teacher involvement and incentives;
• a shift in the role of consultants from technical experts to experts in the process and procedures for managing change;
• the increased importance of curriculum leadership and skills as means to promotion;
• the view of planned change as longitudinal development.

Fullan et al. see these themes as steps in the right direction. However, this position is based more on their belief about what should happen than on evidence indicating that these changes lead to more effective implementation or more effective schools. Also, the authors seem to imply that most change comes from involvement at all levels. Yet Huberman and Miles (1984) found in their study of innovations in twelve school districts that in nearly all cases the innovations were initiated by district personnel, not by school personnel. Once initiated, the successful cases were characterized by strong administrative commitment and support at the district level.

The External Environment
Still other kinds of change, those with greater impact across school districts and provinces, such as French immersion, are the direct result of political pressure on board members from external groups with little involvement in the organization.

The factor of external environment referred to by Fullan (1982) is limited primarily to the effect of government agencies on implementation of change. The difficulties in the relationships between external and internal groups are characterized by a "lack of role clarity, ambiguity about expectations, absence of regular personal forums of communication, ambivalence between authority and support roles of agencies, and solutions which are worse than the original problems" (p. 74).

Other Research

Many researchers and theorists (Berman 1981; Browne and Wildavsky 1984; Fullan and Park 1981; Rossman, Corbett and Firestone 1985) see implementation as mutual adaptation. Browne and Wildavsky refer to two implementation processes. "One is the initially perceived, formally defined, prospectively expected set of causal links required to result in a desired outcome; the other is the unexpected nexus of causality that actually evolves during implementation" (1984 p. 217).

McLaughlin summarized her study of classroom organization innovations by suggesting that a shift in change agent policies from a focus on the delivery system to the deliverer is in order. "Unless the developmental needs of the users are addressed, and unless project methods are modified to suit the needs of the user and the institutional setting, the promise of new technologies is likely to be unfulfilled" (1976 p. 180).

Williams (1976) defines implementation as the stage between decision and operation. It starts with the development of program guidelines or design specifications; moves to what may be a quite lengthy stage of trying to work through a myriad of technical, administrative, staff, and institutional problems that confront a new activity; and ends when the experiment is deemed ready to test or when the non-experimental activity is judged fully operational.

Williams provides an orderly model for implementation analysis (which must be performed before a decision is made) and assessment (which must start early in the implementation process), but cautions that these are heuristic devices used to facilitate exposition. "Implementation is too complicated, and too little is known about it to expect either orderliness or rigor when analysis and assessment are actually undertaken" (1976 p. 271). Williams further states that program objectives are often so elusive as to be difficult to determine at all, much less define rigorously. One could ask: Why undertake the change if the objectives are not clear, if there is disagreement about the objectives, and if there is a lack of rigor in the assessment? Obviously, the answer is that one should not attempt change with unclear objectives if clear objectives are important. However, Williams goes on to support Pincus (1974) in supporting the trial of innovations with proper assessment, rather than pursuing uncertain goals with unclear technologies. He also places great emphasis on implementation analysis prior to decision making. Implementation analysis should investigate the technical capacity to implement, policitial feasibility, and the technical and political strategies for implementation.

The entire question of success in implementation of policy is one that needs extensive deliberation.

Policy Evaluation

The notion that a policy is implemented or not implemented or that a policy succeeds or fails is too precise and absolute to have any real meaning. Given the reality of continuous adjustment in both goals and activities in the policy implementation process, and given the problems inherent in measuring the range of impacts attributable to any particular policy intervention, it is questionable whether many of the policies directed at school improvement can be characterized as complete successes or unmitigated failures (Dutton, Danziger and Kraemer 1980).

Nevertheless, it does seem possible to point to problems in implementation and to suggest what could have been done to reduce the chances for failure — or, stated in a more positive light, to enhance the chances for success. This is possible if we assume that the assessment of the policy implementation, defined here in terms of positive and negative outcome, is not limited solely to the post-implementation assessment. Because of the multiple spillover effects of any significant change, assessment of policy implementation seems appropriate at any point in time and at any phase of the implementation process.

In spite of the apparent success of Furtwengler's (1986) and others' (Glenn 1981; Neale et al. 1981) experience with changes leading to improved schooling, the implementation of policy change is not always easy to assess. "Success and failure are slippery concepts, often highly subjective and reflective of an individual's goals, perception of need, and perhaps even psychological disposition toward life" (Ingram and Mann 1980 p. 12). Because of the "normal" self-interest of individuals and groups, some will see success where others see compromise, and perhaps failure.

Consider some of the potential hazards of the evaluation of policy. First, there are the differing interpretations of the value of the policy. In the case study cited above in which the board passed a policy on language teaching for all teachers, a goodly number of teachers and principals felt strongly that the teaching of language should be the primary responsibility and domain of the language teacher.

Second, there are the problems inherent in deciding when to conduct the assessment. How soon after policy is passed should evaluation of results be undertaken? In other words, when is implementation completed? Obviously, in terms of the formal support given to many program changes, the implementation is over as soon as it starts.

Third, have we asked about alternative policies? What would be the consequences of failing to pass the policy? What alternatives would emerge given this circumstance? Would other solutions to the apparent problem take place? Would the problem change? Although a policy has been implemented, another alternative is offered that would result in greater gain. Has the perceived success or failure of the policy changed?

Fourth, the time frame and situational factors at the time of the evaluation of the policy implementation may also alter the judgment about success and failure. Remember the board policies which led to the building of open-area schools. Evaluation of the effectiveness of those policies when the buildings were first completed differed substantially from the evaluation of several years later. Did a few years difference mean the difference between success and failure? Did the concept of effectiveness change over time? Desired effects vary with the political temper of the times.

The relationship of one policy to another may complicate the judgment about policy success and failure. Consider the policies of "mainstreaming" and specialized secondary schools. One policy is based on the assumption that merged differences are desirable; the other that separation of differences is to be valued. Obviously, distinctions can be drawn between cases. However, how does one distinguish success and failure given the confusion of two apparently polarized positions stated within the policies of the same boards of education?

Finally, there is the situation in which the policy implementation has led to differing effects on various segments of the organization and/or on the population served. How do we assess the effectiveness of the implementation of one policy that caused some negative side effects in other parts of the school system? Do we ignore the side effects or do we take into account all of the effects? For example, assume that policy changes reducing the class size for students with special needs has produced positive outcomes. If this has been brought about by policy changes increasing the size of other classes, and if we assume that this has led to certain negative outcomes, how then do we assess the extent of success or failure of either of the policies?

All this goes to say that the evaluation of policy implementation can be fraught with dangers, at least from the position of those responsible for the success of changes in the school or school district. From a technical point of view, assessment can often be straightforward; one can "follow the book" on various ways of collecting and analyzing data and assessing the perceived and real effects of implementation according to structured criteria. However, in terms of defending the results, the quality of the technique is usually not the primary problem. The key problem is the usefulness (relevance to decision making) of the results in deciding the extent of success and what to do about results that do not support the intentions of the policy. Nagel suggests one way of classifying post-adoption policy failures:

One dimension is in terms of the subjective intent of the decision-makers versus the objective reality. In terms of *intent*, a policy is a success if it achieves its goals, and a failure if it does not. In terms of *reality*, a policy is a success if its benefits minus its costs were intended. A second dimension is in terms of quantity and quality. A policy is a *quantitative* failure if its achievement units fall below an intended or objective standard, even though there is some net achievement. A policy is a *qualitative* failure if it produces more undesirable than desirable results, as measured either by the intentions of the decision makers or by the objective effects regardless of intent. (1980 p. 8)

Conclusion

If we agree with Majone and Wildavsky (1984), then implementation eludes understanding. The confusion arises out of conflicting positions on various aspects of the implementation of policy. One model of implementation focusses on implementation as control; this rational model prescribes clearly stated goals, detailed plans, tight controls and incentives, and indoctrination. In the interaction model, goals and plans are minimized in importance. Since there is little reality in the adopted policies for actual practice, the importance of the interactions among players and between players and the environment is paramount. Policies are seen as dispositions. Hence, implementation begins neither with words nor deeds but with multiple dispositions to act or to treat certain situations in certain ways. This led the proponents of this model to conclude that since policies are continuously transformed by implementing actions that simultaneously alter resources and objectives and since resources and objectives are the major common components of all implementation, it is important to recognize that implementation shapes policy. They also conclude that the assumption that policy shapes implementation is subject to some question, given the extent of failure at policy implementation. Further, their position is that implementation is evolution. "Since it takes place in a world we never made, we are usually right in the middle of the process, with events having occurred before and (we hope) continuing afterward. . . . When we act to implement a policy, we change it" (Majone and Wildavsky 1984 p. 177).

It seems that the potential problems that prevent (or result from) policy implementation might cause one to avoid all change. If it isn't broken, don't fix it. This business world maxim does not apply to schools, however, at least not in any significant way. There will always be identifiable areas (student, staff, program, organization) in need of improvement. Ongoing changes in the environment, in personnel, in objectives, and in a host of other school-related and people-related factors continue to take place, irrespective of what the school is doing. Consequently, persons in positions of responsibility in schools and school districts must continue to seek ways of meeting needs. The key is to set realistic policy expectations and to select the most appropriate means for achieving these expectations. There is enough evidence from research and practice to assist those responsible for ensuring that policy development and implementation can indeed improve schooling.

References

Berman P 1981 Educational change: An implementation paradigm. In: Lehming R, Kane M (eds.) *Improving Schools: Using What We Know.* Sage, Beverly Hills, California

Berman P, McLaughlin M 1978 *Federal Programs Supporting Educational Change,* Vol. VIII: *Implementing and Sustaining Innovations.* Rand Corporation, Santa Monica, California

Bernstein M 1956 *Regulating Business by Independent Commission.* Princeton University Press, Princeton, New Jersey

Browne A, Wildavsky A 1984 Implementation as mutual adaptation. In: Pressman J L, Wildavsky A (eds.) *Implementation,* 3rd edn. University of California Press, Berkeley, California

Corbett H, Dawson J, Firestone W 1984 *School Context and School Change.* Teachers College Press, New York

Cox P 1983 Inside-out and outside-in: Configurations of assistance and their impact on school-improvement efforts. Paper presented at the American Educational Research Association Annual Meeting, Chicago

Cuban L 1984 Transforming the frog into a prince: Effective schools research, policy and practice at the district level. *Harvard Educational Review* 54(2): 129–151

Downs A 1972 Up and down in ecology: The issue attention cycle. *Public Interest* Summer: 38–50

Dutton W H, Danziger J N, Kraemer K L 1980 Did the policy fail?: The selective use of automated information in the policy-making process. In: Ingram H M, Mann D E (eds.) *Why Policies Succeed or Fail.* Sage, Beverly Hills, California

Fullan M 1982 *The Meaning of Educational Change.* OISE Press, Toronto

Fullan M, Anderson S, Newton E 1986 *Support Systems for Implementing Curriculum in School Boards.* Ministry of Education, Toronto

Fullan M, Park P 1981 *Curriculum Implementation.* Ministry of Education, Toronto

Furtwengler W J 1986 Implementing strategies for a school effectiveness program. *Phi Delta Kappan* 67(4): 262–265

Gerstein R, Carnine D, Zoref L, Cronin D 1986 A multifaceted study of change in seven inner-city schools. *The Elementary School Journal* 86: 257–276

Glenn B C 1981 *What Works? An Examination of Effective Schools for Poor Black Children.* Center for Law and Education, Harvard University, Cambridge, Massachusetts

House E R 1981 Three perspectives on innovation: Technological, political, and cultural. In: Lehming R, Kane M (eds.) *Improving Schools: Using What We Know.* Sage, Beverly Hills, California

Huberman A, Miles M 1984 *Innovation Up Close.* Plenum Press, New York

Ingram H M, Mann D E 1980 Policy failure: An issue deserving analysis. In: Ingram H M, Mann D E (eds.) *Why Policies Succeed or Fail.* Sage, Beverly Hills, California

Kritek W J 1976 Lessons from the literature on implementation. *Educational Administration Quarterly* 12(3): 86–102

LaRocque L 1983 *Policy Implementation in a School District.* Unpublished Ph.D. thesis, Simon Fraser University, Vancouver

Majone G, Wildavsky A 1984 Implementation as evolution. In: Pressman J L, Wildavsky A (eds.) *Implementation,* 3rd edn. University of California Press, Berkeley, California

McLaughlin M 1976 Implementation as mutual adaptation: Change in classroom organization. In: Williams W, Elmore R (eds.) *Social Program Implementation.* Academic Press, New York

Miles M B 1977 Planning and implementing new schools: A general framework. Center for Policy Research, New York

Miles M B et al. 1978 Project on social architecture in education: Final report. Center for Policy Research, New York

Miles M B, Schmuck R A 1971 Improving schools through organization development: An overview. In: Schmuck R A, Miles M B (eds.) *Organization Development in Schools.* University Associates, La Jolla, California

Nagel S S 1980 Introduction. In: Ingram H M, Mann D E (eds.) *Why Policies Succeed or Fail.* Sage, Beverly Hills, California

National School Boards Association 1972 *Board Policies on Policy Development: Educational Policies Development Kit.* National School Boards Association, Waterford, Connecticut

Neale D C, Bailey W J, Ross B E 1981 *Strategies for School Improvement: Cooperative Planning and Organizational Development.* Allyn and Bacon, Boston

Odden A, Anderson B, Farrar E 1986 Causal links of local school variables associated with successful implementation of state education improvement programs. Paper presented at the American Educational Research Association Annual Meeting, San Francisco

Pincus J 1974 Incentives for innovation in public schools. *Review of Educational Research* 44(1): 113–144

Rosenblum S, Louis K 1979 *Stability and Change: Innovation in an Educational Context.* ABT Associates, Cambridge, Massachusetts

Rossman G B, Corbett H D, Firestone W A 1985 *Professional Cultures, Improvement Efforts and Effectiveness: Findings from a Study of Three High Schools.* Research for Better Schools, Philadelphia, Pennsylvania

Sieber S D 1968 Organizational influences on innovative roles. In: Eidell T L, Kitchel J M (eds.) *Knowledge Production and Utilization in Educational Administration.* CASEA, University of Oregon, Eugene, Oregon

Splitt D A 1981 Check how policy is set — not just what it says. *Updating School Board Policies* 12(12): 1–4

Trider D 1985 *Factors Influencing the Policy Implementation Behavior of Principals.* Unpublished Ed.D. thesis, OISE, University of Toronto, Toronto

Weick K 1976 Educational organizations as loosely-coupled systems. *Administrative Science Quarterly* 21: 1–19

Wildavsky A 1979 Implementation as evolution. In: Pressman J L, Wildavsky A (eds.) *Implementation,* 2nd edn. University of California Press, Berkeley, California

Williams W 1976 Implementation analysis and assessment. In: Williams W, Elmore R (eds.) *Social Program Implementation.* Academic Press, New York

Zander A 1962 Resistance to change — Its analysis and prevention. *Advanced Management* 15/16: 9–11

6/Effective Schools, Organizational Culture, and Local Policy Initiatives

John Davis

Davis suggests that school culture is profound, unique, and robust. If he is right, major effectiveness reforms will be resisted by many schools if they imply normative change. Some questions to consider include: If culture is so robust, how do some schools change so quickly in certain circumstances? Does change of robust cultures demand clever, manipulative administrative techniques? What are the ethics of such conflict?

Introduction

Within the last decade, the effective schools movement has generated a large amount of literature, much of it descriptive, a fair amount of it evaluative and analytical, and some of it even predictive with respect to the future of the movement. This literature makes it apparent that the extent to which effective school concepts have been implemented in school systems is, to a large degree, determined by the policies of the systems and may range from the giving of tacit approval for a single school's experimentation with effective school concepts to mandating systemwide implementation of attempts to increase the effectiveness of all schools in the system.

The use of the word *policy* implies an allocation of values throughout a system, which, in turn, evokes the currently popular concept of organizational culture, a concept recently used by Goodlad (1984) in his discussion of the effective schools issue. Students of organizational culture note that any institution's culture reflects the pattern of basic assumptions and beliefs supporting its methods of operation. In turn, those assumptions and beliefs are adapted from those of the culture in which the organization is set. Both effective and ineffective schools have their own organizational cultures which have evolved as staffs cope with the problems that are part of organizational life. The concept of organizational culture is discussed more fully later in this chapter.

Policymakers should recognize the power of an organization's culture to facilitate or impede the process of change. The importance of good leaders in creating cultures supportive of change (in this case supportive of effective schools) cannot be overemphasized. Cultures assist members of organizations to cope; they are usually resistant to change. Policies should support efforts to create cultures which, in turn, are predisposed to supporting concepts of effectiveness.

Effectiveness and Goals

Efforts by local systems to improve school effectiveness through policy development are confronted with the hurdle of defining effectiveness. In a review of effective schools, Purkey and Smith (1983) observe that effectiveness has commonly been linked with high academic achievement as measured by standardized achievement tests. At the same time, they question that definition, asking,

> Should school effectiveness be so defined? Is a school effective if there is great variance between its lowest- and highest-achieving students? Finally, what effect would an effective schools program have on the quality of student life in the school, on the "hidden curriculum" of the school, and on the nature of teachers' work in the school? (p. 448)

These questions were addressed in part by a team of researchers (Rowan, Bossert and Dwyer 1983) from the Far West Laboratory for Educational Research and Development. Writing in the *Educational Researcher* they noted that

> the narrow focus on instructional outcomes also has implications for the design of school improvement programs. It has long been recognized that organizational effectiveness is a multidimensional construct, and that devoting scarce resources to an improvement in one domain may lead to decreased effectiveness in other domains. (p. 25)

Ironically, although the effective schools movement seems to concentrate almost exclusively on academic proficiency, most statements of the goals of education are far more comprehensive. One is attracted to the appealing, albeit vague, definition proposed by the National Committee on Excellence in Education. This definition classifies effective schools as those where students perform "on the boundary of individual ability in ways that test and push back personal limits, in schools and in the workplace" (Duke 1985 p. 672). Nevertheless, although the criteria of linguistic and numerical excellence seem to be common in all expectations of excellence, it must be recognized that they are insufficient. For example, in Roman Catholic school systems, the definition of effectiveness includes specific religious beliefs and values.

In deciding which goals their schools are going to emphasize, local policymakers must be aware of and understand the cultural, political, economic, social, and psychological pressures which influence the direction of education in their jurisdictions. The localized nature of policy making is emphasized in this chapter, for although an overarching educational bureaucracy at the state or provincial level may mandate the goals of education, the refinement, articulation, and hierarchical arrangement of those goals is usually left to local school systems. An examination of the policy manuals for those systems shows a wide divergence of opinion with respect to the priority attached to externally imposed goals.

The selection of goals for a school system can be equated with the authoritative allocation of values for the system, an action legally performed in Canada and the U.S. on behalf of the system by school trustees through the creation of district policy. However, the school trustees' role in policy creation varies considerably. Administrators also play an important role in policy development, offering suggestions and information in some systems and actually writing policy in others (Awender 1985; McLeod 1984). Ideally, they work with trustees as a team. In the particular instance of policy setting to increase school effectiveness, team work seems imperative since elected officials and administrators represent important subcultures of the organization whose views must be recognized.

In this chapter, recognition is made of the fact that, for most people, school effectiveness refers specifically to achievement in basic subjects such as numeracy and literacy. However, since the main theme of this paper concerns organizational culture, my ultimate purpose is to examine how cultures may be created, albeit with difficulty, to support thrusts for effectiveness throughout the entire school curriculum.

Organizational Culture

Policy decisions evolve in organizational settings. Such settings are characterized by particular ways of dealing with problems, based upon commonly held values and assumptions. Hence, Schein's definition of organizational culture appears relevant.

> Organizational culture is the pattern of basic assumptions that a given group has invented, discovered, or developed in learning to cope with its problems of external adaptation and internal integration, and that have worked well enough to be considered valid, and, therefore, to be taught to new members as the correct way to perceive, think, and feel in relation to these problems. (1984 p. 3)

Schein (1984) argues that organizational culture is the key to organizational excellence, or, as may be inferred, the key to effective schools. He further suggests that organizational culture can be examined at several levels: (1) the visible artifact level, which is manifested in such physical structures as buildings, technology, and written material, such as policy documents; (2) a values level, which may be analyzed through examining policies or by interviewing people about the reasons for their behavior; and (3) an assumptions level, which is typically unconscious but which is the most powerful determinant of behavior. An understanding of organizational culture is a crucial and necessary factor in furthering our knowledge of effective schools, for each level of culture has a special message for the effective school researcher.

At the visible level, rituals and ceremonies such as school organizational structure, teaching strategies, grade levels, evaluations, and promotions can be noted. Since most of these rituals are of major importance to the proponents of effective schooling practices, two observations seem necessary. Tyler (1985 p. 49) observes that the most prevalent model of school structure today is one characterized by "a loosely coupled system, in which technologies are uncertain, goals unclear" and in which the formal structures "tend towards anarchy." The second observation (Tyler 1985), somewhat in opposition to the first, is derived from the work of T. B. Greenfield (personal communication 1987) — organizations are not loosely coupled and formally defined, but are coalescences of the value orientations of those persons who inhabit the system.

In these observations we find the two historical traditions of organizational study: one with an emphasis on rationality, order, technology; the other with a concern for subjective, value-laden factors. Students of organizational culture today often try to accommodate both viewpoints (Ouchi and Wilkins 1985), although that accommodation is not so noticeable among academically oriented proponents of effective schools studies. A closer examination of the visible artifact level of organizational culture will illustrate this point. What is immediately apparent is that many of the visible manifestations of culture have resulted from the accommodation of most schools to external forces which may emanate from society in general, from the school system, or from political entities such as government education offices. Because these artifacts are tangible things, they either are or are imagined to be susceptible to manipulation. That manipulation rarely considers the values and assumptions underlying the visible artifacts; rather, it is effected through policies and procedures directed toward visible organizational devices. Consider, for example, such artifacts as standards (e.g., an average of 70 percent for admission to certain programs), professional development programs, curriculum development activities, or even evaluation procedures. All too often, the bustle of activity surrounding each of these concerns, although real and pressing, approaches superficiality in nature. The admissions committee may accept a candidate with a 65 percent average this year and one with 63.2 percent next year if there are fewer applicants; the professional development committee fills a slot in next month's program with someone who was recommended by the friend of a friend; the curriculum development committee tries to make sure that teachers feel ownership in the next guideline through becoming "involved"; and the evaluation process is carried out according to the changing values of those who were involved in its implementation. The ritual observances have been met and follow approved district policy, or, in the absence of policy, standard operating procedures. It does not appear to be of much consequence whether these ritual observances are directly related to educational substance. What is important is that the process, rather than the content of that process, has evolved over time into the accepted and standard response of the organization when confronting change.

This suggests that organizations tend to accept behavior at the artifact level as a legitimate response to problems, a response which closely approximates the anxiety-avoidance situation as described by Schein (1984 p. 8):

> Once a response is learned because it successfully avoids anxiety, it is likely to be repeated indefinitely. The reason is that the learner will not willingly test the situation to determine whether the cause of the anxiety is still operating. Thus all rituals, patterns of thinking or feeling, and behaviour that may originally have been motivated by a need to avoid a painful, anxiety-provoking situation are going to be repeated, even if the causes of the original pain are no longer acting, because the avoidance of anxiety is, itself, positively reinforcing.

Of course, schools and school systems perform rituals for reasons other than anxiety avoidance. They may have experimented with various procedures until they found one that worked, and they now continue to use it — a positive problem-solving situation (Schein 1984). Both types of situation exist, but Schein holds that anxiety-reducing procedures are more stable. Therefore, they tend to be used more frequently and become, in effect, standard operating procedures in the system, occasionally even taking on the guise of policy. Moreover,

> Since the basic assumptions that make up an organization's culture serve the secondary function of stabilizing much of the internal and external environment for the group, and since that stability is sought as a defence against the anxiety which comes with uncertainty and confusion, these deeper parts of the culture either do not change or change very slowly. (Schein 1984 p. 10)

The impact of certain external regulatory demands upon schools and school systems is not denied. These forces can legislate changes, such as curriculum revisions, external examinations, and the length of the school day. However, such impositions do little to change the culture of the organization, for the essence of that culture is derived from the relationships among individuals and, specifically, from coping mechanisms engendered through those relationships. The general nature of interactions, such as those between students and teachers, is relatively unchanging over time, thus reinforcing the stability of the culture. Consequently, change within the system will be slow, possibly painful, and will encounter strong resistance. In fact, Schein believes that unless large numbers of people who cling to the original culture are dismissed, it may not be possible to effect change. It is interesting to note that while most attempts to implement change are made at the artifact level, the resistance comes from the deeper, more powerful level of values — a reflection perhaps of the findings of Meyer and Rowan (1977), who perceived beneath the visible artifacts of schools another world whose realities are based upon a quite different value system from that evident at first glance. And yet the rituals are important. Once a new set of values and assumptions emerges in an organization, its visible manifestations will help to confirm and consolidate the new structure.

Yes, change does happen! But, as Cameron (1986) observes, the most effective organizations are characterized by such paradoxes as contradictions, opposing points of view, and incompatible policies and procedures. In education, paradoxes of organizational life are not confined to the system level, for within the broader culture of the system there will exist many subcultures, which may conflict with each other as well as with the pervading culture of the system. Even within schools, organizational behavior may not bear a strong relationship to the professed goals of the system (Rosenholtz 1985). The lack of fit between goals and behaviors, frequently termed "loose coupling," is probably another reason why schools resist change and why implementation strategies are so frequently unsuccessful (Purkey and Smith 1983; Rowan et al. 1983). At the same time, it should be noted that all effective schools do not share identical cultural characteristics.

A lack of recognition of these significant facts and the difficulty in bringing about the fit between goals and behavior are unquestionably the major reasons why the effective schools movement may well have peaked in terms of momentum. In terms of organizational culture, what seems to be apparent is that the majority of effective school strategists are working at the visible artifact level of culture rather than at the more important but also more complex levels of values and assumptions. For the policymakers concerned with making less effective schools more effective there are almost insurmountable challenges ahead and it is to these that the next section of this chapter is addressed.

Challenges and Policy Initiatives

The two major hurdles to be faced by school effectiveness proponents relate, first, to defining effectiveness and, second, to working toward school improvement at more profound levels of organizational culture than those which are readily and visibly apparent. Each of the major hurdles has a concomitant set of smaller problems, resulting in a truly Gordian knot.

Thus far, I have identified a series of interrelated problems, and although various criteria for effectiveness have been noted, the general tenor of the chapter has been cautionary. However, with Purkey and Smith (1983), I can see threads of commonality emerging from the school effectiveness research, even from the faulty research, which may yield promising results.

> Flaws in the original research should not discredit the notion of discovering effective school characteristics — seed for school improvement that can be sown elsewhere. However, the opposite approach — blanket acceptance — would be dangerous. (Purkey and Smith 1983 p. 439)

As indicated earlier, attempts to make schools more effective must be done within the context of a knowledge of, and a desire to work with, organizational culture at both the system and the school levels.

Much current effective schools literature tends to define effectiveness in rather strict academic terms. Interestingly, at the Ontario School Trustees Council conference for new trustees held in Toronto, Canada, in January 1987, the government, university, and lay speakers all emphasized the inadequacy of that concept. What then ought an effective school to look like? In answering the question, school system trustees and administrators will need to consider not only the political and economic realities of the present political scene (the external and internal pressures referred to earlier) but also the sociological and psychological dimensions of the organizational culture (or cultures) of the systems. The process of goal clarification can be lengthy and in some cases never-ending, with systems opting instead to adopt the objectives of supra-organizations such as departments of education. Actual completion of the exercise can bring its own trauma, especially if elected officials and administrators find themselves in philosophically different courts. On the other hand, elected officials waive their right to set system goals if they simply direct their chief executive officers to bring in mission statements for their amendment and approval.

School systems do not have a very good track record for setting goals that increase the effectiveness of their schools, for reasons discussed. As Goodlad (1984 p. 7) emphasizes:

> Because policy makers and many school reformers appear to lack understanding of the school as a culture, they continue to recommend a relatively narrow array of interventions that have little or nothing to do with improving the health of the school ecosystem.

In practice, this narrow array of interventions may foster "best" solutions that are adhered to rigidly, to the detriment of human creativity and development — two accomplishments which may owe more to learning from trial and error than from proven facts (Duke 1985 p. 673). Nevertheless, a general policy expressing an expectation of effectiveness at the system level is a desirable precondition for increasing effectiveness throughout the system; this general statement will necessitate more specific reformulation at the school level. Beyond writing policy, the school board is empowered to engage in very tangible actions such as long-range planning and the allocation of the fiscal, physical, and human resources necessary to support its goals. Moreover, many school-level characteristics felt to promote achievement should also be evident at the system level. For example, system leaders should be seen as setting high standards and as becoming personally committed to encouraging effectiveness. The climate for change within the system must be perceived as supportive and free from recrimination. Within such a milieu, the individual school is seen as the key element in any attempt to improve system effectiveness (Goodlad 1984).

One reason why this may be so is that as systems become large a certain amount of differentiation develops. In a large school this may occur along departmental lines; in a school system, it will be evident in the presence of various school and support services. The nature of the differentiation will help to define the work of the group within each subunit and, as well, create a particular subculture to support that work. Subunits will share some common characteristics which help create a type of generalized organizational culture in the whole system, but they will also possess certain discrete characteristics that create cultures and climates unique to each of them. Among the unique cultural characteristics created are some related to task, as noted above; some to contractual factors such as location and nature of the student body; and some to the composition of the staff. It is easier to analyze, understand, and change the culture of a smaller unit, such as a school, than that of a whole system. Moreover, since achievement seems to be increased where the teachers show a common vision and values and where they participate in shared decision making, the degree to which this is possible seems to be inversely proportionate to the size of the unit. As well, Graham Down, executive director of the Council for Basic Education in the United States, cites research suggesting that efforts to increase school effectiveness are "diluted and diminished when decision making moves away from the individual school and edicts are promulgated from afar" (1985 p. 19).

It is absolutely necessary, then, to recognize the strengths of the cultures within individual schools, and any move to increase school effectiveness should be understood and supported by those cultures. Since support implies a degree of staff consensus, the importance of the nature or direction of that consensus must also be recognized. As Purkey and Smith (1983 p. 442) note:

> Staffs could agree on educationally unsound ideas and practices; consensus could also act as a buffer and prevent critical examination of the school or a proposed change. While staff agreement is important, we do not mean that it should be uncritical.

The school system plays an important role in orienting the direction of school-based change. At the level of the district, consultation, approvals, and sanctions help set the nature of innovations. Coordinated meetings of school-based instructional leaders help set directions for the system and have the potential for use in training leaders to fulfil their instructional role more successfully. One important aspect of this in-service activity should be training in how to work both within the school culture in order to increase school effectiveness and with the school community whose support, rejection, or indifference can powerfully influence school programs. Local policy should permit schools a great deal of program flexibility in order to accommodate the needs of special community groups — possibly, in part, through the provision of compensatory programs (Watkins 1984) and certainly through permitting the development of alternative curricula.

Policy and Organizational Culture

To reiterate the point made earlier, all effective schools do not display common characteristics. Therefore, it is almost impossible for a system to create a policy that applies specifically to all schools; indeed, a fundamental characteristic of policy is that it should be a general guide to discretionary action. Consequently, system policy should encourage policy development at the local school level where it is not only a matter of great importance but necessarily follows from a recognition of the fact that schools have relatively distinct cultures and will operate within boundaries defined by those cultures. Schools developing policies to support goals of increased effectiveness will consequently formulate various and often quite different standard operating procedures to help them attain those goals. Researchers have attempted to draw from these different procedures a list of common factors which must be in place if effectiveness goals are to be realized. Some of these lists will now be examined.

In attempting to create a conceptual model for the development and maintenance of a coordinated school culture, Millikan (1984) creates an extensive list of bases to be considered. His work is especially valuable in that while the bases apply to schools attempting to become more effective academically, they apply equally well to schools embracing other goals as well. Millikan discusses the importance of such factors as leadership (strong, direct, consistent, sensitive, supportive, responsive, and committed); clear, shared goals; vision; frequent evaluation; and school climate. As well, he emphasizes the necessity of strong, important rituals to support the culture. Purkey and Smith (1983 p. 429) isolate five indicators of effectiveness defined in the traditional sense of academic achievement. Their list includes "strong administrative leadership, high expectations for children's achievement, an orderly atmosphere conducive to learning, an emphasis on basic skill acquisition, and frequent monitoring of pupil progress." Duke (1987) emphasizes the overarching importance of strong leadership in the school and, as well, high expectations for students, collegial decision making, and personal commitment. Rutter and his associates (1979) postulate that the individual practices in effective schools are less important than the way those practices coalesce into a particular culture supportive of the students within the schools. Rossman et al. provide a tidy summary of various researchers' opinions:

> Although each author has his preferred list, there is convergence on three categories. Broadly, these include leader attention to desired values and deliberate role modelling; shaping organizational systems to express cultural assumptions; and interpreting the symbolic elements of organizations — the stories, myths, mottos and symbols that both reflect and shape beliefs. (1985 p. 16)

Rossman's summary is probably most useful in that it specifically examines the effective schools movement within the context of cultural change. By expanding it only slightly, however, several policy considerations could be drawn.

Policy Prescription. Effective schools will be driven by policies, developed at the school level, which consider and reflect the culture and history of the institution. These policies should be developed within the rubric of school board policy.

Leadership. Leadership is the hinge upon which school cultures swing. Strong leadership is necessary to implement a school effectiveness program, and although other administrators or groups of teachers may provide this, ideally it should emanate from the principal. Recent research (Leithwood and Stager 1986) shows that highly effective principals possess many characteristics which effective school proponents would recognize as desirable traits in leaders attempting to increase student achievement. For example, effective principals emphasize programs; they set overall school directions; they are concerned about building staff morale; and, even more importantly, they provide a rationale for their priorities. As well, they use deliberative models for problem solving and skilfully use their staffs in such a way as to develop ownership in the arrangement and direction of the school. As Purkey and Smith note (1983 p. 443), strong leadership is especially essential in the early stages of the improvement process when steps must be taken to develop a culture that will support the planned change. Of the various ways by which cultural change may be accomplished, three will be mentioned here, and one discussed in detail.

Rossman et al. (1985) label the three cultural change processes as evolutionary, additive, and transformative. The evolutionary process is slow, with new cultural elements being introduced to replace other, discarded elements. Additive change takes place "when new assumptions arise in a particular cultural domain or paradigm and precipitate changes that eventually modify an entire set of cultural beliefs or values" (Rossman et al. 1985 p. 14). Finally, the transformative process occurs when an individual or group deliberately sets about to change the culture. The second and third change processes need strong leadership. A leader may deliberately act to legislate cultural change, as happened in China's famous Cultural Revolution. On a lesser scale, the leader can effect organizational change by restructuring lines of communication and command as well as by changing staff, thus signalling a change in expectations and creating an awareness of an impending new values and assumption base in the organization. However, there does appear to be strong support for the contention that major innovations such as the introduction of school effectiveness principles are most effectively implemented (transformed) by leaders who create cultures characterized by collegial collaboration.

Goals. Good leaders must have a vision of the effective school and an understanding of the values and assumptions that underlie it; then they must work to gain support for their ideas both within the school and without. They must be aware that the existing culture within the school has emerged as a response to the necessity of contending with the problems of survival in the organization. Attempting to change that culture will create new anxieties and problems. The leaders should know how to address these problems and provide stability within the school until they are resolved. Obviously, great sensitivity to people's feelings will be a desirable personal attribute.

In order to share the leader's vision and goals meaningfully, teachers must be encouraged to participate in goal setting and decision making, a difficult task (Goodlad 1984 p. 8) since few of them regard the school as the unit of improvement and fewer still have had much experience participating in important school-level decision making. Such participation will also raise fears and needs which may be met, in part, through appropriate staff development plans. Where possible, teachers who cannot accept the emerging vision for change should be encouraged to leave the school. System policy should support this element of school policy.

Outside the school, the principal should ensure that the community is aware of the school goals, especially as they relate to the effectiveness thrust, and, within the limits of system policy, endeavor to accommodate parental concerns within the long-range plans for the school. Obtaining parental support will probably affect student achievement positively (Purkey and Smith 1983).

Climate. Millikan (1984 p. 24) observes that

> the underlying ethos of any constructive and coordinated school culture should be one which encourages and supports strong interpersonal empathy, respect, genuineness, and self-evaluation. It will be one in which there is a clear and observable correspondence between the espoused and the actual. If the culture is to be non-conflicting and integrated, then the tangible expressions must be seen to reflect

the intangible values, philosophy and ideology, and the various forms of expressive symbolism must be mutually reinforcing and complementary.

In order to reduce conflict and anxiety, clear expectations for student and staff performance must be set, communicated, and consistently applied. In the spirit of collegiality and cooperation, the involvement in expectation setting by those who will be affected is crucial. The effect of this exercise seems to be greater student achievement (Stallings 1980) and greater teacher satisfaction (Rosenholtz 1985). One commonly expressed teacher concern is to be able to work without uncertainty and interruption; in such an atmosphere, there is more instructional time, an important factor in increasing student achievement. Teachers do not want their classroom time to be broken up by announcements, low priority meetings, and interruptions at the door, nor do they want to engage in such non-teaching tasks as locating materials and routine paperwork.

Symbols. An extremely important component of the climate of the effective school is the presence of visible symbols which illustrate and confirm what is considered to be important in the school. Put another way, visible symbols manifest the school's underlying values and assumptions. The school's curriculum is one obvious declaration of what is considered to be important; another is the award system. What activity is rewarded and the ceremonies during which awards are conferred send important messages to the educational community. School newsletters, statements of goals, behavior codes, rituals, symbols, and legends are all part of the culture of the organization and convey messages of what the school really values. The language mode for the school, the allocation of physical space, and the role-modelling behavior of staff also have been recognized as important symbols of school culture (Millikan 1984) and thus factors to be considered if the culture is to be changed. Indeed, all visible symbols, as manifestations of culture, assume a special importance in "freezing" a newly created culture by confirming what is now considered to be important.

Evaluation. Evaluation procedures may also be considered visible artifacts of the culture. However, since they are such an important aspect of school life, they have been singled out for more detailed comment. If the thrust of evaluation is to monitor the progress of the school toward realizing its goals, much of the trauma associated with that process is reduced. The focus of attaining *school* goals is a major departure for most school evaluation practices and is seen (Neumann 1981) as reducing student alienation as well as actually increasing the chances that the school will be successful. The same focus may be used in principal and staff evaluation, thus increasing satisfaction and skill development and reducing the levels of anxiety and alienation so often produced by less specific evaluation policies (Jess 1984; Rosenholtz 1985). As well, staff evaluation data related to school goals provide a focus for staff development training. School policy should explicitly detail the nature, process, and use to be made of each type of evaluation activity. School staff should participate in the development of evaluation policies (and, in fact, of most policies) since this involvement is so critical in developing a positive school culture.

A positive organizational culture marked by a caring for individuals and a commitment to excellence is an absolute necessity in any plan to increase school effectiveness or, for that matter, the effectiveness of any organization. As Peters and Waterman say, "The basic philosophy, spirit and drive of an organization have far more to do with its relative achievements than do technological or economic resources, organizational structure, innovation and timing" (1982 p. 280).

Development of this philosophy, spirit, and drive does not happen incidentally. Staffs must work consciously and conscientiously to evolve a culture that prepares them not as individuals but as schools to develop the strategies necessary to cope with the problems of internal integration as well as of external adaptation and survival (Schein 1984). Board policies regarding the use of professional activity days may have to be modified in order to provide the freedom and resources to do this. Other policies should facilitate staff transfers in order that compatibility at the school level be maximized. The use of facilitators may have to be funded. Policy creators should also recognize that school cultures exist as subsets of the broader system culture, which must be perceived as empathetic toward the efforts of schools to increase their effectiveness in areas defined by each school as important — within the wider limits imposed by the system and society. To rephrase this, policymakers must realize that efforts and outcomes will vary from setting to setting and that, in fact, the effective school of this year may not be so effective next year.

Conclusion

To support an effective schools movement at the local level, school systems will need to formulate policy with respect to:

- the development of appropriate culture at the school board/administrator level;

- the communication to the community of the board's assumptions and expectations regarding education and educational outcomes;

- the provision of a sufficient degree of autonomy to schools in order that they, individually, can cope with the development of their organizational cultures and feel secure in the knowledge that their processes and outcomes do not have to be identical; therefore, at the school level, there should be freedom and responsibility with respect to:

> *leadership* — a person or group must be clearly identified as having the responsibility for implementing effectiveness-increasing strategies; not only must the leadership be responsible, it must be visionary in its goals and solution seeking, and it must provide security and support for staffs who face the necessity of change to allow those goals;
>
> *climate* — statements of school expectations should be publicized; buffering strategies are needed in order to maximize the time teachers spend on instruction;
>
> *visible artifacts* — the rituals, symbols, and formal statements of the school should accurately interpret the school's value system;
>
> *evaluation* — evaluation practices within the school should be oriented toward the achievement of school goals.

Policy is interpreted as a guide for discretionary action. Little has been documented in this chapter about the procedures to be used in either defining or attaining goals. Questions about the moral worth of those goals or the possibility that organizational culture may be manipulated by administrative sleight of hand have not been addressed directly. However, it has been implied, and the implication bears repeating, that organizational cultures are not easily changed. The culture of an organizational unit reflects aspects of the larger administrative and societal cultures in which it is set. Moreover, since its essential character has developed over time through successfully responding to problems of survival related to fulfilling its ultimate tasks, it cannot be manipulated easily. Administrators may accelerate the pace of change significantly, but only within limits allowed by forces emanating from both inside and outside the organization, forces which vet both the content and process of the change. A successful move to increase school effectiveness probably will have been sanctioned by the senior administration and the school board through policy, by the school community through granting tacit approval of the proposal, and by the school staff through developing consensus about the worth of increased effectiveness as a goal. The desirability and necessity of the tripartite granting of approval, either formally or informally, is probably the reason why school change is so slow; on the other hand, the documentation both of this approval and its resulting successes in many instances raises hope that increasing numbers of effective schools can be a reality.

References

Awender M A 1985 The superintendent/school board relationship. *Canadian Journal of Education* 10(2): 176–198

Cameron K S 1986 Effectiveness as paradox: Consensus and conflict in conceptions of organizational effectiveness. *Management Science* 32(5): 539–554

Down A G 1985 Excellence and equity: The unfinished agenda of the 1980s. *Educational Horizons* 16: 16–19

Duke D L 1985 What is the nature of educational excellence and should one try to measure it? *Phi Delta Kappan* 66(10): 671–674

Duke D L 1987 *School Leadership and Instructional Improvement.* Random House, New York

Goodlad J L 1984 Understanding schools is basic to improving them. *The Canadian School Executive* 3(9): 3–10

Jess K 1984 School reviews: Pursuing effectiveness. *The Canadian School Executive* 3(9): 13–14

Leithwood K, Stager M 1986 Differences in problem solving processes used by moderately and highly effective principals. Paper presented at the annual meeting of the American Educational Research Association, San Francisco

McLeod G T 1984 The work of school board chief executive officers. *Canadian Journal of Education* 9(2): 171–190

Meyer J, Rowan B 1978 The structure of educational organizations. In: Meyer M (ed.) *Environments and Organizations.* Jossey-Bass, San Francisco

Millikan R H 1984 A conceptual model for the development and maintenance of a co-ordinated school culture. Unpublished paper, Faculty of Education, University of Melbourne

Ministry of Education 1984 *Ontario Schools: Intermediate and Senior Divisions.* Ministry of Education, Toronto

Neumann F M 1981 Reducing alienation in high schools: Implications of theory. *Harvard Educational Review* 51(3): 546–564

Ouchi W G, Wilkins A L 1985 Organizational culture. *Annual Review of Sociology* 11: 457–483

Peters T J, Waterman R H 1982 *In Search of Excellence.* Harper and Row, New York

Purkey S C, Smith M S 1983 Effective schools: A review. *The Elementary School Journal* 83(4): 427–452

Rowan B, Bossert S T, Dwyer D C 1983 Research on effective schools: A cautionary note. *Educational Researcher* 12(4): 24–31

Rosenholtz S J 1985 Effective schools: Interpreting the evidence. *American Journal of Education* 93(3): 352–388

Rossman G, Corbet H D, Firestone W 1985 Professional cultures, improvement efforts and effectiveness. Unpublished report, Research for Better Schools, Philadelphia

Rutter M, Mortimore P, Ouston J 1979 *Fifteen Thousand Hours.* Open Books, London

Schein E H 1984 Coming to a new awareness of organizational culture. *Sloan Management Review* Winter: 3–16

Shapiro R N 1982 Excellence: What every school seeks and no one defines. *Independent School* 41(3): 11–15

Stallings J 1980 Allocated academic learning time revisited, or beyond time on task. *Educational Reseacher* 9(11): 11–16

Storey V 1986 The heart of excellence is commitment to people. *The Canadian School Executive* January: 9–11

Tyler W B 1985 The organizational structure of the school. *Annual Review of Sociology* 11: 49–73

Watkins D 1984 The good school — What is it really like? *The Canadian School Executive* 3(9): 11–12

Wergin J F 1976 The evaluation of organizational policymaking: A political model. *Review of Educational Research* 46(1): 75–115

7/Managing Effective Schools: The Moral Element

Edward A. Wynne

Wynne announces the fundamental values on which effective schools should be based. He goes on to demonstrate the ways in which a congenial community, consistent with those values, can be developed. Some questions to consider include: For the implementation of such ideas, how much authority must the school administration wield? What are the implications of Wynne's ideas for schools plagued with conflict and dissent?

For over 15 years, students under my direction have been collecting first-hand information about the operation of schools in the Chicago area (Wynne 1980, 1985). Their observations have been shaped by anthropological principles. As a result, they have collected especially fine-grained data. Furthermore, their focus has been on whole schools, as compared with patterns in disparate classrooms. While this research was underway, I simultaneously followed the developing literature about effective schools and their management. These two streams of study have led me to recognize that effective school management is fostered by the application of relatively traditional moral values (Chubb and Moe 1988).

That conclusion has also been confirmed by my research for a recently completed book, *Traditional Catholic Religious Orders* (Wynne 1987). That research disclosed the many parallels between Jewish and Catholic traditions about community life and the many ways these traditions have affected some principles applied in the Protestant faith. In effect, my historical-religious research has developed new insights into the running of effective secular schools today.

Let me explain what I mean by traditional moral values, how I and other qualified researchers reached our conclusions, and what I see as implications of this research for the operation of effective schools.

By "traditional moral values" I mean values rooted in the Judeo-Christian ethic. I do not mean that such values can only be practiced by Jews or Christians. Undoubtedly, in the schools my pupils studied, some of the persons applying such values were agnostics, probably even atheists. But it is not surprising that persons reared in the United States, a country with a long tradition of Judeo-Christian commitment, should feel affiliation with such values, regardless of their personal religious commitments. Even when considering ghetto schools in disordered environments, we must remember that blacks comprise one of America's most religious ethnic groups.

It is also noteworthy that my support of the Judeo-Christian ethic might be extended to cover other religious groups, for example, Moslems and Hindus. Some modern authorities (Campbell 1975; Skinner 1971), as well as earlier commentators, have remarked on broad parallels among different prominent religions.

The description of values as "traditional" does not mean that such values are extinct or irrelevant — most of them survive, doing relatively well. But the concept of tradition signifies that the values have persisted for long periods of time. Incidentally, I do not suggest that such values have always been universally observed. Presumably, the ancient prohibition against adultery existed partly because adultery had been a recurrent human tendency. But the prohibition does mean that it is a tendency which mainstream society has preferred to repress.

Traditional Values

The following catalogue of traditional values is obviously not exhaustive, but it is suggestive. Despite its limitations, the list does suggest the important parallels between the Judeo-Christian tradition and many of the value patterns which affect contemporary school life.

1. The acceptance of traditional hierarchy. Christ said, "Render unto Caesar. . . ." In the same century, St. Paul directed developing Christian communities to give fealty to existing forms of civil authority. The Jewish tradition gives great emphasis to the deference due elders.

It is true that, on some occasions, there has been some sympathy with the tradition of active resistance to evil. And, in our own era, we have seen the rise of so-called liberation theology. Regardless of occasional variations, the main current of the tradition has been the acceptance of existing, legitimate authority. "Legitimate" has meant that the structure of authority rested on some body of generally accepted principles which placed constraints on those in authority. Justice for individuals was not usually pursued through resistance to authority but more via interpersonal relations, or it was attained in the afterlife.

Throughout Western history, while particular religious groups oftentimes sought justice and freedom for their adherents, intragroup relations were governed more by traditions of charity and tolerance, compared to the adversarial concept of contemporary, legal justice. Thus, we have the theme of Christ as the good shepherd — a benign, solicitous, and loving leader. But the shepherd unquestionably directs the flock.

Hierarchy is a fact in all continuing organizations in our era, including schools — although, often, this reality is treated as a source of embarrassment.

2. The exercise of strong adult control over children and adolescents. The simplest instance is the fourth Commandment: "Honor thy father and mother. . . ." And, beyond the Commandment, Christianity only gradually initiated children into full participation in church life. Judaism followed similar patterns, treating male children as subordinates until they had attained maturity through Bar Mitzvah.

The tradition recognized adulthood as the outcome of both a developmental process and a learning process. Over ten to twenty years, the child completed appropriate rites of passage and became enculturated as an adult. Maturing children found themselves provided with an expanding pool of rights and responsibilities. Final attainment of adulthood, however, involved de facto certification by the adult community.

Today, there is much discussion to the effect that teachers should not properly be "authority" figures. However, parents and children alike recognize the necessary truth that teachers must play an authority role, and they are puzzled by the confusion resulting from attempts to conceal the reality of hierarchy.

3. The priority given to immediate good conduct over more elaborate ratiocination. In the Judeo-Christian tradition, there were proverbs denigrating "words without deeds," and principles focussing on such forms of conduct as charity, obedience, humility, and chastity were honored. All of these principles relate to matters of visible conduct. Visible conduct can be observed and monitored, while words are notorious for masking, as well as revealing, our state of mind. Furthermore, analysis may become a device for avoiding straightforward but uncomfortable action, to the detriment of the persons affected. In any event, this was Shakespeare's drawing of Hamlet.

4. Great emphasis on the life of collective entities. The congregation, the parish, the family (nuclear or extended) were focal points of human life. The persisting assumption was that people would live in diverse forms of groups. It was critical for people to choose to accept commitments and be prepared to sacrifice on behalf of the whole. Considerable thought was given to the mechanics through which families and religious communities recruited and enrolled new members. Our ancestors applied techniques such as marriage, confirmation, adult baptism, and the foundation of religious orders for the enrollment and formation of adult volunteers. All of these concerns have implications for the many communities of choice, including schools and programs in schools, which exist around us today.

5. Reverence for the knowledge of the past. The very idea of holy books and commands from God signifies that certain knowledge has been inherited and must be honored by and transmitted to children. This recognition does not directly ignore the concept of dynamism and change but treats such developments as subordinate to already revealed information. Today, we too often feel awkward or unsympathetic about transmitting and revering such traditional messages. Sometimes this discomfort is excused by criticism of such messages as unscientific, and sometimes we take revisionist approaches to historical materials. These forms of dismissal fail to realize the elements of myth and symbolism which underlie all important bodies of belief — even the popular and possibly ephemeral ideologies of our own day.

6. The reservation of a sphere of life for sacred activities, beyond the day-to-day business of buying, selling, and producing. In the 19th century, the French sociologist Emile Durkheim (1965) gave prominence to the concept of the "sacred," as metaphysically distinct from mundane, material life. His distinction is generally consonant with the spirit of traditional religion. Sacred activities, despite their separation from the secular, materialistic world, provided an important resource for human fulfillment. Sometimes, sacred activities were private, as with individual prayers; but even such prayers were regarded as a dialogue between the individual and God. And many such sacred occasions were group gatherings, typically centering around semi-esthetic activities, for example, Bible readings, hymns, sermons, processions. The activities often solemnized rites of passage or rites of concentration (where groups or individuals symbolically concentrated their energies for some moment of emotional or physical trial).

Once again, in trying to remove sacred ritual and religiosity from our secular schools, we have handicapped our ability to respond to the needs of the young — and also of many of the adults who work with the young. Thus, persons with traditional perspectives are not surprised to discover that some rock and punk musicians, with shows focussing on sadomasochism and devil worship, attract crowds of engaged adolescents. Today, too many responsible adults ignore the basic needs of the young for wholesome symbolic and ceremonial life (Klapp 1969). As a result, we should not be surprised at the appearance of exploiters — modern pied pipers.

7. The equality of all community members as children of God, despite their temporal, material, and intellectual differences. Hierarchy and differentiation prevailed for certain necessary reasons. That hierarchy, however, did not represent some ultimate set of God-ordained values, which finally assessed human worth. As St. Paul said, "Every man among you should not think of himself more highly than he ought. . . . For as we have many members of one body, and all members have not the same office . . . mind not high things but condescend to men of low estate." The necessary judgments of human agencies did not displace the final conclusions of the deity.

In our own times, there is a propensity to justify our belief in human equality on political and ideological grounds. Unfortunately, such grounds are profoundly threatened by the many variations in human competency disclosed both by common sense and by scientific research. Concurrently, there are efforts to develop technologies which provide all members of particular communities with predetermined "equal" shares of benefits. However, such efforts often rely on tendentious definitions of "equality." Thus, so-called competency-based instruction was supposed to permit all students to attain the same level of learning. But such equal attainments, even if feasible, would require some students to receive more instructional time than others. Thus, there would be unequal distribution of instruction, a scarce good, bought by public funds. In trying to create equality in one sphere of life, we have simply shifted the inequality into another, equally problematic arena.

The nub of it is that the concept of moral equality — as proposed by religious tradition — and the concomitant recognition of difference and hierarchy may be a more viable base for egalitarian belief and action. It is my impression that such beliefs, as compared to distorted definitions and intellectual evasions regarding equality, are what prevail in effective schools. In other words, in truly effective schools with populations with disparate skills, there is no great pretention that all pupils will attain exactly the same levels or receive equivalent recognition. There is simply a diffuse appreciation of human difference, a recognition that different levels of attainment and competence are inevitable (and often desirable), and a tolerance of the ambiguity that such patterns sometimes generate.

Applying Traditional Values in Schools

The effective schools research has shown that good schools place great stress on many values and practices which are congruent with the preceding principles. First, consider the matter of hierarchy.

Effective schools are led, we are told, by vigorous principals, who clearly make known their values and policies. When necessary, these principals display determination and courage and press toward their goals in the face of resistance. Furthermore, teachers in such schools respect their principals, follow directions, and expect similar obedience from students. Such leadership does not imply poor communication or disengagement between followers and leaders. The *Rule of St. Benedict* was developed in the sixth century and has been applied since then to the management of many Roman Catholic religious orders, even in our era. The *Rule* prescribed decision making and provided that the monastery abbot exercise complete control over the institution. But see how the *Rule* shaped the exercise of such potent authority: "After hearing the advice of the brethren let [the abbot] consider it in his own mind, and then do what he shall judge the most expedient. We ordain that all must be called to counsel, because the Lord often reveals to a younger member what is best. And let the brethren give their advice with all humble submission and presume not too stiffly to define their own opinion" (Delattre 1921).

Successful leaders must stay engaged with, and sensitive to, their subordinates. Perhaps the distinction is between being authoritative and being authoritarian. But communication and engagement should not be equated or confused with "democracy." That form of governance is appropriate for political entities, where the citizens are adults and, in effect, involuntary members. In schools, the adults are voluntary citizens. Essentially, they express their freedom by choosing to join the school and by being free to leave. The pupils, who are present due to a form of semi-compulsion, are not adults. As at home, they do not have equal power.

In effective schools, adults are unquestionably in control. Fair, firm, and appropriate discipline is applied. Such insistence has nothing to do with oppression. It is simply regarded as an acceptance of traditional, transitional adult responsibility and as a means of transmitting wholesome values to young persons.

In the effective schools my students identified, much emphasis was given to stimulating students to practice good conduct, as well as to maintaining discipline (see also Blase 1986). In almost all such cases, good conduct focussed on immediate, simple acts of helpfulness: acting as crossing guards, fundraising for good causes, tutoring other students, engaging in numerous extracurricular activities where cooperation and helpfulness were important components. There is an important distinction to be made between matters of immediate focus and efforts to enlist pupils in more remote concerns, such as world peace and saving the terrestrial environment. My estimate would be that immediate concerns outbalanced more remote concerns by the order of five-to-one in effective schools. It appears that such an imbalance is consistent with the tradition I have identified. Those who would reform the world should first reform themselves.

Effective schools have identities as schools, and usually their subsystems (classrooms, teams, and clubs) have equivalent vitality. Teachers and students display loyalty to, and have pride in, such entities. Because of such commitments, they care about the other members of these groups. They try to make the groups work, for their own individual self-interest and for the interest of all.

Ceremonial activities are important in effective schools. In part, the ceremonies serve to reward and stimulate academic excellence. But, from my students' reports, it is evident that many educators also see that the ceremonies serve the larger purposes of reaffirming the collective moral values (either religious or secular) of the school and of enhancing the sense of community shared by adults and pupils. Even where legal provisions prohibit the expression of formal religious feelings, celebrations of patriotic memorials and patriotic holidays provide for the enhancement of collective identities and wholesome group values. Many such occasions, incidentally, are times when the members of the school are encouraged to recognize their common ties with external agencies and persons: the nation or state, older persons or deceased generations, or other parts of the world. The occasions are also opportunities to celebrate the school, through activities such as awards ceremonies, pep rallies, and farewell gatherings. It is true that some of the effective schools research has made little reference to ceremonial life in schools. But that is one of the insights which can be generated by an ethnographic perspective.

All children of God are equal before God, if not before man. In effective schools, all children, regardless of their different levels of performance, have the same worth as human beings (Lightfoot 1983). This concept is subtle. It does not exclude the expression — or even the encouragement — of different capabilities in academics, sports, or other areas. And excellence is worthy of recognition. Still, despite such celebrations of difference, all pupils retain a certain basic core of worth. Adults in the school attribute the same high value to this core in all students. Thus, the Judeo-Christian tradition provides a powerful model of an environment in which both achievement and equality are deserving of recognition.

The preceding general remarks may appear to recite the evident. Who is really against hierarchy in schools? Aren't we all in favor of students practicing immediate acts of helpfulness? And don't we all believe in the innate dignity of every human being? In other words, how do my assertions rise above trite truisms?

The distressing fact is that many themes underlying the Judeo-Christian tradition are ignored in too many contemporary schools. To be direct, take the matter of hierarchy. In many schools, it is next to impossible to fire or terminate an unsatisfactory teacher. For many principals, authority over teachers rests on tenuous and uncertain grounds (Bridges 1986). It is true that some principals have overcome such obstacles, by the exercise of determination and ingenuity. However, those exceptional principals make my point. In too many schools, the answer to the question "Who's in charge?" is very obscure.

Turning to the matter of "Honor thy father and mother," it is rare for educators to directly criticize such sentiments. But the pursuit of novelty is a popular pattern with many educators. This pursuit often undercuts the values of parents. Thus, when educators determine to "struggle" against sexism, correct the parochialism of certain adult communities, or otherwise foster certain forms of "progress," they are simultaneously undermining the status of adults who hold such "flawed" values (Franza 1986). Often, those adults are the parents of children in their schools.

Too many educators — or intellectuals who provide them with advice — hold many patterns of responsible life in low regard. Conversely, they display excessive sympathy for forms of disordered conduct. Thus, in the New York City public schools, there was recently much reluctance to introduce a family life course which might suggest to the pupils that bearing children out-of-wedlock was irresponsible. After all, some commentators said, many children in the schools were born out of wedlock and were still living with their parent(s). Thus, there was some solicitude about disordered parent/child relations. However, careful analysts of modern school curriculum have concluded that many materials are profoundly indifferent, even hostile, to traditional family values such as marriage, formal religion, and mothers regularly caring for children (Vitz 1987).

Now, it is true that new information is inevitably discovered in the world. Thus, the process of schooling will sometimes make pupils, on certain topics, more informed than their parents. However, there is a profound distinction between teachers providing pupils with limited factual information which may be unknown to some parents and teachers regarding themselves as licensed to actively undermine basic values which parents want their children to possess. Good schools strive to stay sensitive to this distinction. Too many schools are prone to place themselves in the position of crusaders, striving to mobilize pupils against values crucial to their parents. Perhaps we can imagine parental values (supporting Nazi anti-Semitism, for example) which schools should undermine. However, the tradition emphasizes that such acts of intellectual subversion should be carried out only after grave and open deliberation.

Our less effective schools do not always seem to attack traditional values; but, too often, those values wither in a war of a thousand cuts.

The Case for Tradition

There is a substantial and persisting body of serious thought which has favored the application of traditional approaches and values in schools and other public institutions. Probably its most prominent English-speaking proponent was the late 18th-century statesman and writer, Edmund Burke (1966). His arguments can be easily characterized and they deserve direct consideration.

Human societies, and their subsystems (such as schools), are extraordinarily complex. If any society or subsystem has persisted for a long period of time and displayed powers of adaptability, we should assume that its components and philosophies have peculiar strengths. The relationship among those elements is extremely subtle. Observers frequently cannot divine or forecast what effects novel or dramatic changes may have on such a system. Furthermore, the proponents of analysis and change will rarely be neutral. Instead, they represent parties or forces with their peculiar interests to urge.

Burke's recommendation was that efforts to change systems of long standing should proceed incrementally, giving great weight to the special (though unmeasurable) value of existing precedents. Dramatic prescriptions, and their proponents, should be viewed with special suspicion. For Burke, traditional religion was an important example of an elaborate, persisting institution of notable value.

Schools provide a classic subject for the application of Burke's perspective. Schools have existed in diverse forms for a long period of time — hundreds of years. During most of those years, the principles of the Judeo-Christian ethic pervaded the operation of both private and public schools (Tyack and Hansot 1982). Within a comparatively short period of historical time, perhaps less than 30 years (Wise 1979; Yulish 1980), schools have moved a long way from the tradition lauded by Burke and by most of our forebears. Many of the changes were encouraged by the type of intellectuals and planners critically characterized by Burke. Supposedly, the changes were aimed at producing beneficial effects in education, in relatively short periods of time. Instead of adults passing on the best of their culture, a vague faith in the natural wisdom of children's inner directions developed.

Burke's reactions to such proposals are easily imaginable. He would have predicted that many of the changes would fail or lead to worse situations than previously existed. Furthermore, the changes would give increased authority to the office holders, administrators, and intellectuals who proposed them in the first place — even if they did not work very well. The changes would be only imperfectly implemented, due to their tendentious nature and to growing popular and intellectual resistance. Indeed, in many areas of education, Burke would have predicted that the formally discredited previous doctrines would stay in place or would revive, due to the deficiencies underlying the new approaches. Gradually, the supporters of tradition would gather strength and attempt some form of counterrevolution. Whether and how that effort will proceed cannot be fairly predicted.

The special nature of schools, with their focus on children and adolescents, lends a unique significance to that forecast derived from Burke. Undoubtedly, the proportion of sacred activities has declined over time in Western societies. Occasionally, dire predictions have been uttered as to the meaning of that decline. The preceding discussion represents another example of such predictions. And it may be that the fears underlying such forecasts are exaggerated. Perhaps, Burke to the contrary, quasi-religious values are superfluous in modern Western society.

After all, most major Western institutions — business, trade, agriculture, and war — have been at least semi-secularized for many centuries. And, to some degree, this semi-secularization has succeeded; it has not generated conspicuous adult disorder. But, in contrast to these secularized institutions, education in much of the West, especially the United States and Canada, kept its sacred elements until well into the 20th century. My pupils' research implies that, even today, many formally secular public schools, in covert fashion, still tap important sacred themes. Such schools hold significant ceremonies to demarcate important occasions in their community members' lives (e.g., retirement, the annual school opening); they compose pledges of allegiance to the unique principles of their school, which all students recite daily; and adults talk directly to pupils about matters such as honor, pride, and community obligations.

Maybe there are special characteristics about the education of children and adolescents which dispose educators (and parents) to persist in injecting sacred elements into formally secular education — to strive to transmit patriotism and to appeal to higher values, elevated aspirations, and immediate moral concerns. It may even be that some of the educational reform efforts of the past fifteen to twenty years have had their own priorities affected by some distorted desire to transmit sacred themes to pupils. For example, the concern with "environmentalism" partly represents a semi-mystic fixation on the transcendent elements of our natural environment. Furthermore, some rare or endangered species appear to have taken on sacred elements beyond the rationally useful. And animal worship is a tradition antedating the Judeo-Christian ethic — recall the worship of the golden calf of Baal. But these invent-a-religion efforts are flawed by the utopianism, materialism, and narcissism which pervade much of our secular life. Some evidence of my proposition may be found in the study *Crestwood Heights* (Seeley et al. 1963 p. 224), a careful description of an anonymous suburb in a Canadian metropolitan center during the 1960s. As the authors observed, the upper-middle-class suburb appeared to have made faith in secular education a substitute for traditional religion — but without the anchoring force of long-tried and persisting sacred beliefs.

Evidently, many parties to these contemporary educational controversies realize that educating children is special. It inevitably has certain sacred elements. Unfortunately, the formally sacred has been driven from many other areas of public life. As a result, it has become especially difficult to determine the right mix of sacred and secular to apply in public schools — or even to confront such issues frankly.

The so-called effective schools movement is a classic example of the intellectual power of Burke's overall analysis. Let me try and show how its development follows the lines of the forecast offered above.

The Significance of the Effective Schools Movement

The effective schools movement is a cause that means different things to different people. For Ron Edmunds (1979), an early spokesperson, it meant that children from poor homes could be taught to read just as well (on the average) as children from other environments. For other researchers, such as Michael Rutter (Rutter et al. 1979) and Wilbur Brookover (Brookover and Lezotte 1977), it simply meant that some schools were more effective than others in teaching pupils from equivalent backgrounds. However, such success did not necessarily mean that all family-related factors could be obliterated; it simply meant that some educators, applying the same resources, were more effective than others.

From my own research in the Chicago area, plus a consideration of the literature, I am convinced that effective schools are essentially quite traditional schools. As I said, they apply the Judeo-Christian ethic. Adults act responsibly, accept accountability, and display commitment. They view all pupils as valuable. They set standards, require pupil discipline, affirm good conduct, and treat learning, drill, homework, and grades as important.

The most interesting thing about the effective schools movement is not the discovery of such schools. Instead, it is the very idea that such values and practices should be set aside, or forgotten by some people of prominence. Can anyone be surprised to discover that high demands and standards, firm discipline, and industrious behavior produce higher levels of measured achievement than open expectations, lax discipline, and uncontrolled choice?

The causes for such forgetfulness are as old as the hills. Running effective schools, like living a moral life, is hard work, not always fun. Furthermore, the effective schools approach gives primary emphasis to the educators on the spot — not to the social planners or to the legislators who establish or fund new programs or who offer the electorate the promise of magic, painless nostrums. It does not even favor the progression of novelty. We can surely do some things to increase the proportion of effective schools. It is sobering to realize, however, that good educators must, in general, be people with vital traditional virtues. All common experience tells us that persons with such virtues, while they certainly exist, will always be valuable and probably scarce goods. Perhaps the world would be a happier place if we could invent some improved means of instruction that did not make such strong demands on practitioners; but we cannot. Indeed, one reason secularization is popular among some educators is because it removes from their shoulders the burden of being good examples.

Implications for Practitioners

My general remarks provide a backdrop for a variety of concrete suggestions for practitioners, either administrators or teachers, and for school boards.

- School boards oversee school systems of varying diversity. In more homogeneous communities, especially where only one school is involved, boards should identify principles of supervision that encourage and assist superintendents to apply principles consistent with the proposals I have propounded. Furthermore, boards should apply similar principles in the hiring of superintendents. Where boards oversee more than one school, especially in more heterogeneous communities, they should at least establish principles of management that do not discourage school-based administrators, where there is the likelihood of community support, from applying the proposed principles. Finally, there should be a recognition that the Judeo-Christian ethic, with slightly different "packaging," can have appeal to many non-Western groups. One notable talent of able leaders is to provide for the persistence of transcendent beliefs, while, at the same time, moderately revising their garb to make them palatable to potential new believers. Such acts of moderate revision can gratify both old believers, by protecting their values, and new community members, by facilitating their transition into the environment.

- Running an effective school, or being an effective teacher, is hard work. An important part of the motive for such sacrifice comes from the moral element of the task. That element need not draw upon formal religious belief. However, it is evident that such a belief can be a valuable resource. In effective schools, whether secular or religious, this moral concern is transmitted to the adults involved and, often, to the pupils.

- Educators must work at communicating a moral sense to one another and at defining its substance. This implies frequent formal and informal meetings, appropriate ceremonial occasions, and well-drafted formal and informal documents, addressed to all members of the school community.

- Leaders must lead, followers must follow legitimate authority, and all school community members must recognize that their roles as leaders or followers will vary according to different occasions.

- The Judeo-Christian tradition of equality must be translated into action; it signifies that all community members, including children and parents, have contributions to make to the school, though those valued contributions are still set within a framework of appropriate hierarchy.

• Reward and punishment are inevitable elements of the ethic. Both academic learning and good and bad conduct should be subject to appropriate, vital responses. Obvious as it seems, it must be reiterated that only the good should be rewarded and the bad must be consistently and speedily punished.

• Whether a school is religious or not, tradition, found in the traditional values of either the country, the school, or the classroom, should be viewed as an important source of sanction. The assumption is that many centuries of human experience have gone into refining such tradition. It is unlikely that the pupils' (or teachers') generation has discovered some dramatic, new, and beneficial way of revising that knowledge. Incidentally, as far as curriculum goes, this proposition has evident implications for the teaching of history, as distinct from the amorphous and pretentious subject of social studies. As for the teaching of literature, the material presented should represent the best of our cultural inheritance.

• Ceremonies can be important means of symbolically transmitting school (and social) values and simultaneously stimulating aesthetic expression (e.g., via drama, singing, recitations, costumes).

• Where a school has the legitimate license to express religious values and traditions, that expression should be relatively serious, unabashed, and consonant with the general principles articulated. Religious schools should not popularize and secularize their traditional message (for a dramatic instance of such fidelity, see Peshkin 1986).

• A powerful relationship will prevail between the moral perspective of the school and its formal means of organization. In other words, the school's form of organization — school size, division of grades, terms of the union contract, procedures for hiring and supervising teachers and principals — all have important implications for the practice of the tradition in any school. Space does not permit me to cover this issue thoroughly. But it will be useful to realize that traditional religious communities emphasize small, persisting groups, where entering members are carefully socialized and where intergroup solidarity and universal accountability to concrete moral principles are stressed. Administrators and principals should examine the norms which have evolved in their schools and systems and attempt to diminish the barriers to constructive relationships which may have evolved.

• Something should be said about the tradition of "preaching." By that I mean urging listeners to apply high ideals and making such appeals in an imaginative, forceful, and engaging fashion. For diverse reasons, that tradition has acquired a bad image in our era. But there is good preaching and bad preaching, just like good or bad teaching, or other complex human activities. It is true that some persons (including pupils) may resist even good preaching. However, such resistance is often not as widespread among pupils as teachers think. And, in the tradition, there are innumerable instances of vital and eloquent preachers overcoming audience resistance. Unfortunately, one frequent element of effective preaching is good role modelling — always a cumbersome obligation for adults. In any event, skillful preaching is part of running an effective school.

To sum up, the creation of coherent policies for the governance of a complex, persisting institution like a school is an extraordinary intellectual task. It is no great matter to set down some body of off-the-cuff principles. But great problems arise when such principles must be applied by a group of differing people to a large number of persons for long periods of time. Inconsistencies become evident, unforeseen contingencies develop, and serious conflicts arise within the community.

Beyond questions of religious beliefs, the Judeo-Christian ethic represents a set of gradually refined principles which have been subjected to searching empirical and intellectual examination. People may like or dislike the principles, but they have outlasted the Roman Empire, feudalism, many forms of nationalism, and numerous efforts at raw suppression. Even today, in the highly secularized United States, a national survey in 1982 disclosed that 37 percent of high school seniors attended religious services once a week or more (Johnson, Bachman and O'Malley 1982 p. 17).

The prolonged survival of the Judeo-Christian ethic is a powerful testimony to its efficacy. If the principles of the ethic can be operationally translated, they provide school administrators with a time-tested resource. There are obviously people who believe that they can identify notably different sets of principles, which have never been applied anywhere for long periods of time, and use such principles to manage persisting and more effective schools. But they have a difficult case to make.

References

Blase J 1986 Socialization and humanization. *Sociology of Education* 59: 100–113

Bridges E M 1986 *The Incompetent Teacher*. Falmer Press, Philadelphia

Brookover W B, Lezotte L 1977 Schools can make a difference. Michigan State University, East Lansing, Michigan

Burke E 1966 *Reflections on the Revolution in France*. Arlington House, New Rochelle, New York

Campbell D. T 1975 On the conflicts between biological and social evolution, and between psychology and moral tradition. *American Psychologist* 30: 1103–1126

Chubb J E, Moe T M 1988 *What Price Democracy? Politics, Markets, and America's Schools.* Brookings, Washington, DC

Delattre P 1921 *Commentary on the Rule of St. Benedict.* Archabbey Press, Latrobe, Pennsylvania

Durkheim E 1965 *The Elementary Forms of Religious Life.* Free Press, New York

Edmunds R 1979 Some schools work and more can. *Social Policy* 9: 28–32

Franza A 1986 Does "what works" work in the classroom? *English Journal* 75: 20–22

Johnson L D, Bachman J G, O'Malley P M 1982 *Monitoring the Future, 1982.* Institute for Social Research, Ann Arbor, Michigan

Klapp O 1969 *The Collective Search for Identity.* Holt, Rinehart and Winston, New York

Lightfoot S L 1983 *The Good High School.* Basic Books, New York

Peshkin A 1986 *God's Choice.* University of Chicago Press, Chicago

Rutter M, Maughan B, Mortimer P, Ouston J 1979 *Fifteen Thousand Hours.* Harvard University Press, Cambridge, Massachusetts

Seeley J R, Sim J A, Loosley E W 1963 *Crestwood Heights.* John Wiley, New York

Skinner B F 1971 *Beyond Freedom and Dignity.* Alfred Knapp, New York

Tyack D, Hansot E 1982 *Managers of Virtue.* Basic Books, New York

Vitz P 1986 *Censorship: Evidence of Bias in Children's Textbooks.* Servant, Ann Arbor, Michigan

Walberg H J et al. 1985 Homework's powerful effects on learning. *Educational Leadership* 42(7): 76–79

Wise A 1979 *Legislated Learning.* University of California Press, Berkeley, California

Wynne E A 1980 *Looking At Schools.* Heath/Lexington, Lexington, Massachusetts

Wynne E A 1985 Chicago area award-winning schools, 1984/85. University of Illinois at Chicago, Chicago

Wynne E A 1987 *Traditional Catholic Religious Orders.* Transaction Press, New Brunswick, New Jersey

Yulish S 1980 *The Search for a Civic Religion.* University Press of America, Lanham, Maryland

Part Three

DISTRICT-LEVEL POLICY ISSUES

8/The Role of the School District in School Improvement[1]

Karen Seashore Louis

Louis uses research on a number of school districts to suggest the most appropriate relationship between central administrators and school administrators in a variety of circumstances. Some questions to consider include: Are the personalities and belief systems of the different administrators going to influence the most appropriate type of school/district relations? How strongly can these findings be generalized to different conditions?

Who is in charge of school improvement? Three decades ago the answer to this question would have been rather clear: the superintendent and the district office. The superintendency in the U.S. developed as an educational afterthought, part of the sweeping effort of the '20s and '30s to standardize and make more efficient public agencies of all types (Katz 1971; Tyack 1974). With the growth of public secondary education and the overriding concern with "standards," central management and strong superintendents were perceived as necessary (Callahan 1962). For the period of the '40s and '50s, with the spread of consolidation among rural schools and the growth of district offices in urban areas, the superintendent and his staff reigned supreme. A number of studies (Carlson 1965; Kerr 1964) showed that superintendents, rather than laymen or school-based educators, were the source of most policy initiatives.

Tyack and Hansot point out, however, that this situation has changed drastically in North America, indicating that "at the present time . . . superintendents . . . are at the beck and call of every pressure that is brought to them" (1982 p. 238). The pressures eroding superintendent authority come from many sources. During the mid-'60s, teacher unions and minority and other community groups emerged as potent players in school politics. At the same time, district offices grew rapidly, due in part to the demand for new services and in part to the rapid increase in federal funding for special

ms. The superintendent's job used to be a relative-
out now, at least in the U.S., the tenure of
s is apparently declining very rapidly. In a recent
urban school districts, for example, four had witness-
n which the typical superintendent stayed for only two
ars before being forced out or choosing to move on (Miles
7).

is also a sense that district offices are out of control. School enrollments have declined and teaching positions have been cut, but cuts in administrative and other professional staff in district offices have, in many cases, been less deep. Despite declining enrollments, educational costs have stayed the same or increased, and public criticism of school performance has risen sharply. Some educational commentators have raised serious questions about the effectiveness of bureaucratic efforts to mandate significant educational improvement from a distant central office, when what may be required is creative and professional behavior on the part of teachers (Cuban 1984).

This is clearly a time that requires creative thinking about the role of superintendents and district office staff. But any recasting should draw upon what we know about how improvements are carried out in schools and about the kinds of policymaking and support from outside the school that help or hinder. In the remainder of this chapter I first outline a few assumptions on which the discussion is based and briefly review the existing state of knowledge. I then use a discussion of some research on rural and urban school improvement efforts to explicate the argument that existing generalizations about the role of superintendents and districts are based on the faulty assumption that all districts are more or less alike. Finally, I turn to a review of the general implications for superintendent and district office roles and to a discussion of how these may vary depending on the context.

School Improvement at the District Level

Some Key Assumptions

In clarifying my assumptions about school improvement I draw upon the efforts of more than fifty policymakers, practitioners, and researchers from North American and European countries who struggled with the difficult task of defining a set of core assumptions that can be applied to the development of more effective school improvement efforts in all economically advanced countries.[2] Among the most important assumptions for a discussion of policy making at the district level are the following (Louis and van Velzen 1986):

• School improvement must focus on the school. There are many ways of improving the functioning of educational systems that do not focus on schools (for example, cost-saving approaches to building maintenance or student transportation). However, in this chapter I am only concerned with the introduction of changes that have a potential positive impact on the teaching-learning process or on the immediate school conditions that support better teaching and learning.

• School improvement is a multi-level process. A district's school improvement policy is designed to affect many schools, or at least many classrooms. Thus, it typically requires the cooperation of actors at different levels in the educational system, ranging from teachers, students, administrators, and parents up through policymakers and key educational constituencies, such as teacher unions and representatives of political parties. Of particular importance is the role played by the organizations that provide external support to schools: institutions of higher education, in-service institutes, and other specialized agencies.

• Effective school improvement is a planned process. School improvement does not occur when a new policy is formulated. Rather, the process of school improvement unwinds slowly, often over a period of a decade or more. Policies that do not reflect a relatively self-conscious strategy for managing the slow process of change are less likely to be effective than those that do. Strategies for managing the improvement process — at both policy-making and school levels — are incompletely designed and evolve over time. Thus, the process is inherently unstable and dynamic.

Recent Research Findings

At the beginning of this decade, Fullan (1981) reviewed the literature on the role of superintendents and district office staff in the change process. At that time, the number of studies, and the conclusions that could be drawn from them, was relatively small. This situation has not changed a great deal in the intervening years, in which the focus of most efforts to look at educational reform has centered either on schools (through the interest in effective schools research) or on higher-level policy initiatives emerging out of the many commission reports of the last five years (Fullan et al. 1986).[3] Fullan's 1981 conclusions, supplemented by a few extensions from a non-exhaustive review of more recent research, may be briefly summarized.

Superintendent Roles. Superintendents are important in initiating and supporting improvement, although they are not always the source of the ideas underlying an improvement program. However, most superintendents appear to be more concerned with personnel issues, finance, and legal questions than with school improvement policies as defined above.

Some recent studies have examined the superintendent's role at different stages in the change process. Louis et al. (1981) looked at how "active involvement" of the superintendent contributed to the explanation of organizational change in eighty-five schools and found that it was *negatively* related to the overall implementation effort. However, it was important to have active support from the superintendent at the later stages of an innovation effort when decisions were being made that would affect the allocation of resources for continuation or expansion. Huberman and Miles (1984) found that superintendent pressure and support are critical in maintaining the innovation effort over time. However, the superintendent's role is primarily to maintain a vision for the change effort rather than to be intimately involved. Without pressure from the top, efforts at the school level are likely to wither over time.

These findings suggest a school improvement role for the superintendent that is reminiscent of the relationship between God and Moses. God is available on an episodic basis to give tablets, to inspire, or to judge. For the most part, however, it is the awareness of God's expectations that keeps the Israelites in line. In the words of contemporary organizational policy theorists, there is an apparent distinction between leadership and management: the superintendent plays a leadership role (setting policy and long-term directions) but leaves the day-to-day management of change to others.

District Staff Roles. Fullan (1981) and Fullan et al.'s (1986) reviews indicate that district office specialists and consultants appear to have a moderate impact on school improvement. Teachers tend to prefer other teachers as sources of assistance, but find district staff preferable to outsiders. Where there is an established commitment to using district staff in resource roles, these people can become critical elements. Organized and coordinated efforts to use staff in these roles are the exception rather than the rule, and most district staff have no formal training in how to play the role of change agent or facilitator. Their time spent in facilitating change is often fragmented, working with individual teachers rather than with small groups.

Cox (1983) investigated the role of district staff in more detail and found that internal facilitators from the district play a critical role in implementing change programs that are to affect multiple classrooms and/or multiple schools, irrespective of the level of support from other sources. Their work is most effective when they are involved as a "team" with facilitators and experts from outside the district. This conclusion is supported by Gersten et al. (1986). Louis, Dentler, and Kell (1984) found that most new information that might affect improvement efforts appears to reach local school systems through the district office. District staff play a role in determining what kinds of information about possible innovations reach school-based personnel; in effect, the former control the knowledge base on which the latter may act.

These findings suggest that district staff play important but highly variable roles in facilitating improvement. They screen information, they assist, they train, and they facilitate. However, they typically do all of these things on an ad hoc basis as there is little consensus (either within or between districts) about what a district staff person's role at the school level should be (see also Hall et al. 1985).

A Missing Variable. These conclusions are very limited and they ignore a significant variable that determines the role of the district: the community context. The above studies, like most concerned with educational innovations, focus on "typical" districts — suburban or small city/town. However, two research projects with which I have been involved have convinced me that findings that apply to these districts are not necessarily universal in their truth. When we look at the roles that district personnel play in rural and urban settings some additional critical issues emerge.

Rural and Urban School Improvement Efforts

The Rural Experimental Schools Study

One of the few systematic studies of school improvement in rural school systems was conducted in conjunction with the Rural Experimental Schools Program in the U.S. In summarizing this study, I will draw primarily on the survey analysis of Rosenblum and Louis (1981). However, these results are consistent with ethnographic data collected in the same study (Herriott and Gross 1979).

The first point is that the concept of a district office in rural settings differs from that found in urban or suburban settings. In most cases the office is much smaller. If the district does have a relatively large number of students then the physical boundaries of the district are extremely large, so that getting between the school and the district office on a regular basis is difficult. Thus, the notion of a permanent district staff playing a significant facilitating role in innovation programs is invalid. As Lippitt points out in a review of case material from this study, the roles of these few district staff people are unclear because they carry multiple responsibilities as supervisors, staff developers, and evaluators, and "overlapping responsibilities [make] it difficult to gain credibility or legitimacy as a consultative helper or supporter" (1979 p. 262).

The role of the superintendent, on the other hand, is apparently more critical than in the "typical" district. Rosenblum and Louis found, for example, that

> successful implementation of a district-wide change program is most effectively facilitated by a chief administrator who dominates both the planning process and the administrative decision making in the school system . . . high levels of participation of teachers and principals . . . were not generally associated with higher levels of actual implementation. (1981 pp. 176–177)[4]

The authors conclude that the main problem in creating change in rural school districts is the difficulty of creating a "system" in physically dispersed settings. Within rural districts, the more physically isolated the school, the less likely it was to implement any comprehensive change, even when other factors, such as staff morale, the qualifications of the staff, and collegiality, were controlled. In rural schools many principals teach, coach, drive school buses, or engage in other duties in addition to performing their administrative role. In some instances, two schools share a single principal. The absence of strong leaders at the building level means that, despite the problems of physical dispersion, having a high-authority central administrator is an important means of creating closer structural *and* cultural linkages that permit sustained systemwide change.[5]

The key role of the superintendent in rural systems may be attributable in part to the structural weaknesses of leadership at the building level. But superintendent authority is, of course, not the only factor that affects comprehensive school improvement. Equally critical is a cohesive staff with a high level of collegial interaction, a factor that affects schools in more "typical" and urban settings as well (see Little 1982). In fact, only in rural schools where both collegiality *and* superintendent authority are high does real improvement occur.

Preliminary Results from "Improving the Urban High School"

Over the past year and a half several colleagues[6] and I have been examining the problem of how to create significant change in underperforming urban high schools. Using both surveys of principals in 219 urban high schools and in-depth case studies, we looked at the conditions that permit effective change in unpromising settings (Farrar 1987; Louis and Cipollone 1987a, 1987b; Miles 1987a, 1987b; Miles and Rosenblum 1987; Miles et al. 1987; Rosenblum 1987).[7] The case-study schools all had a history of poor student achievement and of difficulty and disruption. All had been working on improvement efforts for three years or more, although two launched their most recent effort during 1985–86.

Although we sought schools where reasonably successful improvement efforts were going on, there proved to be differences among the sites. Two sites (Agassiz, Alameda) were quite successful; one (Burroughs) had mixed success; and two (Caruso and Chester) were struggling, in part because both were in the early stages of their current improvement programs. These differences permit some comparative generalizations about how the district context affects improvement outcomes.

The influence of both superintendents and district office staff on the planning and design of school improvement efforts tends to be relatively strong but largely indirect. According to the survey analysis, three-quarters of the programs were developed in the context of a districtwide improvement effort. When asked to rate the influence that district office staff had over the development of the plan, half of the principals indicated that they had "some." Despite the fact that slightly more than half indicated that they had strong support from personnel in the district office during planning, this probably did not translate into direct assistance because district staff were represented on less than one-quarter of school-based planning committees.

In urban districts, superintendents are very remote from the improvement process at the school level. Their lives, even more than those of superintendents located in less complicated environments, are consumed with non-educational issues. Although superintendents in the case-study sites often made decisions regarding districtwide program goals and design specifications, neither they nor their associate superintendents were involved in specific school decisions or activities. Furthermore, contact with specialists and consultant staff was also limited. In only one case — Alameda — was communication between district office and school with regard to the school improvement effort relatively frequent. The size of the urban school district does not seem to make much difference: in the smallest of the districts (Chester, which had only one large high school), the superintendent and district office staff were perceived as more remote by both the principal and the teachers than in any district except New York City.

Relationships between urban high schools and their district offices are often like bad but enduring marriages. Although the relationship is rarely uniformly positive or negative, on balance it tends to cause the improving school a lot of trouble. Yet, there is no possibility of divorce, and opportunities for positive mutual influence tend to be very limited.

Data from the survey do not suggest that the district is the source of most problems in planning and implementing school improvement efforts. However, a fifth of the principals interviewed mentioned that some aspect of their relationship with the district caused them trouble during the planning period. During implementation, the problems were often more serious:

- 37 percent reported that "conflicts with the district office" interfered with implementation;
- 40 percent indicated that turnover among district office staff had created problems for their program;
- 64 percent complained that competing requirements from other change programs in the district caused problems during implementation;
- 58 percent indicated that lack of autonomy for school administrators made some aspect of implementing their school improvement effort more difficult.

In our case-study sites, the instances of interference — both direct and because of conflicting demands — are legion in every case except Alameda. To give merely a few examples from Agassiz:

• Increased emphasis on student achievement testing at both state and district levels resulted, in the preceding three years, in externally imposed requirements to administer six major tests between January and April in the English Department alone. In order to improve student test performance, considerable time had to be spent on "coaching," which proved to be extremely disruptive to the implementation of new curriculum efforts in the school.

• The city's new systemwide curriculum was implemented after substantial effort had gone into school-level curriculum work. Not all of the approaches required in the district curriculum were consistent with what the school's staff had been doing.

• At a time when major planning efforts were going into upgrading and modernizing Agassiz's vocational programs, there was a recommendation that these programs be eliminated entirely.

• Two weeks before school was to open in 1986, system economy measures resulted in the loss of several key administrative positions occupied by individuals who had played a major role in carrying out the improvement program.

Whereas direct influence at the state level is usually limited, decisions at the district office *can* make life difficult for schools on a daily basis. Interference is rarely intentionally disruptive to a school improvement effort; rather, it disrupts because it has not taken the school context into consideration.

Another factor to consider is the culture of each district and school, something which dominates the improvement process. Two cultural characteristics, and their relationships with district policies, seem particularly important across cases: (1) staff cohesiveness; (2) the legacy of recent disappointments in school improvement.

Staff cohesiveness was pointed to in both the more successful Alameda and Agassiz cases as very high; both schools managed to gain some control (with assistance from the district) over staffing assignments in order to reinforce cohesiveness. Two schools (Caruso and Burroughs) showed a mixed pattern. In Caruso, a high level of conflict was found within the school's management team (principal, assistant principals, and department heads), but at least some teachers felt a "special sense of community." This, however, was limited to a subset of the teachers because of the very high proportion of instructional staff with temporary per diem appointments who had no expectation of being at the school for more than a brief time. Burroughs encountered a similar problem; the large number of staff who transferred between schools each year made cohesiveness difficult, except among the small stable group of teacher two cases we see strong district effects on staff cohesivenes relating to teacher assignment and transfer resulted in stability. A low degree of cohesion and a lack of mutual among staff characterized the situation at Chester.[8]

The question of disappointing previous improvement results ⌐ less clear, but we may hypothesize that earlier efforts can have two effects. First, a failed program produces a sense of loss. This was explicitly articulated at Chester, where people worked hard and then felt that nothing came through. Heightened expectations were dashed. Poorly implemented or ineffective programs can also produce a "So what?" response to further innovation, which seems to be the case in Caruso. Here a sequence of similar programs produced the sense that there was "no follow through." In both these cases, the failure of previous programs was directly related to turnover and instability of leadership within the district.[9]

Some Lessons and Implications

It is important not to generalize too casually from a few studies to a universe of diverse systems, particularly when national contexts are different. On the other hand, it is worth speculating about some implications of the above discussion. First, I will look at issues applicable to rural, suburban, and urban school systems. Then I shall turn to ideas applicable to one type of school system but not to others.

Stable Policy Environment

Perhaps the most critical feature of the central office and school committee role is to provide a stable policy environment, particularly with regard to school improvement. Rapid changes in district-level improvement programs, no matter how well grounded in research and experience, are inimical to effective change at the school level. This is a particular problem in districts where changes at the superintendent level occur with great frequency, and each new occupant of the position has a different approach to promoting educational quality.

Along the same lines, it is important to consider the possible conflicts between new systemwide efforts to improve the quality of education and activities that are already underway. We often find that schools (of all types) are overwhelmed with multiple new requirements, each of which is, by itself, reasonable. Schools are able to handle the introduction of only a few new programs simultaneously; when more are required, priorities often become unclear and effort is diffused.

A Coherent Strategic Approach

In order to prevent the "over circuiting" that results from many inconsistent efforts to improve, a clear, long-range strategic approach should be developed. Any new systemwide improvement mandate should be reviewed for consistency with the chosen approach, no matter from what office it emerges. This responsibility lies clearly with the superintendent, who should solicit agreement on the strategic approach from all relevant parties (including the school board) to enhance the likelihood that continuity will be maintained.

There are two basic dimensions[10] on which school improvement policy strategies may be classified:

- Is the school improvement effort expected to result in some uniform results across all schools?

- Are uniform procedures or program activities part of the policy?

If we look at the intersection between these two dimensions, we find that there are four different cells. Each of these may be illustrated by a different policy strategy to school improvement, as shown in Figure 8:1.

Figure 8:1
Alternative School Improvement Policy Strategies

	Uniform Results	Non-uniform Results
Uniform Procedures	Implementation Strategy	Evolutionary Planning Strategy
Non-uniform Procedures	Goal-based Accountability Strategy	Professional Investment Strategy

The Implementation Strategy (uniform results and procedures) may be most effective in settings with a clear and relatively narrow program, such as a detailed curriculum, and a smoothly functioning hierarchical organization in which initiatives from the top are likely to be understood and agreed with at lower levels. However, most school systems and improvement efforts (at least in North America) do not meet these criteria. There is ample research indicating that where they are not met, top-down, districtwide implementation strategies or reform efforts may fail to "stick" at the school level and may undermine rather than support efforts to increase the professionalism of the school staff. Research also suggests that even under relatively advantageous conditions, it is important that there be both consensus about the need for the change and support and training provided by the district to help in actually carrying out the program (Fullan et al. 1986).

The remaining three strategic approaches encourage much more

autonomy at the school level. With the Goal-based Accountability
Strategy (uniform results without uniform procedures), the central
office formulates the targeted improvement objectives, but implementation decisions are left to other levels. The role of the central
office during implementation is typically confined to the evaluation
of the policy using the centrally defined objectives or to the provision of support and technical assistance at the school's request. For
example, many recent improvement efforts involve setting standards
for student performance, or teacher accountability. There is no program, however, merely the statement of intent. Schools may be
evaluated on whether they achieve the intent of the policy; there
is no central interest in how they managed to get there, because
there is an assumption that there are many equally viable ways.[11]

An Evolutionary Planning Strategy (uniform procedures without
uniform results) is implicit in a number of decentralized programs,
among which the California School Improvement Program has been
the most publicized (Berman 1984). The government's role is to
stimulate local initiative by providing incentives and to monitor participating schools to ensure that real innovation and improvement
is taking place. These programs are essentially "empty vessels" into
which a school can put its own goals and plans. Sometimes planning
activities and structures are mandated in detail, occasionally they
are entirely voluntary. In any case, the intent of the program is to
induce behaviors associated with continuous self-review and improvement. To talk about measuring success through an assessment
of implementation is often totally inappropriate. Plans may change
quite a lot over the course of a school's improvement effort for very
legitimate reasons. Successful schools often start small and expand
the program with various rather different activities each year.
Although there is a core vision that holds the activities together,
it does not resemble a "project" or a "program" whose implementation one could easily measure. The essence of the improvement
effort is the act of planning as well as the outcomes of planning.

Finally, there is the Professional Investment Strategy (with neither
uniform results nor uniform procedures). In this case, the assumptions are that real school improvement cannot be centrally determined and that the goals for school improvement are best set at the
local level. The best way to promote improvement is to ensure that
the professional staff in the schools have the best conceptual maps
available; improvement work begins at the point where local
educators critically engage with imported ideas. Thus, the role of
government is to provide resources (staff development or other
technical assistance) to support learning and development at the
local level; policies for improvement provide only general frames.
Danish representatives to the OECD have described the overall
school improvement strategy in their country in these terms (Olsen
1986).

Forging a strategic approach at the district level helps to prevent the confusing bombardment of schools with different types of improvement efforts operating under very different types of assumptions. Choices between strategies cannot be based upon purely theoretical grounds, however, but should be realistically matched to the district's context. For example, districts located in a state or province with a tradition of centralized or regulatory control of local schools cannot implement a strong Professional Investment Strategy, because they will be required to help administer centrally designed policies based either on an Implementation or a Goal-based Accountability model. Districts located in a more non-regulatory state, on the other hand, may have greater choice because they are not required to act as the agents for policies developed at other levels.

In general, the Goal-based Accountability and Evolutionary Planning Strategies are probably the most conservative choices for a district office. The logic of an Implementation Strategy is difficult to sustain over time, particularly in a complex or turbulent setting or (as is often the case) where programs and goals are only partially specified. In addition, the costs of maintaining absolute uniformity in both structure and process in many schools simultaneously are very high. At the other extreme, the Professional Investment route is very uncertain in terms of timing and outcomes and, although potentially very effective over the long run, may be more difficult to "sell" and sustain in a period when the public pressures for relatively rapid visible progress are mounting.

The choice between an Evolutionary Planning approach and a Goal-based Accountability approach is more subtle. Evolutionary Planning encourages greater heterogeneity among the schools within a district and is more consistent with some other current reform suggestions, such as school-based accountability. It may be a particularly appropriate choice for districts that support many schools which are different by design (such as open enrollment and magnet schools) or that have a great deal of variability in community catchment areas (such as districts that include both suburban and more rural schools). While Goal-based Accountability also gives some professional autonomy to school administrators and teachers, it exists within a framework of publicly arrived at objectives which, presumably, reflect some consensus within the community. It may therefore be more relevant to systems where the press to raise standards in all schools is great and where there is concern about permitting too many differences between schools. Providing a public benchmark may be a particularly useful policy strategy in settings in which schools are the subject of heated political debate involving diverse pressure groups, for example, systems under more recent court-ordered desegregation. Because Goal-based Accountability supports a stronger decision-making role for the district office, it may also be more appropriate in the kinds of rural settings included in the study reported above, where creating a "system" is a prerequisite to school improvement.

District Resources for Schools

Several of the research reports discussed above point to a common finding: schools need extra help and resources to improve (Crandall et al. 1983; Fullan et al. 1986; Louis et al. 1981; Miles et al. 1987). A large amount of extra money is not typically the key. Rather, resources for staff development and program coordination are critical. These most often come from the district office, either directly (in the form of services provided) or indirectly (in the form of some fiscal autonomy for the school staff or control over staff development resources).

For the most part, schools should have the opportunity to choose among available support resources to fill particular program needs of their school. Some guidelines, however, are appropriate. The research referred to above illustrates the value of sustained training and development support at the school, as contrasted with more typical staff development activities which involve "one shot" exposure to an expert, with little follow-up. Furthermore, few school administrators have much exposure to or training in the kinds of skills that would permit them to develop a long-range improvement plan for themselves, their students, and their buildings. Yet, these kinds of skills may be critical if the Goal-based Accountability or Evolutionary Planning Strategies become a basic system improvement policy. The district office should provide opportunities for school-based administrators to receive technical assistance and training in these areas. Brief sabbaticals, tuition support for attending appropriate courses or seminars, and ongoing, in-school assistance are all part of an effective district support system (see also Leithwood 1989).

Major school improvement efforts should not, however, be based on purely administrative changes. A recent review of the effective schools literature suggests that without improvements in the classroom and in the relationships among adults in the schools, changes in student outcomes are less likely to occur (Rosenholtz 1985). We observe in both the rural and urban studies that many school improvement efforts become "stuck" at the level of instituting administrative and organizational changes and fail to penetrate deeply into the instructional process. Thus, the bias in technical assistance and training should be toward the curriculum and instructional needs of the schools.

Reorganizing Schools to Focus on Instruction

Although a key aspect of school improvement is a focus on the teaching-learning process, I have not addressed that issue very directly here. There is an important reason for this lack of attention: the data discussed above suggest that (1) district offices are too remote from schools to have much direct influence over teaching-learning contexts; and (2) they can have significant indirect effects through the development of policies which support that type of focus.

To be more specific: school staffs are unlikely to grapple deeply with basic issues of teaching and learning in the absence of some preconditions. Perhaps the most critical is cohesiveness among the staff, a factor shown to be strongly associated with improvement in all studies where it is examined. Districts can promote but not ensure cohesiveness through a variety of critical policies, including those affecting teaching assignments and through in-service and technical assistance policies that support team building at the school level.

Many districts feel they have more success in supporting school improvement at the elementary than the secondary level. A significant way of encouraging secondary schools to focus on instruction is to rethink the role and functioning of departments. Focussing on schoolwide instructional improvement in most high schools clearly makes no sense, and the principal in a typical junior high or high school cannot usually play an "instructional leadership" role for the entire staff in the same way that an elementary school principal can. First, the principal always lacks subject matter legitimacy in all departments other than the one associated with his or her own training. Second, it is impossible to keep up with developments in the diverse areas covered within a comprehensive secondary school. Finally, because high schools are much more complex, both in terms of size and structure, the internal administrative tasks associated with making the school run smoothly and dealing with external constituencies take much more time. Thus, the principal may be able to take on a leadership role in orchestrating an improvement effort, but, except under unusual circumstances, the task of providing substantive leadership will be delegated to others.

The department head is located in a key position to take on substantive leadership. Relying on departments ensures both broader participation in planning and improvement strategies that are centered on the content and effectiveness of teaching. This implies, however, a shift in the role of department head from a vaguely defined combination of supervisor and subject-matter specialist to one clearly emphasizing instructional leadership. In this regard, the department head takes on some of the qualities associated with principals in studies of effective elementary schools by providing: strong clarification of goals and vision for individual teachers and the department (consistent with system and schoolwide goals); technical assistance and support for teachers; time spent in the classrooms, not to evaluate teachers but to help them identify and deal with their weaknesses; encouragment of experimentation and sharing among the staff; and other efforts designed to forge and reinforce an emphasis on teaching.

This is not the traditionally defined role of department heads, although many talented individuals work within this framework already. In many districts, the department head position has been used as a consolation prize for aspiring administrators not considered for a principalship or district office position rather than as a reward for leadership among peers. Districts can play a strong role in supporting improvement within secondary schools by giving priority to the development and use of the valuable resources that already exist at this level and by rethinking the expectations held for this role.

Dimensions of District Management

Two separate dimensions affecting the quality of the relationship between school and district are the degree of *engagement* and the level of *bureaucratization*. By engagement, I mean a relationship which has some shared goals and objectives, reasonably clear and frequent communication, and mutual coordination and influence. By bureaucratization, I mean the extent to which control is affected by rules and regulations, rather than by personal relationships. In general, engagement is better for school improvement, and strong bureaucratic rule orientation is worse. Although some level of engagement between district and school would appear to be a good idea, both the rural and urban cases present a dismal prospect of that possibility and provide a cautionary note to more "typical" districts.

Engagement depends on consistency of communication and policies. This is not possible in systems that have high levels of turnover in key administrative positions, as do most urban districts. Look at New York — three chancellors since 1980; Cleveland — seven superintendents since the mid-'70s; Boston — musical chairs at the top between 1974 and 1982 and now another new superintendent, an outsider very different in style and programmatic emphasis from the last one. Only two districts in the Miles et al. (1987) study have the kind of administrative stability that can permit close engagement — and in one of these the option was not exercised. In rural districts, as noted above, communication is made difficult by role overload, lack of full-time administrators, and physical dispersion.

Despite common pressures, we can observe several different modes of district-school relationships in the cases discussed earlier in this paper. The first is a typical urban model, exemplified by Cleveland, Boston, and New York, which is both highly bureaucratic and largely disengaged. In this type of system there are plenty of rules and regulations. In fact, one suspects that with instability at the top, there is rarely an opportunity in this kind of system to "clean up" the rules, to throw out those that conflict with new programs and priorities. The reliance on rules is also exemplified by union contracts and by the vigilance with which the unions often insist on the "letter of the law." Because of the rule orientation, teachers feel they must defend themselves against exploitation, and they develop their own formal system to parallel the bureaucracy. This, in turn, may lead to increased district bureaucracy.

But beyond written rules, these districts and schools often seem to operate in virtual isolation from one another. At an extreme, the district provides no support, no leadership, no new ideas, no programs. In less extreme cases of disengagement there are new ideas and programs, even some support, but these are externally derived and imposed with scant regard for local school conditions. In a disengaged but bureaucratic system, the district context becomes nothing but an irritating set of constraints and conflicting demands; it offers no real support. The principals, even strong ones, don't attempt to exercise influence over the district or to do anything but work more or less within the rules while trying to manage competing programs that are "sent." Passive rule evasion is not rare, a situation that increases disengagement since communication upward becomes a charade.

At least in a rule-oriented, disengaged situation, an effective principal can actively buffer the school and be a careful outlaw with regard to central regulation.[12] An alternative but hardly more promising situation, found in both urban and rural cases, is the engaged and bureaucratic system. In the case of urban Chester, for example, the superintendent's original intent was to combine pressure and support. Each school was to have a central office person act as link between the school and the demands of the mandated change program. But the superintendent, who was to be the link to Chester High School, never really followed through. Communication between the high school and the district office was relatively frequent but poor even before the program began and characterized by mutual distrust. The superintendent insisted on district control over resources; for example, he did not support the principal's requests to use district staff development days for school-specific program work. Later, there was interference in the form of a centrally imposed reorganization in the middle of a major change program. The relationship between school and district actually made it useless for the principal to continue to try to push for program implementation. In exercising any real leadership, she would just be setting herself up for failure.

Engagement is far from being a sufficient characteristic for success. It is possible that negative engagement, combined with bureaucratic rules, is one of the least helpful patterns. To give another example, in a rural district described by Firestone (1979), the superintendent relied heavily on rules and procedures to set standards for teacher and school performance in the districtwide effort to individualize instruction. Personal monitoring and review were relatively heavy, with strong evaluative overtones. Teachers and principals alike increasingly resisted the superintendent's innovative efforts and conformed procedurally rather than purposefully to the new rules. In both this and the Chester case, the outcome of close engagement and bureaucratic control was a marked suspiciousness between district office and school staffs, creating an insurmountable barrier to cooperative activity.

More common in rural school systems, however, is a situation in which the school district relationship is neither engaged nor highly bureaucratic. In an environment with limited staff, a preference for informal rather than formal relationships, and the traditional commitment to high levels of classroom autonomy, instituting any cooperative activity is difficult. In several cases in the rural schools study discussed above, for example, the "districts" were actually organized more like loose confederations; and individual outlying schools simply exercised what they believed to be their option to not participate in the comprehensive change effort. In another system, organized as a "supervisory union" between several schools, the development of a coordinated districtwide effort never really got off the ground.

The only clearly positive district contexts are found in such examples as urban Alameda and rural Oyster Cove, which were engaged but not highly bureaucratic. The district staffing in both these cases was thin — minuscule, compared with others their size. Limited staff meant that any districtwide effort had to involve contributions from other administrators and teachers and, in the case of Oyster Cove, even from community members. Essentially, the picture is one of co-management, with coordination and joint planning enhanced through the development of consensus between staff members at all levels about desired goals for education. Both Alameda and Oyster Cove were among the most effective in their school improvement efforts.

In sum, the best district contexts for supporting school improvement in most cases may be characterized by the adage "less is more," at least on the regulation dimension. It is time to seriously question whether the role of the district should be defined as the direct "manager of school improvement." This is especially so in light of the increasing role of the states in regulation, a situation that simply increases the opportunities for any strong management role from the district to create conflicting demands on schools.

The Importance of Local Community Context
The above review of two studies strongly suggests that prescriptions for superintendents and district office staff should be conditional on community context; the problems are varied, and the available, reasonable solutions vary as well. Some key issues can be highlighted.

Rural Systems. The main issue facing rural districts is their tendency to be extremely loosely administered (i.e., in the language used above, they are both disengaged and non-bureaucratic). Coordinated action in a district with small schools located at some distance from each other and often without full-time administrators is problematic. Even arranging an after-school meeting of principals is not a simple issue when schools are located many miles from the district office and principals are also bus drivers! Superintendents (and the very limited staff typically available to work with them) must overcome these difficulties through a much greater level of personal involvement in the development of both the program and process of change. Because of the general lack of resources at the school level, the superintendents and staff must not only provide the policy frames and support (as suggested in the literature based on "typical" districts), but often have to get involved more deeply as actors in the change process. The challenge is to do so without becoming highly bureaucratic and while supporting the efforts of building staff to develop programs and improvement efforts adapted to their building and local context.

Urban Systems. The problem of communication between central office and school is also a critical one for urban school districts, despite the close physical proximity. Urban systems are typically large, ever-shifting bureaucracies that appear impenetrable to many building staff members. Superintendents are like chief executive officers in other large organizations; they are distracted by public appearances, political crises, broad personnel questions, and the need to deal with a more dynamic range of constituencies. This inescapable fact means that the urban superintendent cannot easily be involved as a key or frequent actor in a districtwide school improvement effort. Yet, there is still a central role for the superintendent's staff in ensuring that all the good ideas for educational reform emerging in a complex system do not become an implementation nightmare at the school level.

The challenge most often facing urban superintendents and their staffs is to unbundle all the layers of previous efforts made to create greater accountability and coordination and to move the focus away from regulation to an understanding of school needs. This is no small challenge because urban systems tend to cling tightly to the idea that good central management leads to good education (Callahan 1962). Unlike the staff in a "typical" district, central office staff in urban settings rarely go out into the schools; they share an incomplete understanding of the individual schools and their needs. Many, in fact, have an unsympathetic view of school staff, which may increase their tendency to prefer regulations to positive incentives for improved performance. Because of blocked communication and low visibility, many schools are able to conform superficially to district requirements while in reality doing pretty much as they please. Others conform to the letter of the law but develop no internal commitment to improving in directions endorsed by the district.

Some urban schools will be able to improve even within these constraints. But the task would be considerably easier if central office reorganization could shift the role of superintendent and staff away from the impossible (central control over student learning outcomes) toward the possible (central policy setting and support for school-based improvement). Reforming bureaucracies is no simple task, and

I shall only presume to emphasize that school-level improvement will not work well in urban settings until some basic principles of co-management, based on deregulation and increased communication, are initiated.

"Typical" Districts. Relationships between schools and districts are generally easier in the "typical" district. But if all the assumptions and recommendations discussed above are to be carried out, there is still a need for action in many cases. First, many "typical" districts do not have major performance problems; they have only a limited history of districtwide improvement programs. The idea of a clearly articulated, long-range strategy for school improvement is likely to be foreign, and educational work will need to be done with various professional and community constituencies to promote the idea of a long-range strategy as opposed to more typical "quick fix" policies to deal with specific concerns. The most critical issue for the superintendent is building sufficient understanding of and support for a more strategic approach so that schools can work independently, but within a common frame.

Staffing issues are also important; the growth of state and federal funding has resulted in the proliferation of "specialist" offices and roles at the district level. These individuals are trained in specific areas (special needs, elementary curriculum development) but are expected to perform numerous tasks, including the facilitation of change, organizational development, and the coordination of groups of teachers involved in development activities. Sometimes staff development is organizationally isolated from ongoing change efforts. District offices are small so it is assumed that bureaucracy and formal role definitions won't get in the way, but they do. Rethinking these roles, and perhaps some retraining, may be necessary in order to use staff time most effectively.

Finally, the "typical" district office should carefully consider its role as a filter through which information relevant to school improvement passes. District staff do not always consider their "information broker" roles to be part of their formal responsibilities; consequently, much information that may be highly relevant to improved school and instructional processes does not actually reach teachers.

Conclusion

Many current debates about the district's school improvement role would find the participants located in two opposing camps. Arrayed on one side are those that advocate "strong central leadership," in which "the key tasks for [district] administrators are finding and developing a practice with a potentially good fit, getting it adopted, providing technical and institutional support, and getting the practice stabilized and extended ... and 'routinized' into existing training, budget and political cycles" (Huberman 1983 p. 27). On the other side are those who would like to see the managerial components of our educational system severely curtailed, such that teachers and "head teachers" are given control over ensuring the quality of education. This chapter has presented arguments that suggest a "middle way," one involving district and school co-management of the improvement process. How the district-school relationship gets played out will vary depending on the size and complexity of the district, as well as other community factors that have not been discussed here. Nevertheless, I may suggest that the co-management scenario would include the following responsibilities for the superintendent and district staff:

• System Building: ensuring that there is sufficient communication and shared understanding of the district's goals, and of how individual school goals relate to them;

• Setting Broad Policies: developing the broad outlines of a semi-permanent policy strategy and how it will be carried out; depending on the strategy selected, this would include setting performance objectives in consultation with relevant parties and/or designing a school improvement process;

• Stimulating: providing easy access to new ideas in ways that permit staff to critically engage with them;

• Enabling: providing administrators and teachers with a staff development model that will permit them to acquire the requisite skills for school development and self-development;

• Supporting: providing technical assistance, moral support, and recognition for schools and individuals with innovative ideas;

• Buffering: ensuring that schools are protected from other demands, such as unreasonable political pressures, new rules, or additional innovative programs that might distract them from the improvement effort, and that they have time lines sufficient to meet new goals.

Notes

1. Throughout this chapter the American term *school district* is used. The term encompasses both the policy-making and administrative functions of the district. No direct attention is paid to the role of lay appointed or elected officials within school districts or boards.

2. This effort, sponsored by the Organization for Economic Cooperation and Development, was called the International School Improvement Project. The full set of assumptions generated by this group is laid out in the volume *Making School Improvement Work* (van Velzen et al. 1985).

3. To give just one example of how districts are ignored in recent research related to school improvement, Lightfoot's (1983) prize-winning book on excellent high schools does not mention the role of the superintendent or district office except in passing.

4. They point out, however, that using power too openly in the change process tends to undermine it: superintendents who were most effective in dominating the planning and implementation process did not "bulldoze" local communities and staff, but persuaded.

5. High levels of collegiality coupled with relatively low levels of decision-making autonomy among teachers were another factor promoting systemwide change.

6. My colleagues are Matt Miles, Eleanor Farrar, Sheila Rosenblum, and Anthony Cipollone.

7. The sampling and survey procedures are described in more detail elsewhere (Louis 1986; Louis and Cipollone 1987b). The schools in the survey represent the universe of urban high schools we were able to locate that were implementing a schoolwide reform based at least in part on the research findings from the effective schools or effective teaching literature.

8. In Chester's staff, cohesiveness seems to be particularly low, although the staff is exceptionally stable; the degree to which district policies have contributed to this condition is unclear. There are many staff conflicts, both overt and covert, and a tendency to blame everyone in sight for the problems in the school and district.

9. Perhaps it is significant that in our five schools we have no instance of a school with a successful innovation history. We may speculate that even temporarily successful reforms are rare in urban high schools.

10. This framework was derived from a comparative review of improvement strategies in the OECD countries, as laid out in Louis and van Velzen (1986).

11. Of course, there has been much speculation that these kinds of policies may result in a wide range of potentially negative behaviors on the part of schools in order to meet the goals — for example, increasing the early drop-out rate of low performing students in order to increase the proportion of students meeting graduation requirements.

12. This cuts both ways, of course. Ineffective principals can block central office initiatives that are well conceived and desirable.

References

Berman P 1984 *Improving School Improvement: A Policy Evaluation of the California School Improvement Program.* Berman, Weiler Associates, Berkeley, California

Callahan R 1962 *Education and the Cult of Efficiency.* University of Chicago Press, Chicago

Carlson R 1965 The adoption of educational innovations. Center for the Study of Educational Administration, University of Oregon, Eugene

Cox P 1983 Inside-out and outside-in: Configurations of assistance and their impact on school improvement efforts. Paper presented at the American Educational Research Association Annual Meeting, New Orleans

Crandall D et al. 1983 People, policies and practices: Examining the chain of school improvement. The Network, Inc., Andover, Massachusetts

Cuban L 1984 Transforming the frog into a prince: Effective schools research, policy and practice at the district level. *Harvard Educational Review* 54: 129–151

Farrar E 1987 Burroughs Middle School: The dilemma of school improvement in the cities. School of Education, SUNY, Buffalo, New York

Firestone W 1979 Butte-Angels camp: Conflict and transformation. In: Herriott R, Gross N (eds.) *The Dynamics of Planned Educational Change.* McCutchan, Berkeley, California

Fullan M 1981 School district and school personnel in knowledge utilization. In: Lehming R, Kane M (eds.) *Improving Schools: Using What We Know.* Sage, Beverley Hills, California

Fullan M, Anderson S, Newton E 1986 *Support Systems for Implementing Curriculum in School Boards.* Ministry of Education, Toronto

Gersten R, Carnine D, Zoref L, Cronin D 1986 A multifaceted study of change in seven inner-city schools. *The Elementary School Journal* 85: 391–421

Hall G, Putman S, Hord S 1985 District office personnel: Their roles and influence on school and classroom change: What we don't know. Paper presented at the American Educational Research Association Annual Meeting, Chicago

Herriott R, Gross N (eds.) 1979 *The Dynamics of Planned Educational Change.* McCutchan, Berkeley, California

Huberman M 1983 School improvement strategies that work: Some scenarios. *Educational Leadership* 41: 23–27

Huberman M, Miles M 1984 *Innovation Up Close.* Plenum Press, New York

Katz M 1971 From voluntarism to bureaucracy in American education. *Sociology of Education* 44: 297–332

Kerr N 1964 The school board as an agency of legitimation. *Sociology of Education* 38: 34–59

Leithwood K 1989 School system policies for effective school administration. In: Holmes M, Leithwood K A, Musella D F (eds.) *Educational Policy for Effective Schools.* OISE Press, Toronto

Lightfoot S L 1983 *The Good High School.* Basic Books, New York

Lippitt R 1979 Consultation: Traps and potentialities. In: Herriott R, Gross N (eds.) *The Dynamics of Planned Educational Change.* McCutchan, Berkeley, California

Louis K S 1986 Reforming the urban high school: Preliminary reports from a survey. Paper presented at the Annual Meeting of the American Educational Research Association, San Francisco

Louis K S, Cipollone A 1987a The slower you go, the faster you get there: A study of the management of change in Dorchester (Agassiz) High School. Center for Survey Research, Boston

Louis K S, Cipollone A 1987b A causal model of the improvement process. Paper presented at the Annual Meeting of the American Educational Research Association, Washington, DC

Louis K S, Dentler R, Kell D 1984 Exchanging ideas: The communication and use of educational knowledge. Center for Survey Research, Boston

Louis K S, Rosenblum S, Molitor J 1981 Strategies for school improvement. National Institute of Education, Washington, DC

Louis K S, van Velzen W 1986 Policy making for school improvement: A comparative analysis of four policy issues. Paper presented at a conference of the International School Improvement Project, Ontario Institute for Studies in Education, Toronto

Miles M 1987a Caruso High School: Reaching at risk students. Center for Policy Research, New York

Miles M 1987b Practical guidelines for school administrators. Paper presented at the American Educational Research Association Annual Meeting, Washington, DC

Miles M, Louis K S, Rosenblum S, Cipollone A, Farrar E 1987 Improving the urban high school: Preliminary guidelines for implementation. Center for Survey Research, University of Massachusetts, Boston

Miles M, Rosenblum S 1987 Chester High School. Center for Policy Research, New York

Olsen T P 1986 Responsiveness, co-operation and school development: A Danish support model. Danmarks Laererhojskole, Copenhagen, Denmark

Rosenblum S 1987 Alameda High School: The big fix. Center for Policy Research, New York

Rosenblum S, Louis K S 1981 *Stability and Change: Innovation in an Educational Context.* Plenum Press, New York

Rosenholtz S 1985 Effective schools: Interpreting the evidence. *American Journal of Education* 93(3): 352–388

Tyack D 1974 *The One Best System.* Harvard University Press, Cambridge, Massachusetts

Tyack D, Hansot E 1982 *Managers of Virtue.* Basic Books, New York

van Velzen W, Miles M, Eckholm M, Hameyer U, Roban (D (eds.) 1985 *Making School Improvement Work.* ACCO, Leuven, Belgium

9/Quality Control: School Accountability and District Ethos

Linda LaRocque and Peter Coleman

LaRocque and Coleman show that the most effective school districts in their British Columbia sample are run by active, policy-minded superintendents who are directly and personally involved in the implementation of policy in the schools. Some questions to consider include: To what extent do the successful districts have qualities that attract the kinds of leaders they have? Will the effect of strong leaders remain after they leave for better things? How can policymakers select people with the desirable qualities?

This chapter derives from a major research project carried out in British Columbia, under the auspices of the Social Sciences and Humanities Research Council of Canada. Our research generally has been concerned with the notion of school district ethos, both as a measure of district quality and as a potential predictor of student achievement. Our interest in district ethos was stimulated by the results of an examination of a number of district status variables and their possible associations with district effectiveness, efficiency, size, and location (Coleman 1986a, 1986b; Coleman and LaRocque 1984).

After controlling for the effects of community educational level, there still remained extensive differences in aggregated student achievement among districts. Resource variables, that is, costs per student, were negatively associated with these achievement variations (Coleman 1986a, 1986b), while the pupil/teacher ratio was positively associated. When the effects of the pupil/teacher ratio variations on costs were excluded, however, no significant relationship remained between residualized costs per pupil and residualized achievement. Thus non-resource district characteristics which might be related to achievement seemed potentially quite important.

We suggest that a positive district ethos consists of a high degree of interest in and concern about six activity and attitude "focusses": taking care of business; monitoring performance; changing/adapting policies and practices; consideration/caring for stakeholders; creating shared values; and creating community support. The first three focusses are task-oriented; the latter three are concerned with values and attitudes. The general nature of these focusses is suggested in Table 9:1, which also demonstrates how they may be linked to parallel issues at the school and classroom level (see Coleman 1986a for more detailed discussion).

Table 9:1
Parallels Between Good Classrooms, Good Schools, and Good School Districts

	ACTIVITY	Classroom Level	School Level	District Level	FOCUS
ACADEMIC PURPOSES	taking care of business	time on task	academic orientation	focus on instruction	**Learning Focus**
	monitoring performance	student accountability	teacher accountability	school accountability	**Accountability Focus**
	changing policies/ practices	instructional practice	continuous improvement	organizational change	**Change Focus**
NURTURANCE PURPOSES	caring for stakeholders	student support	ethos of caring	consideration	**Caring Focus**
	creating shared values	collegiality	consensus on school life	commitment to effort	**Commitment Focus**
	creating community support	parents as partners	parent integration	community integration	**Community Focus**

The notion of school district ethos is displayed more fully in Table 9:2, where each of the six district-level focusses is considered in terms of three broad district tasks. The cells of the resulting matrix constitute descriptions of the work of district administrators and also of a set of beliefs about important features of the role. For us they constitute the heart of the research questions which guided data collection and analysis in our study of school district norms and practices.

In this chapter, we are concerned centrally with policies for effectiveness, so we shall limit our discussion to the issue of accountability. The three research questions are:

• How are schools held accountable for their performance?

Table 9:2
District Ethos and District Tasks

	DISTRICT TASKS		
SIX FOCUSSES (DISTRICT ETHOS)	A. Be Accountable	B. Improve/ Adapt	C. Set Expectations
Learning Focus 1. Focus on Instruction	program effectiveness assessed?	changes to improve instruction?	instructional goals most important?
Accountability Focus 2. School Accountability	schools held accountable for performance?	changes to improve school accountability practices?	monitoring and instructional goals linked?
Change Focus 3. Organizational Change	changes as response to performance data?	changes as response to environment changes?	changes in goals/goal- setting processes?
Caring Focus 4. Consideration	concern for professional and community opinion on performance?	decisions reflect concerns of professionals and community?	emphasis on affective goals?
Commitment Focus 5. Commitment to Effort	commitment to accountability created?	commitment to change efforts created?	commitment to school/district goals created?
Community Focus 6. Community Integration	schools/district involve community in monitoring?	community involvement in change efforts?	community involvement in setting of goals?

• What changes have been made to improve school accountability practices?

• What is the relationship between the monitoring of school achievement and instructional goals?

Perspectives on "Quality Control"

"Monitoring performance" as a general activity (Table 9:1) means an administrative focus on accountability. In particular at the district level it means holding schools accountable for academic and other kinds of success. The notion of holding students accountable for behavior and performance through close monitoring is common in the classroom management and school effectiveness literature (Anderson, Evertson and Emmer 1980; Evertson and Emmer 1982; Mackenzie 1983). Similarly, an emphasis on teacher accountability via supervision is a staple in the administrative literature (Bridges 1986). The notion of school accountability is less common in Canada and the U.S.

Boyd and Crowson (1981) have identified accountability performance, in general, as part of a changing focus in administrative studies. Cuban (1984) has raised the specific issue of school accountability in the context of district improvement. Murphy, Hallinger, and Peterson (1985) have described principal supervision as an important part of the responsibilities of superintendents in high-achieving districts. The emphasis in the districts they studied, however, was on personnel supervision based on personal goal attainment rather than on holding principals accountable for school performance.

Here we describe administrative activities at the district level associated with school accountability, and hence possibly with district achievement levels.

There are currently few instances in the U.S. of district-level uses of monitoring data in comprehensive ways (Kean 1983). In fact, such an approach can be considered inappropriate in either loosely coupled systems (Weick 1976) or professional bureaucracies (Mintzberg 1979), which are characterized by continuing "negotiations" (Corwin and Borman 1988) between schools and central administrators about autonomy and constraints and in which "managing uncertainty" (McPherson, Crowson and Pitner 1986) about means-ends relationships is the critical management problem.

The recent Snyder and Anderson (1986) text on *Managing Productive Schools* contains a chapter describing "The Management Subsystem: Quality Control," but this is interpreted as largely an internal school affair, with only the periodic visits of an external review team to carry the responsibility of holding the school accountable for performance to district-level management. Such approaches reflect a considerable and understandable concern for school autonomy. The strengths of such accountability schemes, however, are also their weaknesses: highly individualized school evaluations make comparative judgments impossible and raise serious problems of validity and reliability. That is, such evaluations do not allow objective performance judgments to be made.

Yet the case for treating the school as the unit of improvement seems strong; Goodlad, a major advocate, asserts that "the most promising unit of selection in seeking to mount and maintain programs providing quality and equitable education is the individual school" (1987 p. 13). Sirotnick has extended this idea to the issue of evaluation and argues that "evaluation becomes the process of rigorous *self-examination,* indeed the process of school *renewal* itself" (1987 p. 42). Schools need district and other kinds of support for this activity, which is essentially the "production of critical knowledge through the process of critical inquiry" (Sirotnick 1987 p. 51). Accountability is transformed into responsibility in this system, and "such level-to-level monitoring as is deemed minimally necessary should focus on whether adequate mechanisms for assuring responsible performance are in place" (Goodlad 1987 p. 13).

Advocates of more traditional approaches to school accountability, such as school-based management and management-by-objectives, argue that school autonomy and "loose coupling" are desirable with respect to means: "Every decision which contributes to the instructional effectiveness of the school, and which can be made at school level, should be made at school level" (Coleman 1984 p. 25). The role of the district is supportive: "The task of central office personnel then becomes to provide support and assistance to these schools, in an effort to help the schools to develop their autonomy, and then improve their quality" (p. 34).

But in the school-based management approach described by Coleman, school autonomy with respect to ends is more limited. He maintains that the support and assistance provided by the school district to schools must include the monitoring of results by collecting data annually on a variety of measures of school quality and providing these data to the schools. He argues from experience that "the longitudinal data are very useful in showing minor fluctuations in school quality" and "the indicators of school quality vary together" (Coleman 1984 p. 34). Thus we envisage broad measures of quality, as does Goodlad, but school autonomy is limited by district goals and expectations. These in turn are limited by the expectations of provincial governments.

As we have noted elsewhere (Coleman and LaRocque 1984) the criteria used by provincial and state governments in assessing school districts have been effectiveness and efficiency, and equity to a lesser extent. Districts unable to meet these criteria have often disappeared in reorganizations. Mitchell and Encarnation (1984) list seven policy mechanisms which state governments use to advance their goals. Very recently in British Columbia, districts unable to meet spending targets were placed under trusteeship, a rather drastic mechanism not listed by Mitchell and Encarnation. The Coleman autonomy/accountability mix is consistent with these constraints. But it is also much less acceptable to teachers than the looser Goodlad approach.

The two approaches to quality control identified in the literature can be labelled "autonomy with accountability" (Coleman) and "autonomy with responsibility" (Goodlad). After the presentation of data regarding current practices in B.C. school districts, these two possible approaches will be reconsidered.

Methodological Considerations

The general methodology parallels that of most of the effective schools research. Given a sample of districts with differing outcomes, we ask if it is possible to identify differences in district ethos and associated policies and practices within the group which might help to account for the variance in outcomes. To be persuasive, such differences in ethos must at least vary across the sample consistently with the variance in outcomes. Just as important, the detailed data on differences in ethos among districts should allow the later development of a conceptual framework linking ethos and outcome which has a predictive rather than an explanatory basis.

Sample of Districts

In British Columbia, Canada's Pacific province, there are 75 school districts, which in 1984 ranged in size from about 400 to over 50 000 pupils. With a few exceptions, each has a locally appointed district superintendent, responsible for the administration of education. Each district also has an elected school board, responsible for decisions on policies such as budget development and some curricular matters. At present, district budgets are established by the Ministry of Education, which also retains some control over curriculum and such operational matters as the school calendar and personnel practices.

Ten districts constitute the sample for this report. They are representative in several respects: residual scores and costs, district size, and type of community (rural/urban location).

Aggregating performance data to the district level raises a number of serious methodological issues, as yet unresolved (Hannan, Freeman and Meyer 1976; Sirotnick and Burstein 1985). The debate concerns use of aggregated student data and the sources of variance in achievement. Bidwell and Kasarda (1975) used aggregated student data in their analysis of district effects. Their critics, advocating the use of individual student data, with school and district identification, argue that the individual is the major source of variance and hence "the appropriate level of analysis." The fact that interdistrict variance is greater than interschool variance in the work of Bidwell and Kasarda illustrates to these critics the errors in using aggregated data (Hannan, Freeman and Meyer 1976 p. 142).

A second critique is that "the variance in student achievement lying between districts quite probably would be substantially less than that lying between schools" (i.e., *attributable* to school districts); it is not "sufficiently large to warrant serious attention" (Alexander and Griffin 1976 p. 145). Yet the data Alexander and Griffin (1976) provide, using an analysis based on individual data, shows that roughly 5 to 10 percent of the variance in achievement lies between districts.

Advocates of the use of aggregated data argue that the use of individualized data necessarily ignores collective sources of variance which are important but not easily identified, such as reading group (which, according to Barr and Drebeen [1983], is the single most important source of variance in achievement in elementary schools) and secondary school track (Alexander, Cook and McDill 1978). Analyses based on individual scores discount variance from such sources. There is a general tendency to undervalue contextual or collective sources of variance (Barr and Drebeen 1983 pp. 22, 41). On the other hand, "The aggregation of learning outcomes to the school level [or higher] biases findings toward the identification of productive conditions at that level" (Barr and Drebeen 1983 p. 68).

For our purposes, we needed an achievement measure which was: modestly longitudinal, since district effectiveness probably fluctuates; broad with respect to both subjects and grades; and relatively independent of provincewide shifts in achievement. Longitudinal consistency in reporting, for example, achievement in mathematics by the students of the province was less important than an accurate representation of the relative standing of districts in the province.

The nine test scores available from provincial test batteries given to all students in the appropriate age cohort between 1981 and 1984 were: science — grades 4, 8, and 12; reading — grades 4, 7, and 10; and mathematics — grades 4, 8, and 12. The cost data were taken from school district budgets (Coleman and LaRocque 1984).

When these data were reported at the district level of aggregation, there were two school districts which were extreme outliers with respect to achievement (and community education level). These were removed from the sample to allow a regression calculation appropriate for the remaining 73 school districts. Our procedure with the achievement data was to standardize and aggregate the test scores and to calculate a residual using community education level (the percentage of families with some postsecondary education) as a predictor. This is the strongest proxy for family environment (Walberg and Marjoribanks 1976) available as a predictor of achievement in B.C. (Coleman 1986a). The resulting measure is residual achievement, a broad and probably somewhat overstated measure of district impact on student test scores.

It was necessary to transform the cost data by using the reciprocal to reduce skewness. The standardized and transformed 1982 per-pupil costs were residualized with district mean grade size, an important predictor of costs over which the district has little control (Coleman 1987; Coleman and LaRocque 1986). The correlation between residual achievement and residual costs was $-.29$ (p = .01). This finding differs sharply from that of Bidwell and Kasarda (1975) and slightly from that of other studies of costs and achievement at the district level, which tend to find no significant relationship (Childs and Shakeshaft 1986). Most other studies use raw cost data rather than discretionary (residualized) cost data.

We then rank-ordered the districts by residual achievement and residual costs, and selected for our sample the ten districts listed in Table 9:3. Table 9:3 also summarizes various characteristics of these districts and illustrates the correspondence between rankings on residual achievement and residual costs suggested by the negative relationship. We have called districts with a high residual score and a low residual cost "high performing" and districts with a low residual score and a high residual cost "low performing." District performance level is given in the last column of Table 9:3.

Table 9:3
The Purposive Sample of B.C. School Districts

District	Size Range[1]	Type of Community	Residual Score	(Rank)[2]	Residual Costs	(Rank)[2]	Performance Rating
R	medium	small city/rural	9.75	(1)	− 330	(6)	high
Q	small	rural/small town	6.67	(6)	− 409	(3)	high
W	large	small city/rural	4.65	(11)	− 217	(13)	high
V	large	city/rural	4.50	(13)	− 260	(11)	high
J	medium	small city/rural	2.93	(21)	− 63	(20)	high
P	medium	rural/small towns	2.48	(24)	− 19	(35)	high/medium
B	large	small city/urban	0.61	(36)	61	(48)	medium
H	small	rural	− 2.13	(51)	541	(70)	low
M	medium	small city/urban	− 6.62	(67)	401	(68)	low
C	small	rural/isolated	− 13.98	(71)	891	(73)	low
			SD = 5.20		SD = 257		

[1]Size ranges: small = 1–2100; medium = 2101–5600; large = 5601–51000; 25 districts per range
[2]Rank of 73 districts: 1 is high for achievement, low for costs

District R serves a small city in the interior of the province as well as the rural area surrounding that city. District Q is a largely resource-based town on a major highway, with most of the schools in town and close together. District W is quite rural, although it also contains a small town. Many of the schools serve small villages some way from any city.

District V is centred on a large city but serves a considerable rural area and has a wide variety of types and sizes of school. District J is in a relatively remote area, with very scattered schools, some of which are quite large. District P serves an economically diverse community with several small towns, some tourist-oriented. District B is suburban/rural, near a major city. The schools tend to be large and close together. The area has grown rapidly and is suffering from planning difficulties.

District H consists of a single high school and a group of small and scattered feeder elementary schools, serving a resource-based community quite near a larger centre. District M is a rather affluent small city, with a long (for British Columbia) history. The schools are close together and quite large. District C is an isolated community, with very small schools and a substantial Native population.

Data Collection

The major method of data collection was the interview. All line administrators in the district — that is, the superintendent, assistant superintendents, directors, and supervisors — were interviewed. This meant one to three individuals in each of the sample districts. All the principals in the smaller districts were interviewed. About one-third of the principals in the larger districts were interviewed, chosen to represent a variety of school types (e.g., elementary and secondary), sizes, and locations (e.g., in-town and out-of-town). Principals with fewer than three years service in the district were excluded on the grounds that they might not be fully familiar with district practices. There were no district administrators with fewer than three years in the district.

The audio-taped interview consisted of 32 relatively broad and open-ended questions, and it took 90 to 150 minutes to complete. One or more interview questions plus some possible probes were developed for each cell in Table 9:2. They were designed to elicit as complete and as accurate a description of district norms and practices as possible. There was an additional question on fiscal decision making and monitoring. Comparable questions were asked of all respondents, although the wording differed slightly for the different categories of respondent. The district and school administrator responses to the following interview questions constitute the data pool for this report:

- How does your district hold schools *accountable* for their performance?

- What important changes is this district presently making in the area of *monitoring* and reporting?

- What are the district's most important *monitoring* goals and what specifically is being done this year in pursuit of them?

The interviewers asked the respondents to clarify, elaborate, and give specific examples whenever necessary. If a respondent's answer to a question was short, the interviewer probed for further information, giving the respondents every opportunity to recall and describe district practices. When the respondents appeared to feel uncomfortable in the face of such probing, it was discontinued. A major inference, basic to the study, follows from this. Since the respondents were given several opportunities to mention relevant district policies and practices in each area, those not mentioned were not salient in the minds of the respondents, and thus not important in the district.

Data Analysis

All the information pertaining to each interview question provided by each of the respondents was compiled into a single file per district. To ensure coding reliability, each interview was coded independently by two coders, neither of whom was one of the co-investigators who conducted all the interviews and wrote the reports.

Next, district summaries reflecting the proportion of respondents to whom each code had been assigned were prepared. In these district summaries, + + indicates that a code was assigned to at least two-thirds of the respondents; + indicates that a code was assigned to one- to two-thirds of the respondents; − indicates that a code was assigned to fewer than one-third of the respondents; and DA indicates that a code was assigned to at least two-thirds of the district administrators but fewer than one-third of the principals. If a code failed either to characterize at least one of the districts or to distinguish between districts, it was dropped from the coding schedule.

Several techniques were used to maximize the "trustworthiness" of the data. One of these was to seek clarification and elaboration of responses throughout the interview session. The main technique, however, was triangulation. This took two forms: the comparison of responses of different respondents and, in particular, of different groups of respondents within a district; and the comparison of interview data with data contained in various documents such as policy manuals, teacher handbooks, and agendas and minutes of administrators' meetings. The greater the consistency in response revealed by these comparisons, the more confident we could be in the inferences drawn about district norms and practices. In addition, inferences made in reference to one cell were examined in the light of inferences made in reference to other cells to see whether or not they made sense, given all the information available about the district.

How Districts Hold Schools Accountable

We were first concerned with the mechanisms by which schools are held accountable by district administrators. Seven different practices were identified from the interview data. School achievement data, particularly test results, were at the heart of each of these practices — whether they involved providing data, discussing data, articulating expectations for the use of data, or monitoring school use of the data. The school accountability practices characteristic of the districts in the sample are shown in Table 9:4.

School Accountability Practices

Providing school-specific test results was the only practice mentioned in all ten districts. The Ministry of Education had just started to report government exam and Provincial Learning Assessment (PLAP) results by school, and in all districts the majority of respondents mentioned that this information was given to the principals.

> The schools receive the same package of PLAP results that we [i.e., the district administrators] receive. (District H)

Table 9:4
District Practices to Make Schools Accountable

	District									
	<Group 1>			<Group 2>			<Group 3>		<Group 4>	
District Practices	R	J	V	B	P	W	Q	C	H	M
provide school-specific test results	+ +	+ +	+ +	+ +	+ +	+ +	+ +	S	+	+ +
indicate relative standings of schools	+ +	+	+	+ +	+	–	+	–	+	–
review internal school assessment report	+ +	+ +	+	–	–	–	–	–	–	–
discuss school-specific performance data	+ +	+ +	+ +	+ +	+ +	+	–	S	–	N
articulate expectations	+ +	+	+	+ +	+ +	+	S	S	N	N
monitor school use of performance data	+ +	+ +	+ +	+ +	+ +	+ +	–	S	–	–
follow up planned school improvements	+ +	+ +	DA	+	+ +	+ +	–	–	–	–
performance rating*	hi	hi	hi	me	hi/ me	hi	hi	lo	lo	lo

Key: + + = mentioned by 2/3 or more of the respondents
+ = mentioned by 1/3 to 2/3 of the respondents
– = mentioned by fewer than 1/3 of respondents
DA = mentioned by district administrators but not principals
N = specifically mentioned by more than 1/3 of the respondents that the practice did not occur
S = practice occurs, but at school rather than district initiative

*performance rating is taken from Table 9:3

In addition, many of the districts administered one or more standardized tests to all students in selected grade levels and the principals were told how their schools had performed on these tests as well.

> We get feedback on the CAT from the point of view of our school. (District B)

> The district administrators give principals their school PLAP and CAT results. (District M)

Frequently, the principals were given not only school-specific test results but also information about how their school performed in comparison to the other schools in the district, or to provincial or national norms.

Each school knows how well it does on PLAP relative to the other schools in the district and relative to the province. And in the light of those results we examine our own programs in the school. . . . And we know how we stand [on the McGinity Test and the Otis Test] with district and national norms. (District R)

We get the statistical analysis on the district tests which includes the mean and standard deviation and distribution of the scores from A through F for our school as compared to the district. Come to think of it, on the district tests we actually get the breakdown for each school, but with the names deleted, so we can see how other schools are doing. (District V)

A concern for school confidentiality suggested by that second quotation was common. Great care was taken to ensure that no one beyond the school staff knew how that school performed — no other educator, and certainly no member of the public.

Only half the districts had a school self-assessment program, and only three of these required the self-assessment report to be submitted for district administrator feedback.

Our school self-assessment report is passed on to the District Office. They usually want to hear about it. We sit down and discuss it with them and follow up on our own recommendations. (District R)

The [self-assessment] report goes to our assistant superintendent and to the director responsible for our zone. . . . The reports are looked at — we've had feedback this year that suggests that each one was looked at thoroughly, because specific points were addressed. (District V)

The SWAT teams [i.e., external school assessment teams] delve into many aspects of the school, and they let you know if you are not on track. The SWAT team comes in and goes through our self-evaluation report, then checks to see if it is consistent with what they find. The SWAT team writes a draft report after their week-long visit to the school. They discuss the draft report paragraph by paragraph with the principal and staff before writing the final report. (District J)

In many districts the principals were not simply sent a report of their school's performance; instead, a district administrator visited the school and discussed the results with the principal, and sometimes with the staff.

Districtwide, the Central Office, with the principals, reviews the results of PLAPs and provincial exams and CTBS — discusses them with the principals as a group, then follows up the nitty-gritty with individual principals in private. So, for example, if there is a problem in my school with algebra or some damn thing, nobody knows about it except B [the superintendent] and me. And then I carry on with the teacher. (District J)

Usually when the provincial exam results come in, then I sit down with R [the superintendent] and G [the assistant superintendent] and we go over them and analyze them for strengths and weaknesses.

> Then I'd take the same information back to my staff and we'd go over it. (District W)

Another common district practice was the articulation of expectations concerning the purposes of monitoring and the intended uses of performance data. It was mentioned in all the districts whose testing program had been operating for at least three years. These expectations are discussed later, in the section on monitoring goals.

In some districts there was a routine procedure to ensure that performance data, particularly test data, were actually considered by the staff in goal setting and decision making.

> There was certainly a concern in the district because some domains in the math PLAP were . . . below the provincial average — they should be at or above the provincial average. There were no specific mandates. The follow up was handled by the Central Office through principals' objectives. . . . We have to sit down and discuss them with the Central Office. It is at this time that they say, "It looks like a district priority for gifted or for improving the math results is not included in your objectives. What are you doing in these areas?" (District W)

> Last year when we sat down to discuss our school objectives, the superintendent had a copy of the school CAT results. If there was something that needed attention that showed up in the test results, [he] looked to see how we dealt with it in our school objectives. (District P)

The seventh practice, and the one that logically falls last, was to follow up implementation of school plans for improvement to see if they had actually taken place and whether or not they were successful.

> I have to answer to the superintendent in April or May as to how we made out, how successful we were in achieving our [school] objectives. (District P)

> We are expected to have a school committee look at our PLAP results and interpret them on a schoolwide basis and submit a report to the superintendent. There are periodic visits from the assistant superintendent assigned to this school. He always has a number of prepared questions, and invariably one of them will be on that particular topic. . . . I show him our report and our recommendations, and then am very specific about what we've done. (District B)

District Approaches to School Accountability

As Table 9:4 shows, the districts differed with respect to which and how many of these practices characterized their approach to school accountability. Some districts did adopt rather similar approaches to school accountability, however, and it is possible to identify four approaches, the first two of which are similar.

Group 1 Approach. Districts R, J, and V were characterized by a strong district presence in the schools. They established a comprehensive set of practices to make schools accountable for their performance. The district administrators provided the principals with a variety of school-specific performance data; they discussed these data with the principals and set expectations for their use; and they monitored, through recognized procedures, how and with what success the schools used the performance data. There are several interesting features of this approach that deserve comment, as they help us understand how these practices contributed to school accountability.

It is possible to imagine these school accountability practices being carried out in any number of ways. For example, principals could have been required to go to the board office to learn their school's test results or they could have been told the results over the telephone, yet neither of these possibilities was ever mentioned. Instead, the school accountability practices invariably were structured so that (a) they involved direct personal contact between the principal and a district administrator and (b) they took place in the principal's office rather than at the board office. In other words, the manner in which the school accountability practices were conducted placed high demands on district administrator time and effort. This feature may have signalled to the other professionals in the district the seriousness with which the issue of school accountability was taken. It may also have conveyed respect for the role of the principal and recognition of the importance of treating each school as a unique entity.

The district administrators used their time in the schools purposefully to engage the principals in discussion on specific topics: school performance data, improvement plans, and the implementation of these plans. This meant that the district administrators had to be well prepared for these meetings, a further demand on their time and effort. But such focussed, well-informed discussion probably served to remind the principals that the district administrators knew what was happening in the schools. As a consequence of the considerable amount of time they spent in the schools, moreover, the district administrators became increasingly familiar with the progress and circumstances of each school, a fact of which the principals must have been aware.

In spite of the emphasis on school test results, the nature of the discussions was collaborative rather than prescriptive. The district administrators acknowledged good performance. They helped the principals interpret the data and identify strengths and weaknesses, and they offered advice and support when necessary. Ultimately, however, plans for improvement were left up to the principal and staff of each school — this point was stressed by the principals — although their progress in developing and implementing the plans was monitored. The features of collaboration and relative school autonomy probably reinforced the perception of respect for the role of the principal and recognition of the importance of treating each school as a unique entity.

Although the school accountability practices were distinct, they were interdependent; for example, school goals were influenced by test data, test data were examined during school assessment, accomplishment of school goals was made the focus of school visits. This meant that there was a cohesiveness to what was required of the schools. Every activity fitted into the overall pattern, and so had meaning beyond the task itself.

In spite of the fact that the district administrators kept the schools under close scrutiny, this approach to school accountability was not seen as oppressive or dictatorial. Instead, one is given the impression of a group of professionals who shared a common purpose and who played different, but complementary, roles in the achievement of the desired outcomes.

Group 2 Approach. Districts B, P, and W were very similar to Districts R, J, and V. They also had established a comprehensive set of school accountability practices — provision of a variety of school-specific performance data, face-to-face discussion of these data, articulation of expectations, and follow-up of use of performance data — resulting in a strong district presence in the schools. The major difference concerned the issue of school assessment. Group 1 districts had successfully instituted a school self-assessment process which provided for an external review of the report prepared by the school staff. In fact, the school assessment process in District J also involved separate assessment by an external team, and Districts R and V were moving in that direction as well. None of the districts in the second group had a districtwide program of school self-assessment.

External review of the school's self-assessment report, especially in conjunction with an external assessment, required considerable time and effort on the part of the district administrators, which might account for its infrequency. It did, however, have a major advantage, as the superintendent of District J explains:

> I like the school assessment process because it gives E [the assistant superintendent] and myself a good chance to have a close look at schools on a regular basis. It keeps us in touch with what is happening in far more detail than we would otherwise get.

The Group 1 district administrators spent a lot of time in the schools anyway, but the school assessment program provided them with another important opportunity to keep abreast of conditions in the schools. Furthermore, it permitted them to examine an array of information (e.g., test data, survey data, program reviews) about one or more aspects of the school at the same time.

There were two other noteworthy consequences of a school assessment program. Not only did the Group 1 district administrators know how a school was performing and the probable reasons for its performance level, but the principal and staff knew that they knew. This probably had an effect on how they conducted the school assessment, interpreted the results, and implemented the recommendations. The school assessment program also provided an additional opportunity for the district administrators to encourage the school in its efforts and to offer support and guidance. Group 2 lacked this important source of focus.

Group 3 Approach. In contrast to the groups already discussed, this group contains both a high (Q) and a low (C) performance district. Both districts were very small and had only one educational administrator, the superintendent, in the central office. This likely limited the district influence at the school level, as one principal explains:

> There is less district initiative here than in other districts I am used to, which I think is due very simply to the factor of size. . . . It is virtually impossible for the superintendent to start much. . . . The principals here tend to take on quite a bit of the role that a superintendent might take on in other places in terms of self-analysis and so forth. (District C)

What influence there was seemed to operate in part through a heavy reliance on test data. In high performing District Q, the superintendent oversaw the annual administration of a standardized test, whereas in low performing District C the initiative originally came from the elementary school principals.

> I think there is an expectation now, since it has been a number of years that both the elementary schools have used the Stanford tests, that this be continued. I think that should anybody stop it, questions would be asked. (District C)

While the principals in District Q did talk about using test data to identify weaknesses and plan improvements, they did so only within the context of the school — there was no reference to monitoring by the superintendent. In District C,

> The board and superintendent are kept advised of the progress of the schools by the principals with test results, staff analysis of test results, general progress reports — that sort of thing is brought to the board's attention. General comments and general recommendations are made, but there is no sort of formal way of doing that at the district level. I think that the schools are very careful to keep the district staff and board consulted all the way along the line.

All the principals in District C and half of those in District Q were recent appointments. Given the severe time restrictions faced by these two superintendents, it was not surprising that their approach to school accountability was to select principals who shared important values, to ensure that they had some reliable school performance data, and then to rely on them to "take care of business." Of these two small districts, Q appears to be a little more stable and to have a little more thrust from the superintendent.

Group 4 Approach. Districts H and M were characterized by an absence of press for school accountability. This was manifested in four ways. First, the district administrators provided the schools with little or no data in addition to what was provided by the Ministry (although this might have been changing). Second, there was little concern for using test data as an indicator of school performance.

> The provincial exams are the only sort of yardstick with any consistency — how our district is functioning compared to others is brought out. (District H)

> The value of test results . . . is not in distinguishing between schools, but to the classroom teacher. (District M)

As long as the emphasis was on district performance or individual student performance, there were no defensible grounds on which to advocate that a school make a particular change.

There were no established structures to ensure that the district administrators discussed performance data with the principals individually. In fact, there was little evidence that this practice occurred.

> The high school results are always discussed [at the administrators' meeting]. Other than that it is very difficult to get specifics. We always spend some time discussing the language arts results but they aren't specific to the school level. Other than that, nothing. (District H)

> The PLAP results were shown to me by a district administrator, with no comment. I discussed them with the appropriate department head, again with no pressure. (District M)

The absence of this practice not only meant that the district administrators missed an opportunity to let the principals know that they knew what was happening in the school, it also meant that they missed an opportunity both to reinforce expectations concerning performance data and to provide support and guidance to the principals in the interpretation of the data and the planning of improvements. It is not surprising, then, that there were no shared expectations with respect to the use of performance data.

Finally, there were no established structures to ensure that the district administrators monitored how and with what success the schools made use of performance data. Couple this with the absence of expectations and it was unlikely that performance data would have had much impact on school staff activities.

District History of School Accountability Practices

We were also interested in recent district changes in school accountability practices. In addition to the substantive nature of the change, both the extent of the change and the time frame of the change (i.e., whether it was a planned change, a change that had occurred within the last year or two, or a change that had occurred within the last three or four years) must be taken into consideration. These three factors constitute a district history of school accountability practices, which is summarized in Table 9:5 for each of the districts in the sample.

Table 9:5
History of District School Accountability Practices

District Practices	<Group 1>			<Group 2>			<Group 3>		<Group 4>	
	R	J	V	B	P	W	Q	C	H	M
administration of standardized tests	****	****	****	***	**	****	****	***	*	**
goal review process	***	****	—	**	****	***	****	—	—	**¹
principal evaluation	****	**	***	****	****	***	—	—	—	—
administration of cross-school exams	**	***	***	—	—	—	—	—	—	—
school assessment process	**	***	***	—	—	—	—	—	—	—
program evaluation	***	—	—	—	—	—	—	—	—	—

Key: * = planned change
        ** = modification or introduction 1 to 2 years ago
       *** = modification or introduction 3 to 4 years ago
      **** = practice established for at least 5 years

¹According to the principals, the follow-up stage of the process is not being carried out because of time constraints

Changes to Promote School Accountability

The simplest and most frequently mentioned change concerned the administration of standardized tests. A district testing program was in the planning stages in District H and some other districts had just recently introduced a testing program.

> We'll be giving CTBS next year. (District H)

> I think that in the last four years there has been a more organized way of collecting test results. . . . The Stanford is not as comprehensive a battery of tests as CTBS. . . . We [the two elementary school principals] wanted to zero in on vocabulary, comprehension, and math skills. (District C)

One district had modified its testing program, and others were planning to expand their programs.

> We changed the type of test, from CTBS to CAT. (District P)

> CAT was started about a year ago. . . . In future it will include grades 4 and 6. We extended CAT to the other grades so that all teachers would be in-serviced on the interpretation of the results. (District M)

Several districts had recently introduced some form of a goal-review process.

> School growth plans have been a focus of our administrators' association for the last year or two. (District B)

> Three years ago the superintendent instituted the idea of a deadline for sending school goals to his office and he in turn reacts to them and comes out and asks for comment. He has done that for three years in a row to my knowledge. That's worked fairly well. (District W)

Principal evaluation was a new practice in a couple of districts.

> In previous years principals were infrequently reported on, whereas now it's one report every three or four years. This was brought in by the new administration, within the last five years. By now each principal has been reported on at least once. (District W)

> Principal evaluations are now going on, and very thoroughly. It's not something this district has had. I went for 17 or 18 years without a report, and now all of a sudden, within the last three or four years, everyone has been scheduled. (District V)

Cross-school exams at the secondary level had been initiated in three districts, and two of them were planning to expand the program.

> Everyone has been put on notice that next year cross-school exams will be applied to the rural grades 8, 9, and 10 as well as to the town schools in the core academic subjects. (District J)

> District tests in selected core areas are new. I mentioned four tests before. Well, that is going to float around now. It will be in each grade, but there will be a different subject each year, just to try to take the temperature. (District V)

> Cross-school final examinations are only in the last two years. (District R)

These same three districts had recently modified their school assessment process.

> Rather than trying to totally assess the school every time, the superintendent decided that we should break it down into a number of areas and we could look at one small area each year. (District R)

> In the last couple of years the major change has been the mandated school self-assessment program. Beause we now have the common language and concept formation from our teacher effectiveness training program, we are trying to superimpose some of those strategies on our school-based assessment. (District V)

> In the early years the school evaluations were done differently. The

external team arrived unannounced — they just swooped down on the school, which is how they got their name of SWAT team. There was no self-assessment. . . . It was a shattering, a hideous experience. I know that one principal had to take a sick leave after one of these evaluations. It was an ugly experience in many regards, but it has evolved into what we have now, which I call a mini-Ministry team. . . . Now there is a self-assessment process which the external team checks. It has evolved into a very thorough, meaningful process, a very worthwhile process. . . . There is no resentment, I don't see it dying or floundering at all. It just continues to be polished a little bit, refined, and that's good. (District J)

Finally, in District R there was an annual program evaluation process in addition to the school assessment process, and it had recently undergone modification.

We changed our system of program evaluation to make it more at the school's discretion which program would be assessed and how it would be done. (District R)

District Change Histories
As Table 9:5 shows, the districts had different histories with respect to school accountability practices. There are some similarities, however, and it is possible to identify four patterns of change.

Group 1 Pattern. Districts R, J, and V had an impressive and very active history. They had a number of established practices, some of which had been refined substantially in recent years. In addition, they were still introducing new practices. Their history of school accountability practices might be best described as continually evolving.

Two threads appeared to run through the changes in practice. One was a concern for acquiring reliable and comparative data. This was reflected in the establishment of cross-grade exams and in the development of the principal evaluation processes, which included examination of school test results and client survey data. The other thread was a movement toward greater school involvement in the monitoring process. This was reflected particularly in the changes in the program evaluation and school assessment processes.

Group 2 Pattern. This group had fewer school accountability practices than did Group 1. Districts B and W, however, had introduced two substantial practices within the last four years and were becoming more like Group 1 districts. Their school accountability practices could be described as emerging.

Group 3 Pattern. District Q (a high performing district) had a history similar to high/medium performing District P (Group 2). District C, in contrast, had a history more like the similarly low performing Districts H and M.

Group 4 Pattern. Districts H and M appeared to be neophytes in the area of school accountability. They either planned to introduce or had recently introduced a district standardized testing program. As simple as this practice was, it appeared to be a significant initial step toward holding schools accountable for their performance. In the words of one principal:

> The principals used to be able to say, "My school's O.K.," and blame poor district results on the fellow down the road, but they can't do that any more because they are given school-level results now. (District M)

In fact, the issue of school accountability in a district may not arise in any meaningful way until there is some kind of district testing program involving school-level analysis of the results. As long as data are analyzed at the district level, responsibility for performance remains diffuse, and there is no compelling reason for change at any particular school.

District Monitoring Goals

We were interested to see if there was a shared understanding of the purposes of district monitoring practices. These findings are summarized by district in Table 9:6.

Table 9:6
Purposes of District Monitoring Practices

	District									
	<Group 1>			<Group 2>			<Group 3>		<Group 4>	
Purposes	R	J	V	B	P	W	Q	C	H	M
identify weaknesses; plan improvements	+	+	+	+ +	+ +	+	+ +	–	–	–
collect reliable and objective outcome data	+	DA	DA	+ +	+	–	–	+ +	–	–
set standards for performance	+	–	–	+	–	–	–	–	–	–

Key:
+ + = mentioned by 2/3 or more of the respondents
+ = mentioned by 1/3 to 2/3 of the respondents
– = mentioned by fewer than 1/3 of the respondents
DA = mentioned by district administrators but not principals
N = specifically mentioned by more than 1/3 of the respondents that the practice did not occur

Many of the respondents alluded to the purposes of district monitoring practices, but there were not many explicit references. Certainly, the most commonly cited purpose was that of using performance data to identify weaknesses and plan improvements.

> We are expected to look at the CTBS results seriously, to assess where there is a significant variance between school and district results, and to correct any discrepancies. (District J)

> We have to do an analysis of test results and take a look at where the weaknesses are and set some goals and objectives for doing something about it. (District Q)

The second purpose was to collect reliable and objective outcome data, to have a good indicator of school performance, particularly in the core academic subjects.

> I want to find out how teachers are doing during the year. (District C)

> There has been an attempt made in this district under board direction and by district administrative leadership . . . to try to develop the notion of having instructional goals and objectives and of administering tests to see if those goals and objectives are being met. (District V)

The third goal refers to performance standards.

> I think accountability is a very high goal in the district. There is an expectation that this school district will do well, and should do well, that we should be above the provincial mean, for example. (District B)

> I think it is academic programs and how we are doing relative to the rest of the province. (District R)

The major distinction, according to Table 9:6, is between Districts H and M (Group 4) and all the others. Not only were no shared goals articulated in these two districts, but according to some of the respondents there simply were none.

> I expected the district to say "Your results were poor in such and such, what are you going to do?" But I have no sense that we were in any way answerable for our results. (District M)

> Expectations of the principals with respect to performance data are not talked about. (District H)

Conclusion

In this chapter, we have focussed on the monitoring performance of school district administrators and its relationship to the comparative academic effectiveness of the district schools. The ten districts in the sample were divided into four groups according to the pattern of practices used to make schools accountable (Table 9:4).

The districts with the strongest and clearest patterns (Group 1) all have a high performance rating. Group 4 districts, with the weakest patterns of monitoring performance, both have low performance ratings. The relationship in Groups 2 and 3 between monitoring and effectiveness is less clear but still evident. When the history of the practices is examined (Table 9:5) the relationship between monitoring and effectiveness is equally evident, with Districts B and

Q being slightly anomalous, the former having a marginally superior history and an inferior level of academic performance. If we turn to the clarity of the purposes of accountability exercises (Table 9:6), the relationship between clarity and effectiveness is rather less clear, with the exception of the districts in Group 4, in which there are few practices to clarify.

We distinguished earlier in the chapter between two approaches to quality control by school districts. We advocated autonomy with accountability, as distinct from the more complete delegation of authority advocated by Goodlad. In our sample of school districts in British Columbia, it is clear that the high performing school districts are characterized by a senior administration very much involved in holding school administrators accountable for quality, while at the same time leaving responsibility and authority for the types and methodologies of change at the level of the school.

References

Alexander K L, Cook M, McDill E L 1978 Curriculum tracking and educational stratification: Some further evidence. *American Sociological Review* 43: 47–66

Alexander K L, Griffin L 1976 School district effects on academic achievement: A reconsideration. *American Sociological Review* 41: 144–151

Anderson L A, Evertson C M, Emmer E T 1980 Dimensions in classroom management derived from recent research. *Journal of Curriculum Studies* 12: 343–356

Barr R, Drebeen R 1983 *How Schools Work*. University of Chicago Press, Chicago

Bidwell C, Kasarda J 1975 School district organization and student achievement. *American Sociological Review* 40: 55–70

Boyd W L, Crowson R L 1981 The changing conception and practice of public school administration. *Review of Research in Education* 9: 311–376

Bridges E M 1986 *The Incompetent Teacher: The Challenge and the Response*. Falmer Press, Philadelphia

Childs T S, Shakeshaft C 1986 A meta-analysis of research on the relation between educational expenditures and student achievement. *Journal of Educational Finance* 12(2): 249–263

Coleman P 1984 Improving schools by school-based management. *McGill Journal of Education* 19(1): 25–43

Coleman P 1986a School districts and student achievement in British Columbia: A preliminary analysis. *Canadian Journal of Education* 11(4): 509–521

Coleman P 1986b The good school district. *Journal of Educational Finance* 12(1): 71–96

Coleman P 1987 Equal or equitable? Fiscal equity and the problem of student dispersion. *Journal of Educational Finance* 13(1): 45–68

Coleman P, LaRocque L 1984 Economies of scale revisited: School district operating costs in British Columbia, 1972–1982. *Journal of Educational Finance* 10(1): 22–35

Coleman P, LaRocque L 1986 The small school district in British Columbia: The myths, the reality, and some policy implications. *Alberta Journal of Educational Research* 32(4): 323–335

Corwin R G, Borman K M 1988 School as workplace: Structural constraints on administration. In: Boyan N J (ed.) *Handbook of Research on Educational Administration.* Longman, White Plains, New York

Cuban L 1984 Transforming the frog into a prince: Effective schools research, policy, and practice at the district level. *Harvard Educational Review* 54(2): 129–151

Evertson C M, Emmer E T 1982 Preventive classroom management. In: Duke D L (ed.) *Helping Teachers Manage Classrooms.* Association for Supervision and Curriculum Development, Alexandria, Virginia

Goodlad J 1987 Structure, process, and an agenda. In: Goodlad J (ed.) *The Ecology of School Renewal: Eighty-sixth Yearbook of the National Society for the Study of Education,* Part 1. University of Chicago Press, Chicago

Hannan M T, Freeman J H, Meyer J W 1976 Specification of models for organizational effectiveness. *American Sociological Review* 41: 136–143

Kean M H 1983 Administrative uses of research and evaluation information. In: Gordon E W (ed.) *Review of Research in Education,* Vol. 10. American Educational Research Association, Washington, DC

Mackenzie D E 1983 Research for school improvement: An appraisal of some recent trends. *Educational Researcher* 12(4): 5–17

McPherson R B, Crowson R L, Pitner N J 1986 *Managing Uncertainty: Administrative Theory and Practice in Education.* Charles E. Merrill, Columbus, Ohio

Mintzberg H 1979 *The Structuring of Organizations.* Prentice-Hall, Englewood Cliffs, New Jersey

Mitchell D, Encarnation D J 1984 Alternative state policy mechanisms for influencing school performance. *Educational Researcher* 13(5): 4–11

Murphy J, Hallinger P, Peterson K D 1985 Supervising and evaluating principals. *Educational Leadership* 43(2): 79–82

Sirotnick K A 1987 Evaluation in the ecology of schooling: The process of school renewal. In: Goodlad J (ed.) *The Ecology of School Renewal: Eighty-sixth Yearbook of the National Society for the Study of Education,* Part 1. University of Chicago Press, Chicago

Sirotnick K A, Burstein L 1985 Measurement and statistical issues in multilevel research on schooling. *Educational Administration Quarterly* 21(3): 169–185

Snyder J, Anderson R 1986 *Managing Productive Schools.* Academic Press, New York

Walberg H J, Marjoribanks K 1976 Family environment and cognitive development: Twelve analytic models. *Review of Educational Research* 46: 527–551

Weick K E 1976 Educational organizations as loosely coupled systems. *Administrative Science Quarterly* 21: 1–19

2480   3890